PRAISE FOR *PEOPLE-FIRST IN* *COMMUNICATION*

What Emma Bridger and Lee Smith have shared with us here will ring in a new, melodic, heart-led way to be people-first about our comms.
Perry Timms, Chief Energy Officer, PTHR

This book captures the essence of what internal communication should always be about: human connection and engagement. The guidance provided will help practitioners to develop exciting new skills and shake off some of the shackles of an over-emphasis on information delivery.
Dr Kevin Ruck, internal comms tutor, researcher and author

Lee Smith and Emma Bridger bring both passion and pragmatism to the future of internal communication, showing us how connection is the true driver of trusted, agile and resilient organizations. A must-read for anyone committed to shaping the future of our profession.
Jennifer Sproul, Chief Executive, Institute of Internal Communication

This is a true masterpiece that propels internal comms into the future of work – where we are integral to putting people at the heart of organizations, right where they belong.
Jo Coxhill, employee experience, internal comms and workplace culture consultant

This book comes at exactly the right time and is a must-read for anyone working in employee engagement.
Nick Andrews, Business Development Director, Sequel Group

With AI it's evolve or die for IC practitioners: it's an extinction event. But this book sets out the new opportunity for internal comms to communicate and lead.
Marc Wright, Founder, Simply Communicate, and Digital Strategist, Gallagher

People-First Internal Communication is the book for strategic communicators of the future. It's the wake up call the profession needs.
Jenni Field, leadership credibility and organizational communication expert

This book lands at exactly the right moment for anyone looking to put people back at the centre of how we communicate. No fluff, just the practical stuff needed to make it work.
Janet Hitchen, international communication leader and strategist

Emma Bridger and Lee Smith have given us more than a book; they've given us a framework for re-imagining our role, reclaiming our value and reminding ourselves why people are – and must always be – at the heart of internal communication.
Priya Bates, ABC, SCMP, IABC Fellow, President, Inner Strength Communication Inc

Easily the best book I've read all year and bang on for such a time as this.
Eduvie Martin, former President, International Association of Business Communicators

Emma Bridger and Lee Smith have written a complete and compelling guide to re-energizing internal communication for the complexities of the contemporary workplace.
Bruce Daisley, *Sunday Times* bestselling author

Packed with examples and case studies, the passion, energy and wisdom of the authors can be felt on every page.
Hilary Scarlett, author of *Neuroscience for Organizational Change*

At a time when technology and AI threaten to strip away the human side of our work, this book puts the people at the heart of communication.
Advita Patel, President, CIPR

Emma Bridger and Lee Smith's insightful book is steeped in experience. It coaches the communicators of today to unlock tomorrow's potential.
Rachel Miller, Founder, All Things IC, and author of *Internal Communication Strategy*

A genuinely inspiring, refreshing and, yes, challenging read.
Belinda Gannaway, Team and Systems Coach, Ocelli XP

AI isn't the end of employee communications. It's the reboot we've been waiting for. This book shows you the way.
Steve Crescenzo, Founder and CEO, Crescenzo Communications

What Emma Bridger and Lee Smith have achieved is the articulation of a blueprint to redesigning a future-ready IC team to leverage our greatest asset, the people we serve.
Frank Dias, Founder and CEO, Ai x Comms Lab

People-First Internal Communication

Communication

*Improving engagement
and retention in the workforce*

Emma Bridger and Lee Smith

KoganPage

First published in Great Britain and the United States in 2026 by Kogan Page Limited

Kogan Page
Kogan Page Ltd, 2nd Floor, 45 Gee Street, London EC1V 3RS, United Kingdom
Kogan Page Inc, 8 W 38th Street, Suite 902, New York, NY 10018, USA
www.koganpage.com

EU Representative (GPSR)
Authorized Rep Compliance Ltd, Ground Floor, 71 Baggot Street Lower, Dublin D02 P593, Ireland
www.arccompliance.com

Kogan Page books are printed on paper from sustainable forests.

© Emma Bridger and Lee Smith, 2026

The moral rights of the authors have been asserted in accordance with the Copyright, Designs and Patents Act 1988.

ISBNs
Hardback   978 1 3986 2308 8
Paperback   978 1 3986 2306 4
Ebook   978 1 3986 2307 1

British Library Cataloguing-in-Publication Data
A CIP record for this book is available from the British Library.

Library of Congress Control Number
2025039342

Typeset by Integra Software Services, Pondicherry
Printed and bound by CPI Group (UK) Ltd, Croydon CR0 4YY

CONTENTS

DEDICATIONS

'People first' has always been more than a concept for me, it's been my guiding force. From studying psychology all those years ago, to writing my first book, to every twist and turn of my career, I've always been obsessed with the people side of things: how we think, how we connect, and how we thrive at work.

This book feels like a full-circle moment for me. I started my career in internal comms, and it was my passion. But I'll be honest, somewhere along the way, the spark dimmed a little bit. The battles, the burnout, and the same conversations over and over – it got to me. But something changed. With new ways of working, thinking and being, I feel genuinely re-energized. Freed up to do the work that really matters – the human stuff. And I hope this book gives others permission to do the same.

To all of you working in IC, the generous, passionate, curious, often unsung heroes – thank you. You are the heartbeat of organizations, and I truly hope you see yourself in these pages, and feel inspired to keep pushing for better. You're my kind of people, and it's been a privilege to learn from, work alongside, and be inspired by you over the years.

A very special thank you to Belinda Gannaway, my co-author on *Employee Experience by Design*. Without that book, and the work we have collaborated on, this one simply wouldn't exist and nor would the People-First IC movement. The foundations we laid in EX by Design – the thinking, the tools, the approach – are woven all the way through this book. Belinda, your generosity, brilliance and collaborative spirit were instrumental in shaping this next chapter, and I'm endlessly grateful for everything we created together.

Huge love and thanks as always to Ted, Harry, Eadie and Teddy. For putting up with the many late nights, book-draft chaos/obsession and conversations hijacked by 'just one more idea.' I couldn't do it without you.

And finally to Lee, my co-author, creative partner and fellow people-first obsessive. Thank you for your brilliance, your patience, and for helping me fall back in love with IC again. I couldn't have written this without you, and nor would I have wanted to.

LEE'S DEDICATION

I've spent a lifetime – over 35 years – navigating the evolving world of internal communication. Along the way, I've seen just how powerful it can be when we put people at the heart of our work. This book is for all those who believe, as I do, that IC isn't just a function, but a force for good.

To the quiet visionaries, the bold leaders, the solo communicators, the C-suite challengers, this is for you. To everyone who believes that work can be more human, this is for you. To those who speak up, show up, and lift others up through the power of communication, this is for you. And to the next generation of internal communicators, this is your moment! Thank you, my tribe, for keeping me grounded, and for your unwavering commitment, curiosity, passion and energy.

Heartfelt gratitude, too, to my long-suffering family. For a while there, I felt a bit like Jack Torrance – the increasingly unhinged writer portrayed so brilliantly by Jack Nicholson in Kubrick's *The Shining*. Trudy, Elliot and Billy – thank you for keeping me sane during my darker moments!

And finally, to the one person who made this book possible: my co-author, collaborator and co-conspirator in all things people-first, Emma Bridger. Without you, this book would never have happened. Thank you for your wisdom, guidance, generosity and patience.

LIST OF FIGURES AND TABLES

ABOUT THE AUTHORS

EMMA BRIDGER

Emma Bridger is a leading employee engagement and experience specialist, psychologist and co-founder of The EX Space – a vibrant professional community dedicated to advancing the practice of employee experience and human-centred design. Through her consultancy People Lab, she has spent more than two decades helping organizations create more engaging, human workplaces. Emma is the author of *Employee Engagement* (Kogan Page), co-author of *Employee Experience by Design* (Kogan Page) and a recognized thought leader in behavioural science, positive psychology and people-first organizational design. With a deep commitment to evidence-based practice, Emma helps clients turn complex challenges into practical, impactful solutions that improve working lives. She is widely respected for her clarity of thought, infectious energy and unwavering belief in the power of communication to shape culture and performance.

LEE SMITH

Lee Smith is an internal communication and employee experience strategist with over 35 years' experience. Working at the intersection of communication, culture and change from the age of 19, he has held senior in-house and agency roles, led award-winning teams and advised leaders globally. As co-founder of The EX Space and Strategy Partner at IC Partners, he continues to work at the cutting edge of internal communication and employee experience. Lee previously co-founded Gatehouse, a leading internal communication agency, and created State of the Sector, the global benchmark for internal communication research. A long-time advocate for professional development, he helped shape one of the first IC competency frameworks and designed and led the IoIC Accelerate programme. He is a Fellow of both the Institute of Internal Communication (FIIC) and the Chartered Institute of Public Relations (FCIPR), a former Chair of CIPR Inside and holds a Master's degree in Corporate Communication & Reputation Management.

Together, Emma and Lee bring a unique blend of strategic insight, behavioural science and real-world experience to the field of internal communication. Through this book – and their shared work at The EX Space – they invite communicators everywhere to reimagine their role and help build better, more human organizations from the inside-out.

FOREWORD

Like all professions, internal communication faces a watershed moment. The advent of enterprise-scale generative AI presents the biggest opportunity since quality and standards were first introduced to the discipline by the establishment of the British Association of Industrial Editors back in 1949.

Industry 5.0 and burgeoning developments in all manner of artificial intelligence will transform the way business information is created, quantified, shared and leveraged within organizations. Routine and repetitive tasks will be automated. Large language models will revolutionize the pace and scale at which existing information can be remixed to create new and improved knowledge and insights.

Overseen with care, AI offers the potential to deliver customized internal communication that meets the needs and context of each internal stakeholder as they navigate their daily workflows. Integrated with thoughtful business and digital acumen, technology innovation will fundamentally reshape the way organizations communicate with colleagues. Time will be freed up to apply much-needed focus to the deeper, nuanced, human elements of communication. The science of AI-enhanced internal communication offers vast efficiency gains.

The art of human-centred internal communication, however, presents the opportunity to rebuild trusted relationships at work, re-establish meaning and purpose, and restore human connection and community at a time when it has never been more needed.

Like many others, I believe technology, in whatever form, is and should always be an enabler. It should complement human endeavour to get things done, ideally with ever-increasing accuracy. Deployed well, enterprise software of any stripe should allow us all to refocus our efforts on the creative, engaging, innovative and uniquely human work that no amount of code can replicate.

From an internal communication viewpoint, there is no shortage of opportunity to deliver strategic value.

We can help restore empathy and trust at work, facilitate stronger human connection and coach senior stakeholders to improve their communication skills. We can create memorable experiences for all workplace contributors, convene and curate gatherings that strengthen relational ties and help organizations harness change agility. These are just some of the many pathways available to deliver next-generation internal communication.

Understanding the forces reshaping work is, of course, the entry point for all successful organizational futureproofing. The interplay between the multiple trends disrupting 'business as usual' requires systems thinking and must be factored into all strategic planning activities.

Organizational strategy – however fluid it might need to become in response to ever-shifting external forces – must be clearly and consistently communicated to all internal stakeholders. As the IoIC's own IC Index research shows, each of us aspires to know what unique part we might play in the delivery of wider business objectives.

While the business media continues to prioritize the benefits of AI, big data and data analytics, delicate balance is nonetheless required. The human brain uses story to make sense of the world and our place within it. No amount of technology will change that.

Applying a people-centred, experience-driven approach to internal communication is therefore a vital shift to counter the rising cynicism, scepticism and disengagement felt by far too many across organizations today. Leveraging the best insights from psychology, neuroscience and behavioural science will help us design and deliver communication that empathically meets the expectations of all internal stakeholders, wherever they are located.

This is where the work of Emma Bridger and Lee Smith makes such an important contribution. *People-First Internal Communication* is a much-needed needle-shift that moves the trajectory of our profession forwards. What makes this book especially powerful is that it does not stop at vision and principle. It is both a rallying call and a practical roadmap, equipping communicators to not only navigate disruption but also to shape the workplaces of the future. By integrating the principles of employee experience with communication practice, it shows how organizations can create environments where colleagues feel valued, connected and inspired to contribute.

At a time when our profession can feel weighed down by uncertainty, this book is energizing and hopeful. It reminds us that the future of internal communication is not something to fear but an opportunity to embrace – an opportunity to reclaim our roots in trust, conversation and community.

As the only professional membership body dedicated to raising standards in internal communication, the IoIC welcomes fresh and dynamic thinking and support at this watershed moment.

Jennifer Sproul
Chief Executive of the Institute of Internal Communication (IoIC)

ACKNOWLEDGEMENTS

Thank you to Carla Draper for the fantastic illustrations in this book, to everyone who contributed their wisdom, time and energy to this project, and to all the organizations and people who have inspired, supported and encouraged us along the way.

Howard Krais	Joe Ferner-Reeves	Chris Manning
Nick Andrews	Archer Ahern	Helen Sierwald
Jennifer Sproul	Riffat Ahmed	Lynsey Davidson
Kirsty Lloyd	Bruce Daisley	Deborah Hulme
Samantha Gadd	Damon Deaner	Alex Graves
Liam FitzPatrick	Sarah Meurer	Tarek Kamil
Monique Zytnik	Sarah Pass	Belinda Gannaway
Katie Austin	Advita Patel	Kerrie Hughes
Shalini Gupta	Andy Pamphilon	Ann-Marie Blake
Prof Michael Heller	Abi Humayun	Sharon Belton
Carla Draper	Kateryna Byelova	

01

It's time to reclaim our roots

Looking back to look forward

Internal communication (IC) didn't begin with apps, intranets or even channels. It started with something deeply human: a belief that people matter. In the earliest days of IC, businesses like Cadbury and Rowntree pioneered ways to inform, involve and inspire employees because they genuinely cared about their well-being. They built communities, not just companies. They understood that great work starts with great relationships.

But somewhere along the journey, we lost our way. As organizations grew and the world sped up, internal communication became less about people and more about process. We moved from purpose to platforms, from connection to channels, from empathy to efficiency. Ironically, just as we perfected the mechanics of internal communication, we began to lose the very humanity it was designed to serve.

And now, just as we're catching our breath, along comes artificial intelligence (AI), with the power to do much of what we've spent years mastering, only faster, cheaper and at scale. AI promises ever greater efficiency, smarter decision-making and makes real the long-held dream of hyper-personalized communication, but it also brings with it massive disruption. Jobs will disappear, new ones will be created and many will evolve in different and unexpected directions. Internal communication will not be immune to all this, new skills and ways of thinking will be required, and the line between human and machine contributions will increasingly blur.

We believe those organizations that embrace AI with a genuinely human-centric approach, prioritizing ethical implementation, transparency and workforce adaptation, will thrive. Those that fail to balance technology with trust, purpose and genuine employee connection risk alienating their people, eroding their cultures and diminishing long-term success. The future won't just be about AI, it will be about how well businesses integrate AI without losing their humanity.

But AI isn't the only force reshaping our profession. The people we serve, our colleagues and employees, are bringing new expectations to the workplace. They want internal communication that's as seamless, intuitive and engaging as the experiences they have as consumers. They expect relevance, personalization, simplicity, interactivity and trust. In short, they expect a consumer-grade experience at work, and this includes their communication experience.

The old models of broadcast messaging and top-down control are no longer enough. People want communication they can connect with, not just receive. They want to be active participants, not passive recipients. So where does that leave us? At a crossroads. And we must ask ourselves, if AI can write the message, build the plan and optimize channels, what exactly is our role?

This chapter takes a look back, not to reminisce, but to reflect and reimagine. Because the roots of internal communication hold powerful lessons for the future. Our profession actually started out as people-first, before becoming more process-led, then evolving into the expert-led practice that dominates today. And now, we believe, it must come full circle, to something richer, deeper and more human than ever before.

We call this People-First Internal Communication. And it's not just a return to our roots, but a reinvention for what comes next. IC is often regarded as a relatively new and emerging field, and yet it has a surprisingly long and rich back story. You might be surprised to learn that businesses first began communicating with their employees in a structured way as early as the mid-19th century, as the second wave of the industrial revolution took hold and organizations began to expand.

Companies like Cadbury, Rowntree and Lever Brothers in the UK, and Hershey and NCR in the US, were among the first to formalize communication with their fast-growing workforces (Heller, 2008). With principled leaders at their helm, these pioneering organizations championed employee welfare and used innovative tools, from factory-floor notices to printed staff bulletins, to keep people informed, build alignment and foster a sense of community.

In the 150 years since, organizations of all shapes and sizes have followed a similar path. What started as a well-intentioned, if somewhat paternalistic, practice has transformed into a thriving profession. At its best, internal communication influences every aspect of organizational strategy, workplace culture, trust and business performance.

From its Victorian roots to today's AI-enabled, hyper-connected workplaces, internal communication has played a crucial role in supporting growth, navigating world wars, strengthening cultures and responding to crises. It has adapted to seismic political, economic, social and technological shifts, and matured into a mission-critical function that seeks to connect, engage, unite and inspire. Yet for all that progress, something has been lost.

Over time, we've become more focused on the mechanics than the meaning, more consumed with channels, content and messaging than with the people at the heart of it all. What was once a deeply human practice has become increasingly process-driven.

In this chapter, we'll explore the rich and fascinating history of internal communication and consider what it means for our future. We'll revisit the roots of the practice, trace its evolution and ask the most important question of all: what comes next?

Because history isn't just a record of the past. It's a guide to the future. And only by understanding where we've come from can we chart a meaningful path forward. In the words of George Bernard Shaw, 'We are made wise not by the recollection of our past, but by the responsibility for our future.'

Together, we'll examine how internal communication has not only supported business success but also shaped society, influencing workplace rights, corporate responsibility and employee well-being. And we'll ask how we can build on that legacy to create organizations where people feel valued, heard and empowered, even as AI moves in.

There is, of course, a newfound urgency to all of this. As we enter what some are calling the fifth industrial revolution – the age of human–machine collaboration – we must step back, take stock of our profession and consider what this new era of work demands from us.

The stakes have never been higher, and the opportunity has never been greater. Employees now expect the same quality of communication at work as they experience in their personal lives; intuitive, personalized and interactive. They want a consumer-grade experience, not corporate broadcasts. At the same time, AI is rapidly reshaping the landscape, automating many of the tasks we've long owned. Throughout this chapter, and the book that follows, we'll explore three critical questions:

- How can we, as IC professionals, ensure that people remain at the heart of organizations, even as AI advances?
- How can we adapt and stay relevant when AI can do so much of what we do – and do it so well?
- How can we move beyond keeping up, start leading the way and start building the new world of work?

These provocations are more than talking points. They're a call to action. And they form the foundation of a new kind of internal communication; one that positions us, once again, as the beating human heart of the organization.

A bright future

It's important to stress that this book is intended as a work of optimism, our aim is to show how we, collectively, can capitalize on these profound changes and carve out a new and exciting future for internal communication. We believe that the future is bright for internal communicators and that this new era of work will open up incredible opportunities for those practitioners who learn to adapt to these momentous changes.

But there is a dark side too. If we don't change, and quickly, it's likely we'll face a quick and painful professional death. We believe that internal communicators are uniquely positioned to not just support, but genuinely enable, the transformation of work in the coming decades. But it will require a significant change in both focus and approach to make this happen. It will require a shift to what we call People-First IC.

To stay relevant into the future, a new kind of internal communicator is required. One who is focused on people, co-creating solutions with employees, rather than simply 'doing' IC to them. One who can partner effectively with AI, using the power of this groundbreaking technology to enable themselves to be more human. One who intentionally designs great communication experiences. Throughout this book, we'll explain how to make this shift and give you the tools and frameworks you'll need to do it. But first we want to explain why we need to change and more importantly, why we need to change now.

The (surprisingly) human roots of IC

Long before the blanket emails, meeting-cluttered calendars, apps and enterprise social networks of today, internal communication was much simpler and much more human. The roots of our profession can be traced back to the late 19th and early 20th centuries (Ruck and Yaxley, 2013). In an age of rapid industrialization, rigid hierarchies and harsh working conditions, a handful of forward-thinking businesses took a different approach. Instead of viewing workers purely as a means to profit, they put people first. They prioritized well-being, introduced new ways to communicate and laid the foundations for what would become internal communication.

In the UK, organizations like Cadbury, Rowntree and Lever Brothers led the way. In the US, it was companies like Hershey and NCR. Their leaders believed that treating employees with respect wasn't just the right thing to do, it was good business. And they built communication practices that reflected that.

Take Cadbury, for example. Known today for its chocolate, the company's deeper legacy lies in how it treated its people. In the late 1800s, brothers Richard and George Cadbury transformed their family business into a model of corporate social responsibility. They didn't just talk about values, they built them into bricks and mortar. On the outskirts of Birmingham, they created Bournville: a village with homes, parks, schools and recreational spaces designed specifically for workers and their families. At a time when many factory workers lived in overcrowded, unsanitary slums, Cadbury offered clean, green, well-planned homes. It was organizational community-building, but with actual communities.

And they didn't stop at better housing. Cadbury also pioneered internal communication long before the term existed. In 1912, they launched *Cadbury Works* (Heller, 2008), one of the UK's earliest internal publications. It shared company news, social updates and welfare initiatives. They also held structured meetings with employee councils and introduced suggestion schemes that empowered workers to share ideas and shape their workplace.

All of this was underpinned by a belief that employees were human beings first. That communication should be a two-way street and that a connected, informed, valued workforce would always outperform a disengaged one.

Up in York, Rowntree was developing a similarly progressive model. Founded in the 1860s and led by Joseph Rowntree, the business took a research-led approach to employee welfare (Roberts, 1995). Rowntree conducted detailed studies on poverty and well-being. What he learnt led to real improvements: better pay, shorter hours, healthier working conditions. The company built libraries, hosted lectures and offered sports clubs, creating a culture that went beyond productivity.

Like Cadbury, Rowntree also introduced formal communication forums. In 1919, they launched Company Councils, bringing together workers and management in a structured way to solve problems and improve working life. These weren't just for show. The councils led to real change: better pensions, paid holidays and housing improvements that made a tangible difference to people's lives. Their approach was guided by principle, not PR. And it reflected a view that communication wasn't about command and control but about shared responsibility.

Meanwhile, in the US, Milton Hershey was putting similar ideas into practice. Inspired by Cadbury, he built the town of Hershey, Pennsylvania, complete with schools, hospitals and public amenities for employees and their families. He introduced profit-sharing and training programmes, and he placed a strong emphasis on open communication. Employees could share feedback, ask questions and stay informed through newsletters and regular meetings.

Then there was NCR, led by the visionary John Henry Patterson. NCR developed some of the earliest formal internal communication tools in America: newsletters, structured feedback systems and a company-wide training manual known as the 'NCR Primer'. One defining moment came in 1913, when a devastating flood hit Dayton, Ohio, home of NCR's headquarters. The company's internal communication systems were repurposed overnight to coordinate rescue and relief efforts, a powerful early example of communication enabling action during crisis.

What we can learn

Across these examples, one clear theme emerges: these organizations didn't treat communication as an afterthought. They saw it as a vital tool for engagement, trust and community. And while their methods were simple, their principles still resonate today.

KEY TAKEAWAYS

1 **Listen and involve**: Communication builds trust, loyalty and shared purpose.

2 **Focus on well-being**: When well-being is prioritized, productivity and engagement follow.

3 **Invest in growth**: Education and clear communication drive both personal and organizational success.

4 **Community matters**: Organizations are made up of people and their lives extend beyond the factory gates.

These pioneers didn't have today's technology or sophisticated strategies. But they had empathy, foresight and a deep belief in the value of people. And that's where our profession began. Today, we're facing new challenges and using new tools, but the core insight still holds: when you treat employees like human beings, everything else works better.

As we step into an AI-driven, consumer-grade future, there's a powerful lesson in looking back: great communication has always been, and will always be, about people first.

From people-first to process-driven

The roots of internal communication were deeply human, born out of empathy, built on trust and designed to create connection. But over the decades, something changed. As organizations grew, so did their need for control. Scale brought complexity, and with it came hierarchy, bureaucracy and a new set of priorities. Slowly but surely, communication shifted from a tool of inclusion to a tool of alignment.

Between the 1920s and the late 1980s, internal communication underwent a profound transformation. What began as a people-first practice evolved into a more formal, strategic discipline. And while this professionalization brought structure, clarity and reach, it also distanced us from our roots.

The end of the First World War marked a turning point for business and for communication. The war had demonstrated the extraordinary power of messaging to rally, reassure and mobilize populations. It wasn't lost on governments or corporations. As soldiers returned home, expectations shifted. People wanted better conditions, fairer pay and a stronger voice at work. Labour movements grew in power, and industrial unrest became a real threat. Companies responded not just with policies, but with messaging.

Internal communication became a means of managing people, aligning them, pacifying them and reinforcing the idea of a shared corporate mission. Corporate storytelling emerged not as a tool for engagement, but as a form of internal PR. It was less about listening and more about loyalty, less conversation and more control (Grant, 1994).

Across the UK and US, this new model took hold. Large employers like London Transport, ICI and the British Overseas Airways Corporation became increasingly sophisticated in their approach, producing bulletins, broadcasts and printed updates designed to inform and influence dispersed workforces.

In the US, Henry Ford doubled down on internal communication through corporate film. His team developed one of the largest motion picture operations in the world, producing training videos, morale boosters and propaganda-style content that reinforced company values (Stewart, 2014).

What had started as a human-centric practice was becoming industrialized. The intention wasn't always cynical, but the effect was clear. Efficiency was the new goal, communication was no longer a conversation, it was a system.

The Second World War only accelerated this trend. Once again, communication was used to rally, coordinate and build morale, this time on an even bigger scale. Governments perfected the art of messaging, and businesses took note. In the post-war years, as economies were rebuilt and globalization began to take root, internal communication emerged as a formal business function. The challenges of scale, distance and diversity made it essential. But they also made it more transactional.

Employee newsletters flourished. So did printed manuals, corporate broadcasts and communication policies. In the UK, the British Association of Industrial Editors (now known as the Institute of Internal Communication [IoIC]) was formed in 1949 to support and professionalize the craft. This was the beginning of the 'channel age'.

From the 1940s through to the 1970s, internal publications boomed. What started as simple factory-floor bulletins evolved into glossy, consumer-grade magazines filled with staff news, corporate updates, interviews and even cartoons. At their peak, employee publications had a higher circulation than the UK's national newspapers (Heller and Fernandes, 1995). They weren't just functional, they were part of the culture.

In many ways, this was a high point for internal communication. It was creative, purposeful and deeply embedded in everyday working life. But even then, the shift from people to process was clear. The publications looked good, and they sounded good, but they were still largely one-way. Feedback mechanisms were limited and while employees were represented to some degree, they weren't always heard.

Technology was also beginning to reshape the landscape. In the 1950s, British Rail experimented with internal radio (Stanton, 2016). Bell Telephone in the US launched its own corporate network. Ford returned to film, using it to train and motivate staff across global sites. All of these innovations increased reach and consistency, but they also reinforced the idea that internal communication was about broadcast, not dialogue.

A changing world of work

The 1960s and 1970s brought wider social change: civil rights movements, gender equality, growing diversity and new demands for employee voice. The world was changing and so were the expectations placed on employers. Internal communication had to evolve again.

Companies started to recognize that people wanted more than information, they wanted purpose, participation and a sense of agency. This led to the rise of employee engagement strategies, corporate storytelling and the early days of what we now think of as listening programmes.

Some organizations introduced structured feedback loops. Others established employee resource groups. In the US, IBM launched one of the first internal networks for Black employees (Haeyoung, 2022), a move that paved the way for future diversity, equity and inclusion (DE&I) communication. Meanwhile, professional bodies like the IABC (founded in 1970), helped define internal communication as a strategic business discipline, with its own tools, standards and career paths.

There was progress, but there was also a paradox. Even as the profession matured and grew in influence, its centre of gravity continued to shift away from relationships and towards reputation. Away from dialogue and towards distribution. We gained professionalism but we risked losing proximity.

By the end of the 1980s, internal communication had firmly established itself inside large organizations. It had titles, teams, budgets and boards. But it had mostly lost its human touch. Communicators were experts in content, channels and campaigns, but not always in connection. They were skilled in alignment, but not always in advocacy. As the function scaled up, it drifted further from its roots. What began as a discipline grounded in dialogue and people became increasingly focused on reach, consistency and control. And while these qualities were, and still are, important, they are not enough.

What can we learn?

It's clear that internal communication didn't just grow, it changed. IC became more polished, more structured and slick, but it also moved further away from the people it was meant to serve. The tools got sharper, but the connection got weaker. And as communication became more about reach and efficiency, we lost sight of the very thing that made it powerful in the first place: humanity.

KEY TAKEAWAYS

1 **Professionalism came at a cost**: As internal communication matured into a formal business function, it gained structure, influence and credibility but often lost its emotional connection to the people it was meant to serve.

2 **The function grew up and moved away**: IC started to earn its seat at the table, but in doing so, it often became more aligned with corporate priorities than employee needs.

3 **Dialogue gave way to delivery**: One-way channels, mass messaging and top-down storytelling became the norm, diluting the role of listening, empathy and co-creation.

4 **We became experts in the process of IC but not always in connection**: Tools and tactics took centre stage, while trust and humanity faded into the background.

The dawn of the digital era and the rise of the IC expert

The 1980s and 1990s ushered in a technological revolution that fundamentally reshaped internal communication. As computers became commonplace, organizations began shifting from print-based newsletters and bulletin boards to email, intranets and early digital media. Communication became faster, more immediate and more complex. With this shift came a new figure that had emerged inside organizations: the internal communication expert.

These weren't the factory-floor editors or values-driven welfare officers of the past. Internal communication had become a distinct professional discipline. This was a new kind of professional: strategic, trained and increasingly influential. They were building comms functions, managing campaigns, crafting narratives and advising leadership teams. They brought with them a sharper focus on behaviour change, brand alignment and employee engagement.

For the first time, internal communication wasn't just about telling people what was happening. It was about shaping what people should think, feel and do. Drawing on behavioural science, psychology and brand thinking, they created sophisticated campaigns designed to shift mindsets and drive engagement. And as the field professionalized, it developed its own language and models, focused on message clarity, audience segmentation, channel strategy and campaign design.

This was an important step in IC's maturity and a huge leap forward in terms of professional recognition and impact. It gave communicators credibility and helped them influence culture. It brought them to the table. But at the same time, communication was still something we did *to* employees, not always with them. And while it was more insight-driven, it was not yet genuinely people-first. The intent was usually positive – to engage, to align, to motivate. But the mindset was mostly top-down. Employees became audiences and communicators were the experts who knew best. The result? A growing gap between the people creating the comms and the people receiving them.

The age of intranets and information overload

One of the biggest game-changers of the 1990s was the corporate intranet. British Telecom (BT) launched one of the UK's first in 1994, designed to reduce information overload and centralize key resources. Ford followed in 1996 with FordNet, offering a digital hub for company-wide information. IBM introduced Blue Pages, an internal directory to help people connect and collaborate, years ahead of modern-day enterprise social networks.

These platforms marked the beginning of self-service communication. Employees no longer had to wait for printed newsletters or announcements, they could access updates on demand. In theory, this was empowering. In practice, it often led to overwhelm. More channels meant more content and more content meant more noise. And the communicator's job? To cut through it.

As the internet matured, so did the internal communication toolkit. Email, intranets, corporate video, CD-ROMs and webcasts gave communicators a growing range of options. With every new medium came new expectations, from employees and from leaders.

Tesco was one of the first UK retailers to combine digital comms with listening initiatives like employee forums and 'listening groups'. Elsewhere, companies began to experiment with internal surveys, forums and real-time feedback loops. The tone was still top-down, but the desire for two-way dialogue was growing.

By the early 2000s, IC professionals were no longer just crafting newsletters, they were managing ecosystems. Coordinating messaging across channels, aligning tone and voice, segmenting audiences and responding to data. The function had matured into a hybrid of strategist, storyteller and systems thinker. But in becoming more expert, we became more centralized and this meant we were less front-line.

By the late 2000s, the next wave arrived: enterprise social networks. Yammer, Jive and Chatter brought the feel of consumer social media into the workplace complete with likes, comments and shares. Companies like Deloitte and Virgin Media were early adopters. These platforms promised a more democratic, employee-led approach to communication. And in many ways, they delivered. For the first time, people could talk back.

But many organizations still used them as another broadcast channel, pushing content rather than facilitating conversation. The opportunity to decentralize communication was there but it wasn't always taken. Even so, something was shifting. The platforms were simpler, more human and more usable and, importantly, starting to mirror the digital experiences employees had outside of work. The first seeds of the 'consumer-grade IC experience' were being sown.

The 2010s brought the mobile revolution. Smartphones became the default way employees accessed information, especially for those in front-line or hybrid roles. Companies like McDonald's and Airbnb launched custom-built employee apps, offering real-time updates, shift scheduling and internal news on the go.

But not every organization kept up. In many cases, employees took matters into their own hands, using WhatsApp groups to coordinate shifts, share information and build their own informal networks. It was practical, and it was fast. But it highlighted a hard truth: communicators were no longer gatekeepers. The power had shifted. Employees were creating their own comms, often more relevant, timely and authentic than what the comms team was producing. This marked a critical moment in the evolution of internal communication and a challenge to the expert-led model.

A pandemic-led reckoning

Then came Covid-19. Almost overnight, digital communication went from 'important' to 'business critical'. Platforms like Zoom and Teams became the corporate lifeline. IC professionals found themselves at the centre of the crisis, enabling remote work, delivering urgent updates and supporting employee well-being through uncertain times.

For a while, it felt like internal communication had finally earned the strategic status it had long fought for. We weren't just supporting the business, we were holding it together. But as the crisis faded, so did some of that recognition. Many IC teams found themselves under pressure once again with budgets cut, roles removed and relevance questioned. And the old tension resurfaced: were we valued for our strategy or just our execution?

The digital age made us faster, more scalable and more precise. But in many ways, it also made us less human. Employees were drowning in email. Zoom fatigue was real. And despite the explosion of channels, meaningful connection often felt further away than ever. In 2023, the World Health Organization named loneliness a 'pressing health threat' (World Health Organization, 2023) – and the workplace wasn't immune.

Technology gave us reach, but it couldn't replace trust. As internal communicators, we became experts in distribution but not always in dialogue. We learnt how to design campaigns, but not always how to co-create culture. And while our strategies improved, our proximity to employees, their needs, their stories, their lived experiences was still not where it needed to be.

What did we learn?

The digital era elevated internal communication. It brought us status, strategy and a seat at the table. It allowed us to influence culture, shape behaviour and support business transformation in powerful new ways. It gave us tools, teams and targets. But it also pulled us away from the people we set out to serve.

We became more sophisticated but sometimes less empathetic, more expert but less inclusive. We learnt how to speak the language of leaders, but we didn't always stay close enough to the voice of employees. The shift from top-down to two-way communication was embraced, maybe giving us the illusion of being people-centred, but we were still a way off being genuinely people-first.

As we look back on this period, it's clear that the digital revolution gave us more than new channels. It gave us a choice: to use technology to connect or to control. To communicate with employees, not just at them. And to remember that behind every click, comment or campaign is a person.

If we want to keep moving forward, we need to take the best of what 'expert-led' era gave us – the professionalism, the clarity, the strategy – and combine it with something older and more fundamental: a deep, human-centred, people-first approach to communication. Because the tools will keep changing, but the need for connection won't.

KEY TAKEAWAYS

1 **The rise of the expert**: IC evolved into a recognized profession, with trained specialists driving strategic campaigns and shaping culture.

2 **From informing to influencing**: IC shifted from simply telling people what was happening to shaping how they think, feel and behave, often drawing from psychology and behavioural science.

3 **Digital tools transformed the landscape**: Intranets, email, video and enterprise social networks introduced new possibilities and new complexities for how employees connected and engaged.

4 **Employees found their own voice**: With mobile tools and informal channels like WhatsApp, employees began creating their own communication ecosystems, challenging the traditional gatekeeper model.

5 **Tech enabled scale but not always connection**: Communication became faster and more data driven, but not always more human. Loneliness, burnout and disengagement emerged as real risks in the digital workplace.

6 **The pandemic showed our potential**: Covid-19 thrust IC into the spotlight, proving its value as a strategic function, but also revealing how fragile that recognition could be.

It is clear from all this that we have reached a critical point in our professional journey. But what does the future of IC look like and does it even have a future in the age of AI? We asked Jennifer Sproul, Chief Executive of the Institute of Internal Communication, to provide her take.

THE HUMAN-CENTRED FUTURE OF INTERNAL COMMUNICATION
By Jennifer Sproul, CEO of the Institute of Internal Communication

Like all professions seeking to deliver stakeholder value in the 2020s, internal communication is at a crossroads.

The range of global, societal, environmental, political and economic forces now in play is unprecedented. There is no playbook for this level of complexity, and if only one thing is certain, it's that all organizations are under intense pressure to evolve and adapt.

Covid-19, lockdowns and social distancing were swiftly followed by worldwide supply-chain issues, inflation and associated cost-of-living crises, extreme weather events and wars in both Ukraine and Gaza. International relations are more fraught than they have been in decades.

In tandem, a burgeoning mental health crisis, escalating inequality, shifting attitudes towards work, a rise in demand for more flexible ways of working and the arrival of workplace AI have fuelled a litany of challenge for organizational leaders who are desperate to resume some semblance of stability and normality.

The pace of change in business today is breathtaking. There's scarcely a profession or vocation that doesn't need to upskill. Continuous disruption is the new normal.

Much contemporary business journalism focuses on the purported efficiencies AI will bring. This is understandable. As far back as 2017, PwC estimated AI had the potential to add $15.7 (ca. £11.7) trillion to the global economy by 2030 (PwC, 2018).

But as workplaces of all denominations become increasingly data-driven and digitized, far less attention is paid to the human skills, behaviours and attitudes that will underpin successful wholesale transformation and organizational agility. These skills – traditionally sidelined as 'soft' – are now crucial for ongoing operating resilience.

Exploring the future of internal communication

The Institute of Internal Communication is the only professional body dedicated solely to internal communication.

Since 2019, it has invested in future of work analysis to better understand the opportunity and likely skills and role evolution for internal communicators.

Understanding the trends reshaping how work gets done is the starting block for all successful organizational futureproofing. The interplay between the many forces disrupting 'business as usual' must be factored into any strategic planning.

For internal communicators, developing an appreciation of what's on the minds of their most senior stakeholders – their C-suite colleagues – is key. Building relationships and rapport and developing situational awareness – the ability to see and make sense of the operating environment as it changes around them – is a surefire way of delivering long-term strategic value. This, in turn, will ensure the ongoing allocation of budgetary and other resources. Only when internal communication is prioritized as mission-critical can the profession deliver robust communication strategies that meet the increasingly divergent needs of all stakeholders.

As the working world embraces the gains offered by big data and data analytics, delicate balance is required. Humans use story to make sense of the world, and this is never truer as our lives become increasingly data-driven.

Organizations seeking to thrive in the coming years are becoming thoroughly acquainted with human psychology and, in particular, the art and science of communication, engagement and motivation. This presents enormous opportunity for internal communicators who are expertly placed to take a centre-stage role.

Moving beyond traditional internal communication

As internal communication evolves, we anticipate a significant expansion of scope for the profession. Some of the current internal comms remit will remain essential for ongoing operating stability. This includes, of course, those activities that prioritize DEI, engagement and culture and access to good work.

Alongside, the opportunity generative AI (Gen AI) presents for internal communication is vast. As the IoIC identified in its AI Ethics Charter, internal communicators are ideally situated to help colleagues in all functions of business uphold quality standards to make sure AI adoption yields optimal benefits for all stakeholders.

But perhaps more importantly, internal communication must expand its focus to prioritize the human experiences that build alignment, community and cohesion. In fast-paced and fluid work futures, this is key.

Gallup's latest State of the Global Workplace report shows deteriorating engagement, most pointedly among those working in management or supervisory roles (Gallup, 2024). Given the influence of managers over the rest of the workforce, it's of utmost importance that manager engagement is prioritized as a business-critical issue.

The IoIC is committed to maintaining a relevant and up-to-date profession map (IoIC, ndb) and standards for internal communicators. Continuous review of the map has identified various areas of skills development for those looking to futureproof their internal comms careers.

New areas of focus for internal communication

Internal communication originated in the 19th century as a means to build trust and community within organizations by way of company newsletters, magazines and social activities. Today's tumultuous operating landscape once again lays bare the need for organizations to prioritize human connection and community.

Edelman's 2025 Trust Barometer reveals the extent of people's concerns about job security and highlights an unprecedented global decline in employer trust (Edelman, 2025). The IoIC's own annual IC Index supports this, showing just how precarious trust at work has become (IoIC, nda).

Looking forward, internal communication must focus far more on the experiences that underpin human relationship and connection at work. Its remit will be to create the 'emotional glue' that sustains sociality, loyalty, goodwill and mutuality between people wherever they are working.

Other areas for internal communicators to evolve their skills and expertise include:

- **Business acumen**: Understanding the broader operating context to enhance C-suite trust and advocacy for internal communication.
- **Business psychology**: Developing a deep interest in why people behave the way they do at work to improve colleague engagement.
- **Empathy**: Putting oneself in the shoes of others to build compassion and enhance connection and community.
- **Influencing**: Leveraging interpersonal relationships to build consensus and alignment around strategic goals.
- **Active listening**: Applying undivided attention to verbal and non-verbal communication to deepen understanding of the meaning others are trying to convey.
- **Scenario planning**: Using the art of narrative to explore alternative plausible futures with colleagues, so as to mitigate risk and leverage opportunity.
- **Critical thinking**: Making sense of, synthesizing and applying information obtained through diverse activities including reading, listening, observation and reflection.
- **Curiosity**: Appreciating knowledge is infinite and remaining open to finding out more about a topic, person or situation.
- **Editorial oversight**: Helping colleagues understand the limitations of Gen AI and review synthetically generated documentation to maintain quality and professionalism.

There is no aspect of business today that is immune from the urgent need to adapt.

In the past, organizations could rely on organizational development experts to foresee and map how skills, roles, departments and business units might evolve. This worked when operating environments were more stable. Now, too much change is happening everywhere and all at once for skills progression to happen in a structured, linear and organized fashion.

This inevitably impacts how we conceive of career pathways. Rather than career ladders, we must think in terms of what Helen Tupper and Sarah Ellis have defined as 'squiggly careers' (Amazing If, nd).

As workplace collaboration expert Harold Jarche has written, the only viable route forward in such fast-paced and complex workplaces is for learning to take place socially and 'in the flow of work' (Jarche, 2020).

This requires internal communicators to think about skills development differently. While, of course, qualifications and structured training will continue to provide credibility, specialist skills and secure foundations from which to springboard, career futureproofing also now depends on a growth mindset, continuous learning and the willingness to participate in communities of practice. In such settings, professionals convene to share and compare notes on their profession, creating good practice as it evolves.

This is, we believe, the future of work. And of course, how we communicate with one another in these high-octane futures is key to our organizations' ability to evolve and regenerate.

The era of experience

We couldn't agree more and we will expand on many of these points as we progress through this book. Internal communication has always been shaped by the times. From factory floor bulletins to global digital platforms, we've evolved alongside society, technology and the changing world of work. Over the past 150 years, we've seen the rise and fall of print, the digital boom and the birth of the IC profession. And now, the dawn of AI era. But with every leap forward, something has quietly slipped through our fingers, that is our closeness to employees.

What began as a human-centric craft, designed to connect, include and support, has too often become a corporate function of cascade comms, content management and channel optimization. In climbing the ladder and gaining professional status, we've somehow lost touch with the people we set out to serve.

Now, a new wave is crashing in. AI is rapidly transforming what we can do, and what we no longer need to do. Content creation, personalization, planning, research, distribution, these are all squarely in the AI wheelhouse. And it's just getting started.

We're not being alarmist, we're being honest. If we define our value by how efficiently we send messages, manage channels or craft comms plans, we risk becoming irrelevant. These are the tasks AI already excels at and soon will outperform us in. So we have to ask the hard question, what is our core value in the era of AI?

This is not the end of internal communication but the beginning of a new era, where our role is no longer just to inform, but to inspire. Not just to communicate, but to design and deliver brilliant communication experiences.

Because while AI can optimize a message, it cannot create meaning. It can replicate tone, but not trust. It can mimic empathy, but it cannot feel. That's where we come in. The future of internal communication isn't about fighting AI. It's about embracing it and focusing on what it can't do. And what it can't do is be human.

Our value now lies in something far more meaningful than message control or campaign execution. It lies in designing communication experiences that feel intuitive, personal and human, experiences employees actually want to engage with. That means taking our cue from the outside world, where consumer-grade experiences are the norm.

We expect clarity, simplicity and responsiveness in the apps, services and brands we use every day. Why should communication at work be any different? As IC professionals, we have a unique opportunity and responsibility to create this same quality of experience inside our organizations. To move beyond content calendars and cascade plans, and start shaping communication that's as seamless, relevant and engaging as anything employees encounter outside of work.

This is our moment to reposition internal communication not just as a function, but as an experience. One that connects people, builds culture and drives performance. But to truly design and deliver this next-generation IC experience, we need to re-centre our work around people; their needs, their expectations, their lives. That's where People-First Internal Communication comes in.

It's not a nostalgic return to the past, but a bold leap forward, using all the power of AI, technology and behavioural insight but anchored in empathy, trust and human connection. So let's use AI to free us up for what really matters: listening deeply, designing intentionally and creating workplaces where people feel they belong. This is our moment – our chance to reset.

We can go back to being the voice of the organization. Or we can step up to be the voice *for* employees.

We can continue to be custodians of content. Or we can become architects of culture.

We can keep chasing the next comms tool. Or we can build the future of work around trust, empathy and shared humanity.

CHAPTER IN SUMMARY

- **AI is changing everything**: From planning and personalization to content creation and analytics, AI is automating many core IC tasks and will only accelerate.

- **Human connection is our edge**: While AI handles the mechanics, only we can foster trust, belonging and a sense of shared purpose.

- **The future is experience-led**: Internal communication is no longer just a function, it's a workplace experience. And employees expect it to be consumer-grade: seamless, personal, intuitive and human.

- **People-first is the way forward**: To design great experiences, we must centre on people – not processes, platforms or performance metrics.

- **We're not here to fight AI**: We're here to do what it can't – to lead with empathy, listen deeply, co-create culture and make work feel more meaningful for everyone.

Welcome to the next era of IC, we call it People-First Internal Communication and we're excited to share it with you.

References

Amazing If (nd) *Books*, Amazing If, www.amazingif.com/books (archived at https://perma.cc/5LS4-Q2PL)

Edelman (2025) 2025 Edelman Trust Barometer, Edelman, www.edelman.com/trust/2025/trust-barometer (archived at https://perma.cc/M687-PQQN)

Gallup (2024) State of the Global Workplace 2024: Understanding employees, informing leaders, Gallup, www.gallup.com/workplace/349484/state-of-the-global-workplace.aspx (archived at https://perma.cc/F3E4-4TG6)

Grant, M (1994) *Propaganda and the Role of the State in Inter-war Britain*, Clarendon Press, Oxford

Haeyoung, A (2022) The activist legacy of the IBM Black Workers Alliance, *WIRED*, www.wired.com/story/tech-organizing-labor-ibm-history (archived at https://perma.cc/S87C-2WQ9)

Heller, M (2008) Company magazines 1880–1940: An overview, *Management & Organizational History*, 3 (3–4), 179–96

Heller, S and Fernandes, T (1995), *Magazines: Inside & out*, Rockport Publishers, New York

Institute of Internal Communication (nda) IC Index: Exploring the state of internal communication, IoIC, www.ioic.org.uk/knowledge-hub/thought-leadership-research/ic-index.html (archived at https://perma.cc/CC6M-EDAD)

Institute of Internal Communication (nd) IoIC profession map, IoIC, www.ioic.org.uk/learn-develop/the-profession-map.html (archived at https://perma.cc/B46J-DZW8)

Jarche, H (2020) Learning in the flow of work, 2 February, jarche.com/2020/02/
learning-in-the-flow-of-work (archived at https://perma.cc/3W3A-TQFU)

PwC (2018) AI predictions: 8 insights to shape business strategy, PwC, www.pwc.
com/gx/en/issues/artificial-intelligence/publications/artificial-intelligence-study.
html (archived at https://perma.cc/D46H-76TS)

Roberts, D (1995) *Paternalism in Early Victorian England*, Routledge, London

Ruck, K and Yaxley, H (2013) Tracking the rise and rise of internal communication
from the 1980s, *International History of Public Relations Conference*,
Bournemouth University, June, www.researchgate.net/publication/275657118_
Tracking_the_rise_and_rise_of_internal_communication_from_the_1980s
(archived at https://perma.cc/69XK-2UWT)

Stanton, P (2016) Farewell to the NRN, *Rail Engineer*, www.railengineer.co.uk/
farewell-to-the-nrn (archived at https://perma.cc/3SXN-RA5P)

Stewart, P W (2014) Henry Ford: Movie mogul? *Prologue Magazine*, 46 (4),
www.archives.gov/publications/prologue/2014/winter/ford-film (archived at
https://perma.cc/VX6E-WSEZ)

World Health Organization (2023) WHO launches commission to foster social
connection, 15 November, www.who.int/news/item/15-11-2023-who-launches-
commission-to-foster-social-connection (archived at https://perma.cc/G4QG-QUED)

02

What is People-First Internal Communication and why do we need it?

The wake-up call

The old models of internal communication (IC) are no longer fit for purpose. We've had decades to prove our worth, but the evidence we'll share in this chapter clearly shows that we're still fighting the same issues. We're grappling with the same challenges: a lack of influence, disengaged employees, information overload, managers who struggle to communicate effectively and more. We might have hoped that more tools, channels or campaigns would move the needle, but it's clear this is not the case.

If we're honest, IC has never quite been able to realize its full potential, but we believe this is about to change.

There's a revolution happening in work. Employees expect more, they want a consumer-grade experience. And AI is rewriting the rules. But now is our moment; this is not a gentle nudge to evolve but an ultimatum: evolve or die.

If we don't radically reimagine how we communicate with our people, if we keep treating them as 'audiences' instead of human beings, our profession will become irrelevant. We have the tools, evidence and momentum to build something better, to stop doing communication to employees and start doing it *with* them. It's time to ditch the old ways of working and design truly human communication experiences. It's time to lead.

The good news? There is a better way. One that puts people, not processes, platforms or even PowerPoint, at the centre of everything. It's called People-First Internal Communication.

This chapter is where it begins.

We'll expose why traditional internal communication is failing, still rooted in broadcast thinking and expert-led control, while the world around us has radically changed. We'll show how internal communication has struggled to evolve, stuck in outdated patterns despite decades of effort and countless engagement initiatives. And we'll ask the tough question: what's really stopping us from fulfilling our potential?

But more importantly, we'll set out a bold new path forward.

We'll introduce People-First Internal Communication, a transformative, experience-led approach that puts empathy, co-creation and connection at the heart of everything we do. We'll share a powerful model that redefines the role of IC in the age of AI and rising employee expectations. And throughout the rest of this book, we'll show you how to apply it.

You'll discover how a shift in mindset, methods and tools can move IC from being seen as a functional service to a strategic force, driving trust, engagement, innovation and culture from the inside out. By the end of this chapter, one thing should be clear: the time for small changes is over. The world of work is changing fast and so must we. This is your opportunity to lead that change, to redefine the future of internal communication and to reclaim your role as a catalyst for meaningful, human connection at work.

A profession in crisis: an industry stuck on repeat

As authors of this book, between us, we have spent nearly 60 years working in the IC and employee engagement space – it's our life's work. During this time, we have both been lucky enough to work with some incredible leaders and truly progressive organizations. We've been part of multi-award-winning teams, have consulted with senior leaders in some of the world's biggest businesses, we've led epic campaigns, undertaken groundbreaking research and been recognized by our peers. But somewhere along the way we fell out of love with IC, growing increasingly frustrated with the profession. Let us explain.

As we discovered in Chapter 1, IC started out as a human-centred endeavour, developed by the most visionary and principled leaders of the day to make their world of work better. But this early human-centred approach soon made way for channels, content and process. Over the years, while the channels and job titles may have changed, the overall approach has moved on very little. IC has lost its way. The reality is many organizations still rely on communication models developed in the early 20th century. At worst, hierarchical, command-and-control approaches treat communication as a one-way street. Leaders speak, employees listen and feedback loops often fall short of driving any real change. At best, expert-led approaches seek to inspire behaviour change but often fall short despite being well-intentioned.

Today's 'head of internal comms and engagement' may be using e-newsletters, apps and enterprise social networks, but much of what they do remains similar to the industrial editors of yesteryear. In fact, we'd argue that the proliferation of channels has made the communication experience *worse* for employees, not better, contributing to the noise and clutter so many now complain about. The truth is job titles and shiny new tools have not altered the fundamentals. Much of what we currently do as professionals is long past its sell by date. We may think we are operating in a progressive, human-centred way, but the reality does not reflect that.

A look at Gallagher's annual State of the Sector survey, a piece of research originated by one of the authors and now in its 17th year, shows that many of the same issues remain today as they did at the turn of the millennium. Nearly two decades later, we still find a lack influence in the boardroom, issues with line manager comms capabilities, restrictive budgets and poor leadership. While other themes have emerged more recently, such as change fatigue and the increasing impact of technology, these key challenges have remained stubbornly persistent. It's disappointing to see that in the 2024 *State of the Sector* report, 72 per cent of IC professionals said 'line managers not communicating effectively' remains a top challenge (Arthur J Gallagher & Co, 2024). Exactly the same issue was highlighted in the very first version of the survey nearly two decades ago. Despite the evolution in tools, the profession is stuck on repeat.

According to the IoIC's *Voice of the Profession* 2023 report, just 38 per cent of IC professionals feel they are 'influencing strategic decisions'. And just 12 per cent feel their function is 'well understood' by senior stakeholders. This reflects a profession that is not only underperforming, but often misunderstood (The Institute of Internal Communication, 2023).

There's plenty of evidence that builds a picture of an unperforming profession. IBM's global study *Making Change Work* (2008) states that only 41 per cent of change initiatives fully succeed, while 59 per cent either underperform or fail outright, with poor communication being cited as a major contributor (IBM Global Business Services, 2008, p 10).

The current way we do IC is also incredibly time-consuming, and very often it simply adds to the noise. During our years of running focus groups and auditing the internal communications of organizations all around the world, one of the most consistent themes has been a plea from employees for less, not more. We are overwhelming our people, with multiple channels to contend with, more and more information to attend to. According to Cross et al (2023), 38 per cent of employees say they receive an 'excessive' volume of communications at their organization.

The failure of traditional internal communication is also evident in employee engagement statistics. According to Gallup's *State of the Global Workplace 2024* report, global employee engagement dropped to just 21 per cent, marking only the second decline in the past 12 years. And this isn't just an HR problem, it's a communication problem. One of the key drivers of engagement, according to Gallup, is whether employees feel informed, connected to purpose and aligned with leadership; all outcomes internal communication can directly influence. When IC fails to create emotional connection, clarity of direction and space for authentic employee voice, it undermines trust and contributes to the disengagement crisis. In short: you can't have engagement without communication that works.

Another issue is that too often we treat employees as audience not actors. Audience is probably the most over used (and abused) word in the IC lexicon, and its use says a lot about how we currently operate. An audience is a group of people who gather to watch a performance or who consume content. It's a term borrowed from the worlds of theatre, TV, film and marketing, with their focus on entertainment, persuasion, telling and selling. Its use reinforces the idea that internal communication is about broadcasting to the masses. And it suggests that employees are simple homogenous groups we can easily target, rather than complex individuals, each with their own motivations, needs and wants.

When you look at the absence of progression and growth with the IC profession, it's clear something needs to change. The picture painted above is a big part of the reason we (the authors) became frustrated with IC. But no more, because we believe we have a way forwards – this is where People-First Internal Communication comes in.

This chapter is your invitation to step into a new story, one where IC is not just a function, but a force. One where empathy replaces assumption. Where communication is designed *with* people, not simply delivered *to* them. Where connection becomes the measure of success. Because this isn't about saving IC, it's about transforming it, so it can finally become what it was always meant to be: a catalyst for trust, energy and change at the heart of every organization.

The burning platform: why IC must evolve now

The world of work is changing, and employees today have far greater expectations for their experience at work than they did some 20 years ago. Gallup talk about employees as now being the 'consumers of the workplace':

> Today's employee is a consumer of the workplace. Employees are no longer satisfied with clocking in and out and receiving a paycheck. They are looking for meaning in their work, a supportive, collaborative environment, and an employer that can match the lifestyle they want. (Gallup, 2018)

We believe this is a mindset shift we, as internal communicators, must embrace to ensure we stay relevant. Employees today expect more than information; they want meaning, clarity and empathy. In short, they want communication that feels as good as the best consumer experiences they have outside of work on Netflix, Spotify and TikTok.

They want to be heard, involved and inspired, not just informed. And yet, too often still, internal communication operates in a top-down, channel-driven and often broadcast mode. We measure clicks and fixate on outputs. We revert to tell and sell despite our best intentions. But what if our role isn't to send more? What if our role is to design better? This is where the opportunity lies, by leaning into what makes us uniquely human.

We're not just comms experts anymore. We believe IC pros must become **experience designers.** The discipline of human-centred design can give us the tools to do just this. It means putting employees, not platforms or processes, at the heart of every communication moment. It means using empathy to uncover what people really need. It means co-creating communication journeys that feel personalized, intuitive and emotionally resonant. This is the shift from communication as output to communication as experience.

But it's not just about the need to deliver consumer-grade IC experiences. AI is one of the main catalysts for the transformation of work we are now experiencing. Between 2022 and 2025, the adoption of Gen AI has seen remarkable growth. According to McKinsey & Company (2025), AI adoption by organizations increased from 55 per cent in 2023 to 78 per cent in 2024. Meanwhile, a Pew Research Center (2025) survey found that about one in six US workers (16 per cent) reported that at least some of their work is currently done with AI, although this work is often below the radar rather than employer-sanctioned.

For IC, AI isn't on the horizon, it's already embedded in the tools we use every day. From Microsoft Copilot to GrammarlyGO and ChatGPT, AI is reshaping the way work gets done.

At the time of writing this book, we're only just beginning to understand the scale of this change. For years, IC pros have worked hard to establish themselves as the go-to expert, but the world is changing and fast. Let's take a look at some examples of what AI can do:

- Draft clear, concise and engaging internal communications at scale.
- Develop a comms plan in seconds.
- Write an engaging CEO script in the correct tone of voice.
- Personalize messaging to different employee segments, roles or locations.
- Summarize employee sentiment in real time.
- Automate channel scheduling.

You might be asking 'where does that leave me?' But before you lose all hope, here's the transformative opportunity AI presents to IC. AI will never be truly human-centred; it will never replace skills such as curiosity, empathy and creativity. AI can optimize processes, but it can't create connection. The future isn't about competing with AI; it's about working with AI to design and deliver the kind of internal comms we used to dream about, if only we had the time and budgets! AI can free us up to:

- Ensure communications reflect diverse employee experiences and needs.
- Develop communications that authentically reflect organizational values and foster trust.
- Coach leaders to communicate with empathy, emotional intelligence and authenticity.

Yes AI can write messages, but it can't build meaning. While AI is brilliant at automating tasks and optimizing outputs, it lacks one thing IC cannot survive without: humanity. It can draft a leadership blog post, but it might struggle to make it feel authentic. It can summarize employee feedback, but it can't feel the nuance of trust breaking down. It can push out updates, but it can't create a sense of belonging. AI can be your co-writer, your insights analyst, your production assistant, but it will never be your connector. That's your superpower as an IC pro and it's never been more needed.

Which is why we believe that the future of the IC profession is a human-centred, people-first approach – because it's not only right for our people, but it ensures the longevity of the IC profession. The World Economic Forum's Future of Jobs Report states the most in-demand skills are shifting from technical knowledge to human-centred capabilities. The question isn't if AI will change work, it's how we prepare ourselves, and we'll explore this further in later chapters.

We know from our own research, The EX Report 2024, that AI for IC is a growing area of interest for practitioners (The EX Space, 2024). We heard loud and clear that practitioners are increasingly prioritizing the use of AI to gather and analyse actionable insights for employee voice. In addition, the IOIC has published a white paper, 'AI and the Future of IC', which features insights from leading experts in internal communication across diverse sectors. The paper emphasizes the transformative potential of AI in internal communication.

And there's no shortage of IC commentators sharing views on how AI is going to change the face of IC as we know it. For example, Staffbase highlights how AI can help manage everyday communication challenges while boosting employee engagement with targeted, relevant communications. They outline the ways AI can assist, such as content creation, personalized comms, language translation, data analysis, chatbots and workflow automation. A blog post from Cleary, meanwhile, discusses the dual-edged nature of AI in internal communications, citing a significant and positive impact on content creation but also highlighting the need for ethical considerations. Their blog mentions that 68 per cent of communicators believe AI will have a significant impact on internal communications in the next five years.

The extent to which AI impacts our day-to-day work remains to be seen, but what is clear is that we will all need to learn to partner with the bots. As Monique Zytnik, author of *Internal Communication in the Age of Artificial Intelligence*, says: 'The most successful of us in communication roles will need to become the puppet masters of whatever the current AI platforms offer and be able to work with them effectively' (2024, p 45).

We believe that the rise of AI, and the shift in employee expectations, aren't a threat but a much-needed turning point. We now have a chance to reposition internal communication as a vital, strategic force in shaping employee experience, culture and trust.

To do that, we must:

- Embrace AI, not as a threat but as a tool to elevate our work.
- Use human-centred design to shape communication experiences that connect and inspire.
- Shift our identity from experts and broadcasters to facilitators and co-creators.

In the following pages you'll learn what People-First IC means, why it matters now more than ever, and throughout the rest of the book you'll discover how you can build the mindset, skills and tools to lead the change and the future of our profession. Because one thing is certain: if we don't change how we do internal communication, someone or something else will. This may sound like hyperbole, but our view is that this is a pivotal moment for our profession. If we do not reimagine the role and contribution of IC to organizational success, and reinvent ourselves as professionals, then internal communication, at least how we currently conceive it, will likely face a quick and painful death.

AGENTIC AI

The next disruption for internal communication

Gartner (2024) predicts that 33 per cent of enterprise software applications will include agentic AI by 2028. So far, much of the conversation around AI in IC has focused on tools that assist with content creation, personalization and automation. But the next wave is already here: agentic AI.

Agentic AI refers to systems that don't just respond to prompts; they act with autonomy. These agents can plan, execute tasks, monitor outcomes and adjust their actions based on feedback and all without constant human direction.

In internal communication, this means AI agents could soon:

- Monitor sentiment trends and automatically flag risk areas to leaders.

- Identify gaps in communication flow and generate real-time content to address them.

- Personalize entire employee comms journeys based on role, behaviour or engagement data.

- Orchestrate omnichannel campaigns, optimizing timing and format based on employee habits.

- Even facilitate 1:1 nudges for managers; for example, 'It's been 10 days since your team last heard from you. Here's a personalized update suggestion.'

These aren't hypotheticals. Agentic systems are already being piloted in marketing, operations and customer experience. The implications for IC are profound. We are moving beyond automation into orchestration, where AI not only drafts comms but also decides what, when, to whom and *why* based on live data.

This presents big opportunities and even bigger questions. If AI agents can manage campaigns, channels and optimize messaging in real time, what becomes the role of the IC professional?

The answer lies in design and direction. While agents can execute, they still need a human-centred vision to execute toward. That's where People-First IC comes in. The future IC pro won't just manage outputs, they'll architect experiences. They'll guide the strategy, set the ethical guardrails, define what 'good' looks like and ensure that IC remains emotionally intelligent, trustworthy and culturally resonant. The rise of AI agents won't replace us, but it will redefine our role; IC pros will become curators, designers, coaches and protectors of what makes communication human.

Defining 'People-First IC'

Before we set out to define People-First Internal Communication, let's first clarify what it is not:

- A new communication strategy: This isn't about tweaking existing methods and approaches but rather fundamentally rethinking the role and professional practice of IC.

- A rebadging of employee experience: This isn't a rebranding of employee experience (EX), though it does utilize some of the powerful tools and techniques already used by pioneering practitioners in this space.

- About generating more or richer content: This isn't about crafting content in a different way or utilizing the power of AI to personalize material but about radically re-engineering how we interact with employees, emphasizing connection over content.

- About introducing new channels: The focus isn't on the methods of communication but the very nature of communication and interaction inside the organization.

- Improved audience segmentation: This isn't about 'slicing and dicing' your audience, though it does rely on deeper insight and developing empathy with employees.

People-First Internal Communication is an employee-centred, experience-driven approach to IC that prioritizes human connection and emotional engagement over information delivery. It transforms internal communication into an interactive, co-created and highly personalized experience.

Let's break that down into its core components:

- **Employee-centred** means internal communication that is designed with the needs, perspectives and experiences of employees at its heart. It doesn't treat employees as vague groups or discreet 'audience segments' but as individuals, each with their own unique needs, wants and expectations. It starts with empathy, involving a deep understanding of what makes people tick. These insights are gathered through listening, feedback, input and dialogue. It aims to enrich their experience of work and empower people to be their very best, treating them as human beings, rather than human resource.

- **Experience-driven** means seeing the communication experience as an integral and central part of the wider employee experience. Instead of focusing on delivering information, it considers how communication makes employees feel and how it impacts their day-to-day work and behaviours. It elevates the moments that matter for them, including key stages of the employee life cycle like onboarding, career development and even exiting the organization. And it supports the 'everyday experience'. It recognizes that emotions play a key role in shaping and defining experiences, giving them personal meaning and making them more impactful and memorable. It is consistent and integrated across multiple touchpoints. It utilizes storytelling as a powerful means to capture and convey emotions and connect employees with the organization's purpose and values. An experience-driven approach to IC isn't just functional; it makes employees feel valued, informed, involved and connected.

- Prioritizing **human connection** over information delivery means shifting the focus from transmitting information to fostering meaningful human relationships. This creates 'social glue' by connecting employees, building trust and creating a sense of belonging for employees. Instead of viewing internal communication as one-way, or even a two-way flow of information, facts and updates, it emphasizes empathy, dialogue and emotional engagement across the organization. It recognizes that how people feel about their work, their colleagues and their organization is just as important as the information they receive. It is conversational, authentic, inclusive and social. It goes beyond ensuring employees know what's happening, to ensuring they understand why it matters, what it means for them personally and how they can best support it.

- People-First IC is **transformational** rather than transactional. It has a long-term outlook and is focused on shaping culture, driving change, unlocking engagement and creating the climate for innovation. It delivers behavioural change by creating emotional connection and encouraging employee participation. Think actors, not audiences. It drives organizational performance and delivers improvements across a wide range of organizational outcomes, from productivity to profitability.

- **Interactivity and co-creation** are at the heart of People-First IC – this is IC done *with* rather than *to* employees. Employees are actively involved in shaping *their* desired communication experience, rather than it being dictated by senior leaders and expert communicators. It's built on a collaborative process where employees provide input and help test ideas, give honest feedback and engage in a dynamic dialogue, rather than being passive recipients of information. This 'co-created' approach builds a sense of ownership, trust and engagement and reinforces a psychological safety.

Figure 2.1 summarizes what we see as the key differences between People-First IC and traditional IC.

FIGURE 2.1 Traditional IC versus People-First IC

Traditional IC	People-First IC
Expert-led	Employee-led
Internal communicator as expert	Internal communicator as facilitator
Transactional	Transformational
Employees as audience	Employees as actors
Information	Emotions
Segmentation	Personalization
Leadership-led	Employee-centred
Shaped by IC experts	Facilitated by IC experts, shaped by employees
Communication as output	Communication as experience
Telling and selling	Engaging
Information distribution	Meaningful interaction
Employees feeling informed	Employees feeling involved
Engagement as metric/score	Engagement as one of many positive outcomes

To switch to People-First IC requires a fairly radical reimagining of our profession, and we recognize that this could be a big leap for some practitioners. But we believe that leap is vital. As AI begins to disrupt our world of work, there's a limited window of opportunity to reshape IC, recalibrate our careers and reinvigorate our value.

For many years, building a career in IC relied on being a deep subject matter expert. The best practitioners were the go-to people when challenges arose: the intranet experts, the killer copywriters, the events gurus, the change experts. But AI is already changing the game. If the bots can draft copy, craft comms plans, manage channels and personalize content, what's left for us? How can we ensure we stay relevant and valued into the future? Better still, how can we reposition ourselves at the heart of the reinvention of work?

The answer lies in human-centred design. Harvard Business School describe human-centred design as: 'A problem-solving technique that puts real people at the centre of the development process, enabling you to create products and services that resonate and are tailored to your audience's needs' (Harvard Business School Online, 2020).

This is an approach that focuses on designing solutions based on the needs, behaviours and experiences of the people who will use them. Its goal is to create products, services and systems that are useful, usable and meaningful to users, by directly involving them in shaping those solutions. And it sits at the very heart of People-First IC.

WHAT CAN WE LEARN FROM THE MARKETERS?

Like us, you'll no doubt be fairly sceptical about the world of marketing and the parallels between it and what we do as internal communicators. We have to confess that, for much of our careers we saw marketing as a lesser discipline, and we would do our level best to distance ourselves from what 'they' did. Marketing is selling and persuasion, right? Well yes and no. Recently we've had something of an epiphany, and we now believe there's a huge amount we can learn from our marketer cousins. Let us explain.

Over the past 30 or so years, marketing has undergone a complete transformation. It has evolved from being primarily sales-driven, to a practice that is genuinely customer-centric, with an emphasis on relationship building and enhancing customer experience. This shift has been enabled by changes in technology, consumer behaviour and expectations, and, of course, market dynamics.

In the 1990s, when we first entered the world of work, marketing was essentially about sales. It was heavily focused on advertising and promotion, typically through mass media like TV, radio, print and more targeted direct mail. Its primary goal was to drive sales volumes and the 'four Ps' of the marketing mix – product, price, place, promotion – were king. Customer feedback was passive – the more enlightened organizations (and those that could afford it) conducted occasional market research, mostly consumer polls and surveys.

Around the turn of the millennium, we began to see the rise of digital marketing and personalization. The e-commerce boom had begun, the internet was fuelling the rapid growth of new businesses like Amazon and eBay, and we moved into more of a data-driven era. Online marketing and search engine optimization (SEO) became critical in driving traffic and visibility, customer relationship management (CRM) systems emerged to enable brands to track customer interactions and build more targeted campaigns. The rise of digital delivered data by the bucketload, and marketers began using web analytics and customer data to more accurately segment audiences and personalize content.

The 2010s saw the emergence of customer experience (CX) as a field, recognizing that customer relationships are multi-faceted, and every interaction shapes their perceptions of a brand or business. This was the era of social media, with platforms like Twitter, Facebook and Instagram becoming marketing machines. Marketers talked of 'omnichannel experiences' as consumers began demanding a more seamless experience across digital and physical touchpoints. There was a refocusing on content and inbound marketing, as brands moved from pushing product to creating connection with consumers through blogs, videos and social content. The rise of the smartphone forced marketers to optimize for mobile and use push notifications and apps to drive direct engagement. And the age of the influencer was ushered in as brands sought to create deeper, more authentic brand associations through people.

As we progress through the 2020s, we are very much in the era of customer centricity, where experience is the key differentiator. Brands now compete on CX more than they do on product or price. AI is automating the work of marketers through AI-based tools like chatbots, predictive analysis and hyper-personalized recommendations. Engagement happens increasingly in real time. At the same time there's been a shift towards purpose-driven marketing, as consumers increasingly expect brands to align with social and environmental causes, and community building through user-generated content (think TikTok).

Over the course of three decades, marketing has transformed from a one-way sales-driven model to a dynamic, customer-centric approach focused on delivering long-term value through relationships. While selling remains an important goal, customer experience (CX) has become the foundation of modern marketing success. The brands that get this right are driving customer engagement, loyalty and market advantage.

When you think about it, the parallels between the evolution of marketing and our own professional journey as internal communicators are quite profound. Internal comms is on a similar trajectory. We have seen the rise of the employee advocacy and activism – information has empowered employees and given them more choice and higher expectations, Tools like Glassdoor, the Tripadvisor of employment, have driven transparency, making the reality of the workplace visible to all. We have seen the emergence of the employee experience movement, though take-up has been slow.

Technology has driven massive shifts in what we can do and how we do it, from personalization to using data to better understand our people and demonstrate our impact. Like the marketers, we have realized that information sharing is no longer enough – we need to build deep emotional connections through positive experiences and superlative storytelling. We now appreciate the vital importance of listening, employee voice and psychological safety.

There are downsides to all this, of course. In a world of big data, it's easy to lose sight of the human being we're seeking to engage – an over-reliance on marketing automation, for instance, can create distance rather than connection. In an era when algorithms guide so much of what we consume, creativity can take the back seat. The same goes for automated internal comms.

The lure of AI is obvious, and the marketers have been quick to utilize this technology to deliver more personalized content – though it often lacks authenticity, which over time can erode trust. But what the marketers have done brilliantly is demonstrate value through precise measurement and evaluation – an area we internal communicators still struggle with. Marketing is hardwired to revenue and that alone is guaranteed to make senior leaders sit up and listen!

With hindsight we feel we can learn an enormous amount from the successes and mistakes of our early-adopter cousins. Indeed, we would argue that we need to think much more like marketers – viewing work as a product to be designed for customers (employees) who have real choices, with their input, taking a long-term, relationship-based approach, focusing on value creation and outcomes, and using technology to deepen human connection.

All this is at the heart of what we mean by a 'consumer-grade experience' – employees are now demanding the same quality of experience they are used to outside work. From the ease with which we can interact with our favourite brands, to our experience listening to music or watching a film on our mobile devices, from how we consume news, to how we shop, our experiences outside work increasingly influence what we expect as employees.

People-First IC means getting to know your people

The early days of IC laid the foundations for taking a people-first approach. In Chapter 1, we shared stories from companies like Cadbury and Rowntree, who placed their people at the heart of their approach. However, the evolution of IC has relegated this focus and instead turned up the dial on IC process, for example, channels and messages, with a cursory mention of the 'audience'. We have taken some inspiration from Herzberg's hygiene-motivation model (Herzberg et al, 1959) to help understand why this might be the case and what we can do about it.

Herzberg first developed his model in 1959, and in summary it makes the distinction between what he calls hygiene factors and motivators at work. Hygiene factors are those elements of a job or work that are necessary foundations for satisfaction – the basics if you like. Examples of hygiene factors might include pay, physical working environment and fringe benefits perceived to be part of the job you do. While the absence of hygiene factors results in dissatisfaction at work, the inclusion of hygiene factors alone merely results in satisfaction, nothing more. This is not the same as being motivated or engaged at work. In short, hygiene factors on their own do not deliver a great experience that engages people. Motivation factors are much more innate, including elements such as achievement, growth, responsibility and meaning. And it is these motivation factors that unlock engagement and are at the heart of a great experience.

This model is useful to understand employee experience and engagement, and in particular why companies tend to focus their energy and investment on the hygiene factors rather than on the motivators. Hygiene factors are visible; they are above the 'waterline'. Focusing on areas, such as the physical working environment, hosting a great Xmas party or offering free yoga sessions, for example, give the illusion of doing something positive about employee experience and engagement. Of course we aren't saying that the hygiene factors don't matter; ignore them or get them wrong and you'll know about it! Companies should ensure employees get paid the right amount, and on time, work in a physical environment that is right for their job and much more. However, while the hygiene factors are important, on their own they are not enough. We need to take time to understand what is beneath the waterline: the motivators. It is these motivation factors that elicit positive emotions and are the foundation for positive experiences and engagement. It is the motivator factors that are the hallmarks of a 'people-first' approach, given that they rely on a deep understanding of the people within our organizations.

So what has this got to do with taking a people-first approach to IC? We can take inspiration from Herzberg and apply this thinking to understand where we have come from in IC and where we believe we need to get to.

Figure 2.2 visualizes the evolution of IC we explored in Chapter 1 and outlines where we are heading now. Let's take a closer look at the three ages of IC:

1. PROCESS-LED IC – TRANSACTIONAL AND BROADCAST MODE

In the early days, IC was largely transactional and process-driven. It focused almost exclusively on channels and messages, with a basic, surface-level view of the 'audience'. The aim was simple: push out information to employees. Communication was predominantly one-way, sharing news and announcements with little thought given to how people might feel, what they might need or how they might respond. During this stage:

- The priority was visibility and volume: getting the message out was seen as success.
- Employees were treated as passive recipients, not active participants.
- There was no real focus on understanding employee emotions, motivations or experience.

In short, communication was done *to* people, not *with* them.

2. EXPERT-LED IC – CHANGING BEHAVIOURS AND ENGAGEMENT

Over time, IC pros began to recognize that communication is really about facilitating behaviour change and helping to engage people. IC pros began

FIGURE 2.2 The three ages of IC

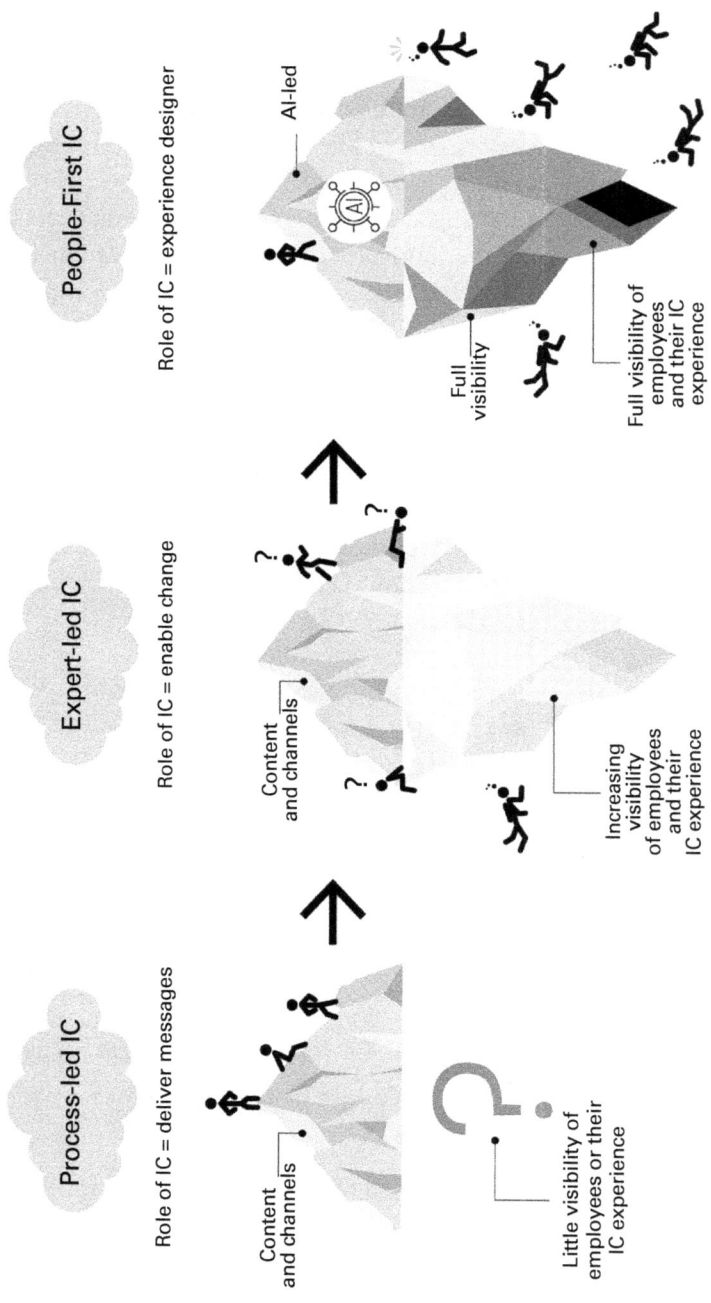

Process-led IC

Role of IC = deliver messages

Content and channels

Little visibility of employees or their IC experience

Expert-led IC

Role of IC = enable change

Content and channels

Increasing visibility of employees and their IC experience

People-First IC

Role of IC = experience designer

AI-led

Full visibility

Full visibility of employees and their IC experience

asking what do we need our people to think, feel and do? And we began building comms around these insights.

This was a pivotal realization. Communicators began to dive beneath the 'waterline', aiming to understand employees better and drive meaningful outcomes like behaviour change, engagement and trust.

Practices at this stage of our evolution included:

- annual IC audits
- surveys and focus groups
- building basic employee personas
- gathering feedback.

However, despite these good intentions, IC remained fundamentally expert-led. This was the age of the gatekeeper, with IC pros deciding what employees needed, rather than truly co-creating with employees.

Key limitations of this expert-led approach include:

- The right intentions were there, for example, wanting to personalize IC, but the execution was limited by bandwidth and resources.
- Understanding was still surface-level: employee personas were developed, but often not meaningfully embedded into communication strategies.
- Personalization remained low: comms were still broadly targeted rather than tailored to individual or group needs.

This was a step forward, but IC was not yet truly people-first.

3. PEOPLE-FIRST IC – HUMAN-CENTRED, AI-ENABLED AND FUTURE-READY

People-first IC is the new frontier. This approach demands that we go beyond thinking about employees as an 'audience' and start designing communication *experiences* that are rooted in deep empathy, curiosity, co-creation and trust.

Let's take a deeper look at our people-first approach to IC here.

As we've outlined, taking a people-first approach to IC means genuinely understanding employee needs, motivations, emotions and daily realities. It's about designing with and for employees. In practice, this shows up when we personalize communication journeys based on real insight, not assumptions. And it means getting comfortable and competent with tools like journey maps, empathy maps and co-creation workshops to build IC experiences that are meaningful, intuitive and emotionally resonant.

Importantly, in a world where AI will increasingly take over expert-led tasks like drafting copy, segmenting audiences and automating workflows (World Economic Forum 2025) the human-centred skills of IC, such as building trust, empathy, connection and creativity, become our unique, irreplaceable advantage. We believe that this is the future of internal communication and it is no longer optional. Much of what AI can and will do fits into the 'expert-led' space, focusing on IC process factors. But in our new people-first model of IC, we combine IC process factors with human factors and ensure we ground AI in human needs.

In Figure 2.3, you'll see that above the waterline we are in familiar territory, here we're focusing on what we're going to refer to as 'IC process factors'. In this space we are taking an 'expert-led' approach. This is where we are using our IC expertise to craft messages that stick, develop channels that reach employees and design visuals that grab attention and align with our brand. And of course, understanding the psychology and neuroscience in the 'expert-led' space helps us to do a great job. It goes without saying that we need to write engaging copy, reach remote audiences and communicate in ways that work for our people. But in this space, it is all about 'us' as IC pros, doing what we do best and making good use of our expertise. It makes perfect sense that this is where the IC profession has tended to focus for many years; it's visible, it feels familiar, it demonstrates our value and it's what we know as IC experts. And of course, it is absolutely critical to get the IC process factors right; this is the foundation for great IC practice.

But taking a genuinely people-first approach to IC requires more. We need to dive beneath the waterline to genuinely understand what a great communication experience looks and feels like for the people we want to communicate with. We need to deeply understand our people, their needs, motivations and emotions, and use these insights to inform our practice. In this space it is no longer about us, as IC pros; it is about the people we want to communicate with. In this space we are taking a 'people-first' approach, taking the time to put our people at the front and centre of our thinking and delivery. When we take a people-first approach, the outcome is a superior IC experience, one that is more likely to be consumer-grade, which is where we need to get to, given the changing expectations people have at work.

Let's be clear here, taking a people-first approach is holistic, it is the sum of both the expert-led space plus the people-led space; *we need to do both*. The IC process factors must not be ignored but considered alongside the human factors. And in taking this 'people-first' approach to IC, we are also future-proofing our careers as we move quickly into a world where AI can outmatch us in many of the areas we built our expertise in.

FIGURE 2.3 People First IC

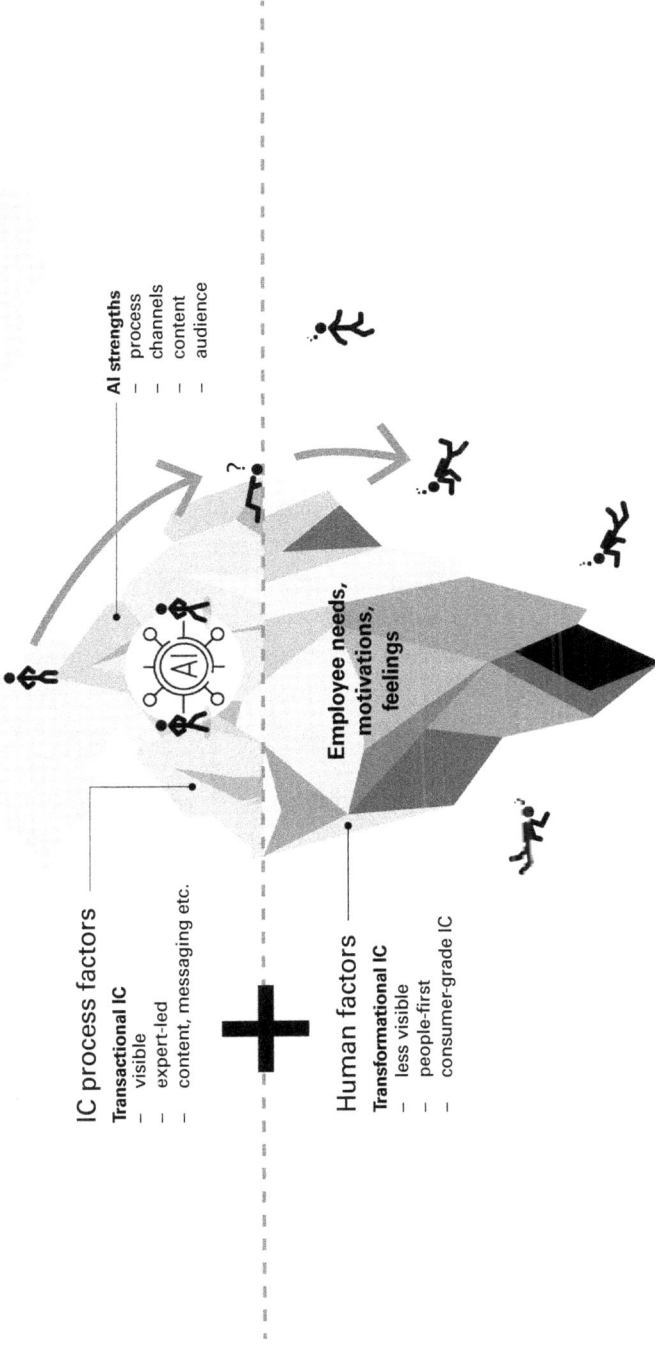

IC process factors

Transactional IC
– visible
– expert-led
– content, messaging etc.

Human factors

Transformational IC
– less visible
– people-first
– consumer-grade IC

Employee needs, motivations, feelings

AI strengths
– process
– channels
– content
– audience

Future-proofing IC

The need for a people-first approach to IC is no longer just a philosophical argument; it is a strategic necessity. Recent insights from Microsoft's *2025 Work Trend Index Annual Report* strongly reinforce the case we make throughout this book and the approach we advocate for. In summary, one that balances technical excellence in IC process factors with a deep, sustained focus on the human factors that create genuine connection, trust and engagement.

According to Microsoft's research, the future of work will be characterized by 'human-agent' hybrid teams, where AI will increasingly perform operational and technical tasks. IC pros will be valued for uniquely human capabilities: empathy, creativity, curiosity, emotional intelligence and moral judgement. The report highlights that as AI transforms work at every level, organizations that succeed will be those that blend machine intelligence with human leadership. This mirrors our People-First IC model, which advocates for combining expert-led communication processes with people-led, human-centred design and delivery. In short, what AI cannot replicate the deep human capabilities that sit *beneath the waterline* of our model: empathy, creativity, curiosity, meaning-making and emotional connection. It cannot truly understand the emotional context of a message, build authentic trust or create communication experiences that resonate with people at a human level.

Microsoft's research highlights that the organizations thriving today are those that intentionally combine machine intelligence with human leadership. In these 'frontier firms', humans are no longer simply transmitting information, they are designing experiences that foster connection, trust and belonging, while AI handles much of the operational load. Internal communication must evolve in the same way. To future-proof our function and our organizations, we must leverage AI to strengthen our processes but invest deeply in human-centred communication. As we move into a future shaped by AI, it becomes clear that the opportunity for IC is not to compete with technology but to complement it. Table 2.1 summarizes the division of strengths between AI and human-centred IC.

In short, the People-First IC model is not simply a philosophy for better communication today, it is a strategic blueprint for the future of work. The question is how we ensure that human connection, creativity and empathy remain at the heart of everything we do. We will now explore what this looks like in practice.

Let's take the example of an intranet project, something that many IC pros have had some experience with. Let's imagine we have a legacy intranet

TABLE 2.1 Where AI adds value in IC versus where humans add value in IC

Where AI adds value in IC	Where humans add value in IC
Drafting clear, concise internal communications at scale	Building emotional connection through authentic communication
Developing comms plans quickly and efficiently	Using empathy and emotional intelligence to design meaningful experiences
Personalizing messaging based on role, location or data segments	Understanding the real, often unspoken, needs and emotions of employees
Automating workflows, updates and scheduling	Creating trust, credibility and psychological safety through communication
Providing 24/7 availability for basic queries (chatbots, FAQs)	Fostering belonging, shared purpose and cultural connection
Analysing patterns and providing insights on channel usage	Exercising critical judgement creativity and ethical decision-making
Scaling communications across diverse, global workforces	Coaching leaders to communicate with authenticity and humanity

that is not fit for purpose, the content is poorly written by multiple authors, it's not aligned with our tone of voice guidelines, there's way too much on there and it's impossible to find what you need. The intranet doesn't sync with other apps our people need to access and the overall user experience is poor. In addressing these challenges, we of course need to address the IC process factors. For example, overhaul the content, copywrite it to align with our tone of voice, address the visual design and rework the site architecture. In doing this we will deliver a cleaner, fresher-looking intranet, with better navigation and more organized content. But these steps alone would not necessarily create a great IC experience. We haven't taken the time to understand what employees really need from the intranet, and how they feel using it. And we've made assumptions about what we, as IC experts, believe the solutions are. We have taken an 'expert-led' approach – which in previous times served us well – but will not deliver the consumer-grade experience we want for our people. There is a very real risk of the new intranet feeling generic and likely disconnected from what our people need day to day. And we have missed the opportunity to create a great user experience. Taking this approach might result in a satisfactory intranet that does what it needs to do, but not a solution that facilitates a great experience per se.

Interestingly, when approaching an intranet redesign project like this, it's possible that a people-first approach might be taken, given the adoption of 'user-centred design' for digital projects to create a great user experience. User-centred design emerged from the fields of human factors, cognitive psychology and design thinking (Norman, 2013). Its origins can be traced back to a focus on 'human factors engineering' during the Second World War, but it really gained traction in the 1990s, as the web and software boom prompted companies to prioritize the user experience. Why? Those companies that got the user experience right thrived and outpaced their competitors. It is now a well-practised approach in the design of digital products, which often includes intranets.

So what might a people-first approach in relation to an intranet redesign project involve? This approach doesn't begin with solutions or assumptions, it doesn't start with the selection of a platform, it doesn't involve rewriting copy or briefing a graphic design agency. It starts in the 'people-first' space focusing on the human factors. This means spending time with different intranet users, observing how they currently use the intranet, mapping their current experience, asking lots of questions and gathering insights. At this point, we are seeking to understand the current experience from multiple perspectives. We are also asking questions about what good might look like. In the second part of this book, we'll share practical tools and examples to support you to do this; the tools are dynamic and involve much more than running a few focus groups or a survey. For example, you might expect to map the current journey from a range of different perspectives, unearthing the 'moments that matter'. Then you might map the desired future experience and generate a range of 'how might we' questions to give a clear steer on where to develop solutions. These tools enable clarity on the problem you are trying to solve and provide the space to get clear on the scope and define the destination.

Getting beneath the 'waterline' to augment the IC process factors is all about taking a people-first approach. Here we use tools to help us empathize with the user experience, such as employee personas and empathy maps to better understand employee pain points and desires. These insights can then be used to inform the 'process factors' from content to navigation. But they will also help us to understand what a great intranet experience looks like and feels like for our people and then design solutions that will make the difference. Taking this approach moves your intranet towards a consumer-grade experience for your people.

Table 2.2 summarizes the difference between an expert-led approach to an intranet project and a people-first approach. This comparison shows why taking a people-first approach to IC moves the intranet from basic fixes to a consumer-grade experience.

TABLE 2.2 Expert-led IC versus People-First IC

Aspect	Expert-led IC	People-First IC
Core focus	Basic functionality and aesthetics (copy, branding, architecture)	Deep understanding of employee needs and emotions
Methodology	Standard upgrade process with IC pro/expert-driven decisions	Iterative, collaborative process using design thinking/service design methods
Primary objective	Employee satisfaction with intranet as a channel	Create a brilliant employee experience
Potential outcome	Meets minimum expectations; functional but generic	Intuitive, personalized and emotionally resonant, exceeds basic expectations
Considerations	Overlooks personal and emotional challenges	Requires more time and effort; without it, the intranet may feel disconnected

REAL-WORLD EXAMPLE

Bupa's journey towards consumer-grade tech to unlock a brilliant digital experience

Setting the scene

Bupa are a global healthcare organization with 82,000 employees worldwide. Offering a range of services, including health insurance, dental care, aged care and clinical care, Bupa have a purpose to help people live longer, healthier, happier lives and make the world better. They are on a mission to become the 'most customer centric healthcare company' in the world.

Internally, the mission is to provide a market-leading digital experience for their people, enabling them to connect with each other and interact effortlessly. This involves three pillars of focus:

- active listening
- continuous improvement
- human-centred design.

The challenge

In-depth internal research revealed that the current approach to the Bupa digital experience just wasn't making the grade. The legacy approach had become too focused on providing 'professional grade' experiences, with multiple products servicing different professional requirements in isolation. That is tech focused on subject matter experts (professionals) rather than the end users, in this case, employees. In short, it felt chaotic and the experience was a long way from where it needed to be.

The solution

Riffat Ahmed, Head of People Technology and Digital at Bupa UK, and his team set about changing this, taking a human-centred design approach to genuinely understand what employees need and want from their digital experience.

They began by taking the time to understand exactly what makes a digital experience 'consumer-grade'. The team spent a great deal of time and energy distilling this complex question into some clear and simple design principles. In summary, a consumer-grade digital experience at Bupa needs to:

1 Be simple: Streamlined processes, which get users to what they need via limited steps.

2 Look good: Users' comfort and confidence in a product is improved when it's visually engaging and appealing.

3 Be intuitive: Can users get to grips with the product easily? With little need for direction and training?

4 Be accessible: By anyone, anywhere and can be integrated across platforms without loss of usability.

Riffat and his team then used employee personas to help them view the experience from different perspectives and understand the different users' needs. From this research, they identified a range of opportunities to improve the digital experience for their people:

- Personalization: Relevant content, 'pushed' to people when they need it.

- 'Intelligent search': Search engines that work. Bringing content and information about colleagues together.

- Automation: Reduce manual input required to trigger processes and acquire data and insight.

- Artificial intelligence: Predictive AI, which uses 'natural language models' to answer questions, alongside generative AI 'co-pilots' which assist someone in their role.

- Integration: All systems plugged-in to one 'layer', allowing everything to be accessed in one 'window'.

In summary, the key opportunity was simply to make things easier to use! This led Riffat and his team to ask themselves what they could give to employees to improve their digital experience. The team are now on a transformational journey to improve the digital experience their people have and the improvements they are making have not been designed in isolation but in response to the robust discovery work undertaken.

One of the most fundamental changes they are making is to provide a 'single entry point', kind of like a front door that provides access to the various tools and resources available. So, rather than having to search for and then sign into different tools and apps, the single entry point takes employees through to what they call the 'The Experiential Layer', which they describe as 'where our people live'. This layer involves personalized homepages and content, search engines that work, access to data and insights, the ability to connect with colleagues, conversational AI bots which trigger automated processes alongside 'co-pilot assistants' which support them with their role.

The journey is still work in progress, but here is an update of where they are at the time of writing:

- An understanding that neither technology nor employee experience stands still. With the highest number of older people in work, as well as early entry pathways into work, the employee experience needs to work for all. As a reference, Bupa have developed two phrases that hold true to their intent:

  o Don't force the user into the technology; take the technology where the user is.

  o No matter which technological door the user steps in from, the experience should be consistently the same.

- This meant that they reached the crossroads of collaboration versus services, or as Riffat calls it, desktop versus needs-based. They reached this crossroads earlier than expected, which resulted in a lot of discovery and thinking work with their employee personas. They asked what tools do people use for collaboration, to get started on their working day, and what tools do people look for when a need arises. For example, in Bupa's case, someone has a people, procurement or property need.

- They are also working on a review of their knowledge strategy. Previously, they had worked with 'user-journeys', understanding where a user begins with knowledge, then how they might continue to fulfil their need through a transaction. This work involved a separation (at least conceptually) between collaboration and services, and the work continues to preserve this concept.

- The greatest outcome of this knowledge work has been the launch of an AI-powered intelligent search that is personalized to the user and returns not only the relevant knowledge to them but also summarizes them for the employee.

- The second greatest outcome of their evolution has been the launch of an AI-powered, intelligent chatbot, which converses in natural language, can take advantage of the intelligent search mentioned before, but can also transact on the user's behalf. This cuts down filler time significantly from each transaction and need.

- Next up in their continuous evolution is further integration into core systems through the collaboration versus needs concept. This will involve the introduction of live chat and a specific focus on onboarding journeys as listening indicated people would really value improvements in this space.

This brilliant case study from Bupa highlights just how profound the people-first shift can be. It also underlines that there are pioneering practitioners out there, just like Riffat, who are already utilizing the power of human-centred design and a people-first approach to deliver greater value and enhance the overall employee experience.

We want to make it really clear that many of the tools and ideas we highlight in People-First IC are already in use out in the field, and in some cases, have been for some time. For example, design thinking, a human-centred, iterative approach to problem-solving, which we'll explore in more depth in later chapters, dates back to the 1960s and was popularized in the 1980s and 1990s. Our aim here is not to propose some new or radical methodology but rather to present a tried and tested set of tools, frameworks and mindsets in a coherent way to help increase adoption in the world of IC.

People-First IC builds on the employee experience movement and learns from the experiences of the pioneers already operating in this space. It's a response to the fast-changing world of work and charts a new course for our profession as we enter the AI era. It recognizes that organizations are fundamentally social systems made up of individuals working towards a common goal and that effective communication is the glue that holds such systems together.

This is our moment

We have a once-in-a-generation opportunity to reinvent our profession for the greater good. We are standing at a crossroads. For decades, IC has struggled to prove its value and fought for a seat at the table. But the world has changed. AI is moving into our space and fast, becoming the go-to experts for many areas of IC. And our people are quite rightly demanding better experiences at work, wanting parity with the way things work in their personal lives. And everyone is searching for trust, connection and meaning in an increasingly complex world.

This is our moment as IC pros, not to double down on outdated methods, but to rise. Because the reality is this: if internal communication doesn't evolve, it will become irrelevant. If we don't redefine our value, others, be it EX, AI or marketing, will step in to fill the gap. But if we seize this moment, we can lead. We can transform IC from a functional service to a human-centred, experience-driven discipline that drives culture, trust and performance.

We truly believe that the opportunity has never been greater. We have the tools, the insights, the evidence and most importantly, a compelling reason to make the change. Now we need the courage.

This is the moment to:

- Stop broadcasting and start co-creating.
- Stop chasing outputs and start designing experiences.
- Stop waiting for permission and start leading the change.

Because what we do next doesn't just shape the future of internal communication, it shapes the future of work. Let's be clear: this isn't evolution. It's transformation. So the question is – will you be a bystander in that shift or will you lead it?

CHAPTER IN SUMMARY

- **The old models of internal communication are broken:** Despite decades of effort, the same challenges of disengagement, a lack of influence and ineffective leadership communication still persist.

- **The world of work has changed – radically:** Employees now expect consumer-grade experiences, authentic connection and personalized communication. The rise of AI is reshaping roles, tools and expectations at speed.

- **Internal communication must evolve or risk irrelevance:** Broadcasting to audiences is no longer enough. We must shift from expert-led output to co-created experience.

- **People-First Internal Communication is the new frontier:** It's a human-centred, experience-driven approach that works with AI to enable the IC pro to dial-up human skills including empathy and curiosity.

- **AI is not a threat – it's an amplifier:** Used well, it can free IC professionals from low-value tasks, allowing us to focus on what only humans can do: build trust, create meaning and design powerful experiences.

- **Human-centred design provides the tools to make this shift:** Using tools like journey mapping, personas and empathy interviews, we can design brilliant IC experiences that work for our people.

- **This is a once-in-a-generation opportunity:** By embracing People-First IC, we can reposition our profession as a strategic driver of trust, culture and performance in the AI era.

- **The time for incremental change is over:** If we want to stay relevant, we must transform. This isn't evolution, it's revolution. And it starts with us.

References

Arthur J Gallagher and Co (2024) State of the sector 2023/24: Internal communication and employee experience, Gallagher, www.ajg.com/employeeexperience/-/media/files/gallaghercomms/gcommssite/state-of-the-sector-2024.pdf (archived at https://perma.cc/TW6A-QVSA)

Bupa (2025) About Bupa, Bupa Group, en.wikipedia.org/wiki/Bupa (archived at https://perma.cc/K6EK-ZSFX)

Cleary (2023) AI in internal communications: Innovate with integrity, Cleary, gocleary.com/blog/embracing-ai-in-internal-communications-a-path-to-innovation-and-integrity (archived at https://perma.cc/XV8W-6K38)

Gallup (2018) Gallup's perspective on designing your organization's employee experience, Gallup, https://www.gallup.com/workplace/355601/employee-experience-paper.aspx (archived at https://perma.cc/X5C5-XAGK)

Gallup (2024) State of the Global Workplace 2024 report, Gallup, www.gallup.com/workplace/349484/state-of-the-global-workplace.aspx (archived at https://perma.cc/Q59R-XV3B)

Gartner (2024) Intelligent agents in AI really can work alone, here's how, www.gartner.com/en/articles/intelligent-agent-in-ai (archived at https://perma.cc/5MHA-JVZ6)

Harvard Business School Online (2020) What is human-centered design? https://online.hbs.edu/blog/post/what-is-human-centered-design (archived at https://perma.cc/6DBX-6UTS)

Herzberg, F, Mausner, B and Snyderman, B B (1959) *The Motivation to Work*, 2nd ed, John Wiley & Sons, New York

IBM Global Business Services (2008) Making change work: Practical recommendations for leaders who want to make change stick, IBM Corporation, public.dhe.ibm.com/software/be/Making_Change_Work_eff.pdf (archived at https://perma.cc/7S72-MVWH)

McKinsey & Company (2025) The state of AI: How organizations are rewiring to capture value, www.mckinsey.com/~/media/mckinsey/business%20functions/quantumblack/our%20insights/the%20state%20of%20ai/2025/the-state-of-ai-how-organizations-are-rewiring-to-capture-value_final.pdf (archived at https://perma.cc/NX5F-MUBU)

Norman, D A (2013) *The Design of Everyday Things: Revised and expanded edition*, Basic Books, New York

Pew Research Center (2025) Workers' exposure to AI, www.pewresearch.org/social-trends/2025/02/25/workers-exposure-to-ai (archived at https://perma.cc/J2ES-ES8S)

The Employee Experience Space (2024) The EX Report 2024, The EX Space, mailchi.mp/ba7520959fe7/exs_exreport2025 (archived at https://perma.cc/U9HS-D349)

The Institute of Internal Communication (2023) Voice of the Profession 2023, IoIC, www.ioic.org.uk/resource/ic-index-2023-press-access.html (archived at https://perma.cc/87MY-J8UZ)

World Economic Forum (2025) Leading with purpose: Why human-centric strategies are vital in the AI era, 17 January, www.weforum.org/stories/2025/01/leading-with-purpose-why-human-centric-strategies-are-vital-in-the-ai-era (archived at https://perma.cc/776R-9725)

Zytnik, M (2024) *Internal Communication in the Age of Artificial Intelligence*, Business Expert Press, New York

03

The science of internal communication

Internal communication (IC) has always been about people. At its core, it's there to help shape behaviour, so when we talk about IC, we're really asking: *what do we need people to think, feel and do?* That's why the fields of psychology, neuroscience and human behaviour are so useful; they help us design communication that actually works.

In Chapter 2, we introduced our People-First Internal Communication approach, where truly understanding your people is the starting point. With that in mind, it makes sense that having a solid grasp of the science behind how people think, feel and behave will not only strengthen your IC practice but also build your credibility as a strategic communicator. This is about more than instinct, it's about bringing an evidence-based mindset to your work.

There's a lot we can take from the science of human behaviour, and many experienced IC pros have been applying these insights (consciously or not) for years. But being truly people-first means going deeper. It's not just running an IC audit or a few focus groups, or checking analytics every now and then. And it's not just knowing that visual content lands faster than text.

It means making a real investment, of time, curiosity and empathy to understand the people you're communicating with. What matters to them? What motivates them? What's getting in their way? When you take the time to step into their world, you get far better at creating communication that resonates, sticks and makes a difference.

Of course, this is a huge area; we could write a whole book on the science alone. But in this chapter, we'll focus on a handful of models and concepts we've found most helpful in supporting a people-first approach to internal communication.

The science of IC: revisiting the psychological foundations

Internal communication can sometimes feel more like an art than a science. We often rely on gut instinct and experience, and sometimes that's OK. But over the years, our understanding of how people process information, make decisions and change behaviour has grown significantly. And when we apply these insights intentionally, the impact can be transformative.

There's a wealth of behavioural science out there, but in this chapter we'll focus on some of the most relevant ideas you can bring into your everyday practice. Especially now, when many of us are working with generative AI, understanding the science of communication can help you get better outcomes, from your tools *and* your teams.

To unpack these ideas, we've invited behavioural change expert Deborah Hulme to share her perspective. Deborah is an experienced organizational effectiveness, communications and employee engagement professional with over 25 years' experience of working on business transformations to deliver change and improve performance. With a deep focus on the human aspects of change, Deborah specializes in creating dynamic, brain-friendly sessions that support effective transformation. At the core of Deborah's work is a commitment to effective leadership and the latest insights from neuroscience. She is a Fellow of the Institute of Internal Communication and a Master Neuroplastician, recognized by the Institute of Organisational Neuroscience. Internationally, Deborah is a highly respected speaker and facilitator on neuroscience, change, engagement, communication and leadership.

The future of internal communication: a neuroscience perspective (contribution from Deborah Hulme)

Neuroscience theory offers insights into how internal communicators can overcome engagement and change challenges by respecting cognitive limits and crafting messages that resonate. However, to be of value within an organization, the neuroscience theory requires an additional layer of strategic thinking for effective application. The skill of the internal communicator is in understanding the nuances and layering of organization-informed strategic insight over the research.

This then affords the opportunity to grow and enhance capabilities by developing knowledge of the human system and how it responds to pressure, ambiguity, overload and change. With the ongoing research into mindset, behaviour and emotion, we know much more about the human system and what it needs to stay well and perform well through change.

Therefore, the internal communication professionals who take the time to learn the fundamentals of human behaviour will become the advisors of the future, able to coach leaders and function as guardians of the mental and emotional bandwidth of the organization.

While the topic is vast, there are three neuroscience-informed pillars that internal communicators can leverage to drive engagement and resilience: cognitive capacity, threat response and emotion-driven communication.

Cognitive capacity

Internal communication today isn't just about the tools we use, the timing we choose or how we frame a message. It's also about whether people have the capacity to process what we are sharing.

The human brain is estimated to absorb up to 11 million bits of data every second (Wilson 2002); however, people only have the capacity to consciously process up to an estimated 120 bits, which is the equivalent of three people talking at the same time. And even that is a stretch.

Today's workplaces, with the constant distractions, interruptions and continuous change, mean that cognitive capacity is often operating to the maximum leaving us feeling exhausted and overwhelmed. When this happens the prefrontal cortex, the area of the brain responsible for focus, reasoning and decision-making, tires quickly, and we lose the ability to think strategically, to be creative, solve problems or even adapt and pivot when needed.

Instead, to conserve precious internal energy, we operate on more automatic thinking systems, relying on embedded routines and habits. We slip into familiar ways of thinking and behaving and, when this happens, creative thinking, problem-solving and innovation diminish.

This means that important messages can be missed, not because people aren't interested, but because their minds are already full due to limited cognitive bandwidth. Neuroscience highlights that the brain favours information that is easy to process, familiar and emotionally safe. The importance of message fluency and alignment for engagement, therefore, should never be underestimated.

Practical application

Less is always more. Balance what must be communicated with what the audience can manage, use plain language, reduce complexity and aim for no more than three key points, to avoid flooding working memory.

Align messaging. Contradictory or disconnected messages stimulate a sense of threat; therefore, alignment and coherence are essential for a brain that craves safety and understanding.

Repeat often. Slow down because people need time to absorb, reflect and act. Repetition reinforces the formation of new mental pathways and consistent messaging increases retention and understanding over time.

The more cognitive limits are respected with communication approaches and plans that emphasize clarity and fluency, the easier it is to reduce overwhelm and foster engagement.

The threat response

The threat response, rooted in evolutionary survival mechanisms, plays a critical role in how employees process information and incorporates key brain regions such as:

- **The amygdala**, which detect threat, triggering fight/flight and activating the release of cortisol and adrenaline.
- **Pre-frontal cortex**, which manages rational thinking and emotional regulation and whose functionality becomes impaired when under stress.
- **Hypothalamus and brain stem**, which activate many physiological and, when under stress sets off a cascade of activity, such as increasing the heart rate and narrowing focus ready for fight/flight.

When the threat response is triggered, the human system will always prioritize survival over logic, impairing problem-solving and creativity. Negativity bias is amplified, which means negative perceptions, mindsets and behaviours are processed faster and remembered for longer. In addition, social sensitivity is heightened, meaning events such as exclusion or unfairness create sensations that are experienced in a similar way to physical pain.

In today's workplaces, perceived threats like ambiguity, overload or poor communication can quickly push people into a threat state. When this happens, thinking narrows, trust is eroded, creativity collapses and collaboration suffers. Individuals and teams shift their focus away from performance towards survival, causing engagement and productivity to drop dramatically.

In such circumstances even the most carefully crafted communication will not land well and, if poorly planned and executed, may even contribute to heightened resistance. Understanding the importance of cultivating a culture of safe space, what this means for communication and leadership, and how to work with neuroscience informed tools, designed to mitigate threat, are now all core internal communication skills.

One such tool is the SCARF model, developed by David Rock (2008). The research identified five social domains, Status, Certainty, Autonomy, Relatedness and Fairness that, when triggered, activate a threat (defensive) brain state:

- Status: do I matter in the eyes of others?
- Certainty: do I have clarity now and in the future?
- Autonomy: do I feel I have choice and influence?
- Relatedness: do I feel I belong?
- Fairness: am I being treated fairly and equitably?

These domains, sometimes referred to at the five primary colours of engagement, play a crucial role in emotional safety and, when two or more of the domains are negatively impacted, people enter a heightened state of threat. This severely compromises logical thinking, collaboration and engagement.

As communicators it is important, therefore, to consider what we can do to mitigate rising threat if we want to engage colleagues.

Practical application

- **Encourage dissent**: Create forums for constructive feedback, which reduces resentment and advise leaders on active listening techniques.
- **Provide autonomy**: where possible, offer choices to engage the brain's reward system and reduce helplessness.
- **Careful messaging**: use empathic language, align with SCARF where appropriate, and maintain consistency to reduce threat and foster psychological safety.

Emotion-driven communication

To sustain attention and resilience through change, internal communication must reach colleagues beyond logic alone. Facts and data may well appeal to a logical brain; however, it is the emotional hook that propels people into action. For this, it is necessary to engage the brain's reward system, which plays a critical role in shaping motivation, engagement and behaviour.

While the reward system comprises various neural structures, the most important pathway is the dopamine pathway, which plays a role in regulating emotion and is responsible for reward-driven learning. Every type of reward that has been studied increases the level of dopamine transmission in the brain. This is powerful and can also create unintended consequences such as oversaturation and reward fatigue.

The skill of internal communication is to create environments that motivate without overwhelming, activating the reward system through clear purposeful messaging, celebrating progress and offering positive feedback. All of which strengthen motivation and encourage continued engagement. At the same time, there should be monitoring for impulsivity, disengagement or unhealthy behaviours, indicative of reward systems backfiring and course correcting when necessary.

Storytelling is another vital tool. Well-told stories activate the amygdala and hippocampus, enhancing emotional recall and stimulating the release of oxytocin, which deepens empathy, trust and a sense of belonging. Facts and data alone rarely move people, but when data is framed through human stories, resonant visuals, or emotional narratives, it becomes memorable and meaningful. Storytelling transforms information into experience, helping people see themselves in the change journey.

Practical application

- **Celebrate progress:** Design programmes to build long-term engagement, not just short-term dopamine hikes, for example, actively recognize small wins, contributions and milestones.
- **Combine logic and emotion:** Pair factual updates with emotional framing to ensure messages appeal to both rational and emotional processing.
- **Avoid overload:** Keep recognition meaningful – credibility matters.

Combining clear facts with emotional framing, whether through personal stories, shared goals, or compelling metaphors, allows communication to reach both the analytical and emotional centres of the brain. It's this blend that builds connection, sparks energy and helps people find meaning, even in times of rapid transformation.

In summary

The future of internal communication is human at its core. Internal communicators who understand human behaviour will be uniquely positioned as strategic advisors in their organizations. By protecting cognitive capacity, training leaders in de-escalating threat responses and crafting emotionally resonant stories, internal communication professionals are uniquely placed to make that future a reality.

Applying the science: start with understanding your people

Understanding the science gives IC pros an advantage, not least when collaborating with AI. Ultimately though, applying the science without understanding the people you are communicating with at a deeper level means we are still being expert-led, not people-first. We are still making assumptions about what will work, albeit informed by some science, and what good looks like for our people. Of course, there are many examples of best practice where an expert-led approach has achieved the right outcomes, but we would argue this is more by accident than design. Even with the best psychological insights, there's a risk: we assume we know what employees need. When we rely on expert knowledge alone, we design based on what we think will work, rather than what actually does. Taking a more holistic, people-first approach to IC will deliver a superior experience for your people. Let's share an example.

Back in 2020, we were asked to work with a client on their new behaviours roll-out. A key component of their approach to embed the new behaviours involved a recognition scheme. This scheme was not just about recognizing those people bringing the new behaviours to life but about communicating the behaviours in action, using employee stories to showcase where the behaviours were lived day to day. The problem? The approach just wasn't working, with a lack of engagement and interest in the scheme, there were very few nominations coming through and therefore a lack of stories to showcase the behaviours in action.

The solution the team had developed was expert-led and covered the 'IC process' factors. At first glance it looked great. The behaviours had been developed by involving employee representatives, and the initial communication launch was well received, which was backed up via survey findings. The data showed that the behaviours were understood and supported from the board through to front-line managers and employees. To build on these initial wins, the team had developed a peer-nominated behaviour recognition scheme, supported by a slick recognition app. The plan was to showcase the winners' stories to help their people understand how to bring the behaviours to life to facilitate the culture change required. They had rightly used and understood some of the science that helps IC to land well. The campaign didn't overload employees; it was simple and easy to understand the ask. The team also understood the power of emotions in IC, using stories to help bring the behaviours to life. But something wasn't working.

We used a design sprint to understand the problem and what might need to change. This began with an 'experience mapping' activity to get clear on what was happening today. We mapped the experience with employees from a range of different perspectives: employees who were nominated, those doing the nominating and those responsible for administrating the scheme. We ensured we heard voices from different parts of the organization, most notably online and offline employees.

This simple activity alone immediately highlighted a number of issues with the current approach. For example, many employees were offline and had problems accessing the app. But the lightbulb moment came when those who had designed, and now administered the scheme, heard first-hand how others liked to be recognized, or not, as it turned out. The idea of being formally called out and spotlighted to the whole company as someone living the behaviours filled the majority of employees with horror. The experience-mapping activity enabled the team to quickly understand that they had, in fact, designed something that worked for them, but few others. The design sprint process highlighted other factors which contributed to the failure of the scheme, but in summary if the team had started by seeking to understand what worked for their people in terms of recognition, they would not have designed and launched the scheme in its current format. The outcomes of the design sprint enabled the development of prototypes for a new approach, which were then tested and iterated with groups of employees, and the resulting solution looked very different. It involved a more personalized approach, with the option for employees to state how they liked to be recognized and even choose to stay anonymous if that was preferred. Other improvements were made to the nominators' experience, as well as creating options to get involved for 'offline' employees. This new approach was a success and the team was able to gather many stories which were then shared, helping to embed the new behaviours.

PUTTING THE SCIENCE INTO PRACTICE

Behavioural science offers a wealth of insight that can help us become more effective, people-first communicators. Developing our understanding of how people think, feel and make decisions gives us the tools to design communication that doesn't just inform, but truly influences behaviour in a way that feels human and supportive.

There's no shortage of great theories to draw on, and we share several in this chapter. One of the most practical is the Theory of Planned Behaviour. It provides a clear and simple framework for thinking about what needs to happen for people to say 'yes' to change. Here Kateryna Byelova shares how it comes to life in internal communication. Kateryna is a communications professional with 15+ years of experience. She has built internal communication functions for organizations during major transformations, focusing on shifting employee behaviour to support business goals and she holds a Master's in Communication from Johns Hopkins University.

Application in practice: using the Theory of Planned Behaviour in internal comms

Driving behaviour change is a common goal in internal communication, but the path to action isn't always clear. Most teams know *what* needs to happen (using the new system, following the new process), but struggle with *how* to get people to actually do it.

This is where behavioural science comes in, and the Theory of Planned Behaviour (TPB), developed by psychologist Icek Ajzen (1991), gives us a useful framework. It breaks down intention into three factors:

- Attitude: Does the employee believe this change is worthwhile?
- Subjective norm: Do they believe that others expect or support the behaviour?
- Perceived control: Do they feel confident and capable of doing it?

Let's look at how this translates into practical, people-first communication.

Attitude: help people *see the value*

If people don't understand why something matters, they're unlikely to engage. Comms should make the benefits of any change crystal clear, not just for the business, but for *them*.
Tactics that work:

- Show how the change makes their life easier (e.g. saves time, reduces hassle, improves day-to-day work).
- Link the behaviour to familiar frustrations it helps solve.

Avoid:

- Vague promises or abstract 'strategic' benefits that don't feel personal.

Subjective norm: *show it's already happening*

People take cues from those around them. If they see the behaviour is already supported and expected by trusted peers, teams or leaders, they're more likely to follow suit.

Tactics that work:

- Share quotes and stories from real employees who've already made the change.
- Highlight visible momentum ('85 per cent of teams are already using it').
- Use praise and peer recognition to reinforce the behaviour.

Avoid:

- Making it sound optional or like it's still being decided.

Perceived control: *make it feel doable*

Even if people believe in the change and feel social pressure to act, they won't do it if it feels hard, confusing, or risky. Communication needs to reduce friction and build confidence.

Tactics that work:

- Break things down into clear, simple steps.
- Use visuals, demos, or peer quotes ('It took five minutes – way easier than I expected').
- Offer just-in-time support: guides, tools, or manager help.

In summary, if we want people to act, we need to do more than just tell them what's happening. We need to help them *believe in it, see others doing it,* and *feel they can do it too.* That's what makes the Theory of Planned Behaviour such a powerful tool for People-First IC.

How to create great experiences: unlocking a consumer-grade IC

To design and deliver a brilliant IC experience, we need to consider not only the science of IC, but the science of a great experience as well. This understanding helps to elevate our practice, add greater value and enable the delivery of a 'consumer-grade' experience. Let's start by taking a look at the nature of 'experience'. Put simply, an experience is any event or occurrence that leaves an impression on an individual (Bridger and Gannaway, 2024). Ultimately, an experience is grounded in emotions, it makes you feel something; whether good or bad! So, from an employee perspective, experiences can be anything that happens to the employee in a work context that leaves an emotional impression on them. And a quick glance at any employee survey will tell you that IC is an incredibly emotive area at work. A poor IC experience is a sure-fire way to frustrate and disengage your people.

So what do we mean by a consumer-grade experience? We are all consumers so we likely have a good understanding of what a good experience looks and feels like in our everyday lives. There will be brands and companies we love because of the way they treat us and how they make us feel. And for the most part, the experiences we have inside organizations, including the IC experience, are a long way from our ideal! There are some key attributes that make up a consumer-grade experience and they include being:

- *Intuitive*: Meaning the experience is frictionless, easy to engage with and doesn't demand serious cognitive effort on our part.
- *Engaging*: Meaning we have a positive emotional response to the experience itself.
- *Personal*: Meaning the experience feels like it is designed around our own personal wants and needs.
- *Relevant*: Meaning the experience delivers value to us at the right time.
- *Empathic*: Meaning we feel seen, heard and understood (Kalbach, 2020).

When considering what we mean by a consumer-grade experience, there are obvious parallels to the insights shared earlier by Deborah. Ultimately, consumer-grade experiences are designed around our people and at their core are emotional. The case study example we shared illustrates why the application of the science of IC alone is not enough to facilitate a great experience. In this example, the missing piece of the puzzle was the lack of real-world empathy to design a solution that was people-first.

What is empathy and how can it help IC?

Designing brilliant IC experiences for our people should involve a deep, empathic understanding of them. Personas and empathy maps are tools we can use to help us to achieve this, which we'll share in later chapters. But what is empathy and how can we use it in our people-first IC approach? There are many definitions that exist, depending on the lens you adopt.

DEFINITIONS OF EMPATHY

Psychological definition (Baron-Cohen, 2011)

Empathy is the ability to understand and share the feelings of another.

Design thinking definition (Brown, 2009)

Empathy is the capacity to step into other people's shoes, to understand their lives, and to guide decisions based on their feelings and needs.

Leadership definition (Goleman, 2006)

Empathy means considering employees' feelings and perspectives and using that understanding to guide your actions as a leader.

In essence, empathy is the ability to stand in someone else's shoes and see the world through their eyes. Empathy helps us to challenge what we believe to be true, as well the assumptions we hold about the IC experience. As IC pros, we often experience this when a senior stakeholder has very particular views and ideas about IC; what needs to happen and the way it should be done.

Being empathic enables us to design and create solutions for the things that really matter to people, not the things we might *think* are important. This is true for the IC experience as well. Let's go back to our case study example of recognition to bring this to life. For example, a company's engagement survey suggests that employee recognition is an issue. In response, HR and IC spend six months and a lot of time and money designing an employee of the month programme, a new platform to support it and a glittering event to celebrate winners. However, in the next engagement survey, the score has not improved. It turns out, what people really wanted was for someone to say thank you for a job well done. The solutions looked good on paper, but they didn't address the root cause of why people felt a lack of recognition. Taking an empathic approach to this challenge would have avoided this scenario.

Psychologists debate precise definitions of empathy, but what is interesting is that there are different ways we can view empathy: we can think of empathy as not one thing, but many. It is a collective noun for a range of ways people respond to other people's feelings. For example:

- **Cognitive empathy**, sometimes called intellectual empathy, is when we can rationally understand the perspectives of others. We can understand their thoughts and feelings towards something, and this helps us get to the core needs and motivations of the people we're designing for and overcome our own assumptions and biases.

- **Emotional empathy** is when we take on the feelings of others. This is where we are able to actually experience the emotions of others and is a deeper level of empathy than cognitive empathy. This is really powerful in IC design, helping us to really connect to the lived experience of others.

- **Compassionate empathy** goes beyond understanding others and sharing their feelings. This type of empathy actually motivates us to take action. This is not only useful for IC pros when designing IC experiences but it's worth considering how we unleash compassionate empathy in leaders, managers and colleagues (Goleman, 2006).

Empathy isn't a trait, it isn't something that is fixed at birth, but something that can be worked on, nurtured and developed. In the book *Employee Experience by Design*, Emma and Belinda Gannaway share the inspiring work of Jamil Zaki, Associate Professor of Psychology at Stanford University and author of *The War for Kindness: Building Empathy in a Fractured World* (2019). Jamil argues that just knowing it is possible to build empathy can inspire individuals towards empathy. And we are more likely to exercise empathy if we have a sense of belonging or connection with another person or group. This background is incredibly useful knowledge when it comes to IC and can help us to understand how we might work on the IC experience.

Why empathy is vital for a people-first approach to IC

Empathy is at the heart of the shift from an 'expert-led' approach to IC to a 'people-first' approach; it forces us to move from 'what we think' to 'what they feel'. In the absence of empathy we will deliver IC solutions based on assumptions rather than lived experience and reality. For example, we might assume that our regular newsletter is simple and clear, but an overwhelmed employee might find it irrelevant and confusing.

Empathy also unlocks the real problem we need to get to grips with. This is something we see time and again, IC teams working to fix a surface-level issue without really understanding the root cause. For example, an IC audit we conducted for a client indicated that employees didn't feel like they had a voice. Developing employee voice is often a key part of our remit as IC pros; enabling 'two-way' comms or dialogue means we move beyond broadcast comms and establish a culture where employees can talk, share and feel listened to. An obvious response might be to implement more channels to enable people to share their concerns or ideas: listening sessions, ask the CEO, an ideas scheme and more. But an empathy-led approach might uncover the root cause of the problem lies with a lack of psychological safety, cynicism that anything will actually change and leaders who discourage open dialogue with sometimes dismissive responses. And throwing more channels to try and fix employee voice wouldn't work when we understand the root cause of the issue.

We know that when IC makes people feel seen, understood and valued, the experience will be better. This is something colleagues in customer experience are very aware of, tailoring their approaches to the needs, motivations and emotions of customers to deliver a more personalized experience. Focusing on empathy in IC enables us to do the same and create more meaningful communication. An empathy-led approach ensures that IC feels relevant, personal and emotionally resonant. It's doubtful anyone would argue against more personalized comms. When we demonstrate we have taken time to know and understand our people, it also builds trust, connection and ultimately engagement. By embedding empathy into our IC approach, we ensure we create IC experiences that don't just work logically, but feel intuitive, natural and human. Because at the end of the day, great IC experiences aren't just designed, they are felt.

From theory to practice

We previously shared some of the key neuroscience and psychology that should be considered in IC practice (thanks again to Deborah and Kateryna for their contribution). We explored the idea of moving IC towards a consumer-grade experience and flagged empathy as a key enabler of this shift from 'us' to 'them'. Combining empathy with the established science really helps to elevate our practice and make a significant difference with IC in our organizations. In addition, there are some further psychological and neuroscientific concepts that are useful to share and consider in pursuit of a more consumer-grade IC experience.

We can learn much from the world of customer experience and consumer brands when it comes to designing and delivering a better IC experience for our people. There are a number of well-established theories and concepts that are tried and tested in the pursuit of creating engaging and memorable experiences for people and we'll share some of the relevant ideas here. Consumer brands have used these principles such as belonging, psychological safety, autonomy and purpose, to create engaging, memorable and intuitive experiences for decades (Neumeier, 2005).

In addition, over the past decade, Emma, through her work at People Lab, has gained insight into the workings and experiences of thousands of employees across diverse, global organizations. Insights from hundreds of 'Best Experience' workshops enabled individual perspectives on what truly makes a great experience at work to be unearthed and understood. Analysis of the data collected from these workshops was then analysed to assess common themes. Categories of similar meanings were distilled from the data and used to inform what exceptional employee experience is, and the conditions that make it possible. The EX Lens provides an overview of these insights and the 'universal themes' highlighted by the model are the same concepts and theories used by consumer brands over the years. This thinking can be applied successfully to the design and delivery of an exceptional IC experience, albeit you'll see that some of the themes are more relevant to IC than others. Let's unpack the universal themes one by one, starting with those themes that have an obvious link to IC practice.

Trust

A great experience is built on trust. Trust is a two-way thing, it happens from being trustworthy and another has to grant it. It's difficult to have a good IC experience without trust. Amy Edmondson, in her book *The Fearless Organization: Creating Psychological Safety in the Workplace for Learning, Innovation, and Growth* (2019), explains why trust supports psychological safety, which in turn, supports effective communication and well-being at work. In short, trust helps to build psychological safety and empowers us to be our best selves at work. It's difficult to have a good experience at work if we don't believe that we are trusted by others, or if we don't trust others in return. How many of us have, over the years, been involved in comms around the regular employee engagement survey? It's often the case that we are designing communication to increase responses and assure people that the survey is confidential, or that something will happen with the results. These issues are in fact all issues of trust, or rather a lack of it.

Trust exists at various 'levels' inside an organization, for instance, trust in senior leaders, trust in your line manager and trust in your colleagues. Being trusted is linked to morale and motivation, which is good for building teamwork and collaboration. Edelman has been researching the nature and role of trust for over 20 years, and their latest 'Trust Barometer' (Edelman, 2024) research is well worth a look for IC pros. Interestingly, their research has consistently found that employee trust cements the employee-employer relationship.

Meaning

'We're not sure exactly where meaning comes from, if it is inherent, or if it is "real" at all; what we do know is that humans flourish when they have it and suffer when they don't' (Irvine 2013).

Meaning is present when employees share their 'Best Experience' stories. Meaning is subjective to our own individual experience. However, Viktor Frankl, in his seminal book, *Man's Search for Meaning* (2004), proposed that we can discover meaning in life in the following ways:

- creating something or accomplishing a task
- experiencing something fully or loving somebody
- the attitude we adopt towards unavoidable suffering.

We're hardwired to search for meaning in our lives. And finding meaning in our experiences at work is a key feature of a great experience. Employees consistently talk about meaning when they reflect on their best work experiences. Whether it's through purpose, accomplishment, relationships, or even resilience in the face of challenges, meaning matters deeply. And internal communication has a powerful role to play in helping employees connect their day-to-day work to something bigger, whether that's organizational purpose, team goals, or customer impact.

When IC clearly connects strategy to personal contribution, and when it communicates more than just the *what* but also the *why*, it helps employees find meaning and that's a huge contributor to a great IC experience.

Connection

Connection creates social identity, something consumer brands have been using to create great experiences for many years. Inside organizations, connections can come from interactions with your manager, with company leaders, team-mates, colleagues or even people from outside the organization. The nature of these connections is personal to individuals and their own context. For some people, connection involves support from a colleague, for others it might be a social connection from a fun experience. As social creatures, feeling connected is rudimentary to our well-being.

The biological foundations of this are tied to oxytocin (Zak, 2017) and its impact on serotonin. When oxytocin is released through any type of social connectivity, it triggers the release of serotonin. Serotonin then activates the reward circuits in our brain, resulting in a happy feeling. It's no surprise that a great experience features connection.

IC is one of the main enablers of connection at scale. Creating opportunities for peer recognition, humanizing leadership, or simply facilitating meaningful conversations all build connection, and with it, a better employee experience.

Belonging

Building on the work of Maslow et al (1995), in their foundational research, they argued that the need to belong is a fundamental human drive. A feeling of belonging at work is a place where we can be ourselves. It is associated with alignment between personal values and organizational values. IC has a role to play to promote belonging at work, which helps our people not only feel safe but also able to bring their full selves to work. Research also shows than belonging at work drives a significant increase in employee net promoter scores. A report from BetterUp (2020) found that a strong sense of belonging at work is linked to a 56 per cent increase in job performance, 50 per cent reduction in turnover, and 167 per cent increase in employee Net Promoter Score (eNPS).

IC plays a critical role here, particularly in reinforcing cultural norms and shared values. When IC reflects the true voice of the organization, rather than a polished corporate script, it helps employees see themselves in the narrative. That sense of identification strengthens belonging and ultimately, commitment.

Appreciation

Appreciation and gratitude are also key features of a great experience according to our research. When we experience appreciation, it releases positive emotions and all the benefits this brings (Achor, 2011). Being appreciated leads to positive feelings, great memories, higher self-esteem, feeling more relaxed and more optimistic.

What is interesting though, is that the person showing us appreciation also gets a boost. Showing others appreciation is linked to a range of positive outcomes too, including well-being, increased and better sleep habits, increased metabolism and lower stress (Hamilton, 2017). IC often plays a behind-the-scenes role in amplifying appreciation, through shout-outs, recognition programmes, stories of success, or celebrating milestones.

Autonomy

Direction and control of our own lives is important and a key feature of intrinsic motivation (Pink, 2009). In work, autonomy brings with it flexibility, another key feature of a great experience. Autonomy also promotes a feeling of respect; respect for individual abilities within the organization, which would otherwise be missed. Autonomy sets employees free from limiting micromanagement and demands good communication within the organization. This instils freedom for employees and communicates a level of trust, both of which are associated with great experiences.

While autonomy may seem more operational than communicative, IC has a subtle but significant role to play. Clarity is an enabler of autonomy. When people are well-informed, when expectations are clearly set and when communication is two-way, autonomy can flourish. Internal communication can reduce ambiguity, support decision-making and reinforce trust, all of which create the conditions for autonomy to thrive.

The following universal themes may not at first glance seem as relevant for designing great internal communication, but when we dig deeper, they are still valuable to consider. Understanding these deeper drivers of experience can help us elevate our practice as expert IC experience designers – because IC doesn't exist in a vacuum. It shapes how people engage with their work, the organization and themselves.

Growth

As humans we have an innate need for personal growth (Dweck, 2006), and the 'best experience' data always involved some element of growth. This may involve more traditional and intentional learning and development at work. Or something less tangible, such as a feeling that we have grown as a person in response to an experience. Growth is also linked to challenge; we often find ourselves experiencing personal growth when we have a challenge to overcome, provided we are given the right level of support to do so.

So how does IC support growth? Great internal communication provides clarity, context and access. It connects employees to opportunities for learning – whether that's a new project, a stretch role, or a development programme. But more than that, IC can spotlight growth stories – sharing how others have developed, overcome setbacks, or learnt something valuable. This helps normalize development, celebrate progress and inspire others to invest in their own growth journeys.

Impact

Having a positive impact is also a key feature of our best experiences at work research. The stories we collected involved the idea of 'making a difference'. This links to the concept of meaning, but it is different: it is more visible and external to the individual. It is possible to find meaning from an experience without having a positive impact.

When we have a positive impact and make a difference, it stimulates a rush of positive emotions: we feel good about that experience. When we experience positive emotions, our serotonin and dopamine levels rise. These chemicals make us feel good, and they enhance our ability to learn and absorb information. Having an impact also teaches our brains that our actions matter (Achor, 2011).

Internal communication can amplify this by helping employees *see* the ripple effect of their work. Case studies, user feedback, customer testimonials, community updates and performance outcomes all help connect the dots. IC plays a vital role in showcasing success and reinforcing the idea that every contribution matters. In doing so, it helps boost positive emotion, pride and motivation across the organization.

Challenge

Overcoming a challenge elicits positive emotions, but developing purposefully hard experiences is not the answer. Challenges require problem-solving; they bring novelty and demand personal growth. Challenges provide us with intrinsic motivation (Ryan and Deci, 2000). Building experiences into workplace practice with an element of challenge engages the essence of employee well-being in organizational culture. An experience with the right amount of stretch provides opportunity for personal development and freedom to tackle challenges creatively features in creating best experiences (Fredrickson, 2001). Challenge and support go hand-in-hand when it comes to creating great experiences.

Internal communication helps create the environment in which challenges can be faced constructively. IC can demystify complex changes, break down big initiatives into understandable steps and provide frameworks for problem-solving. It can also shine a light on stories of perseverance – showing that challenge is not a sign of failure, but of learning. When IC encourages open dialogue, constructive feedback and support-seeking, it makes space for people to face challenges with confidence.

The EX Lens overview

Figure 3.1 is a useful summary of the EX Lens model.

FIGURE 3.1 The EX Lens

THE EX LENS

The visual metaphor of a camera lens is deliberate. First, the EX Lens is something you, the IC pro, interact with and control. Like a great image, a great experience is not something that happens by chance; it's intentional. Just as a photographer decides on the composition of their picture before clicking the shutter, IC pros need to make a deliberate choice about what to keep in-frame and what to leave out. The photographer cannot capture everything; they make a series of very conscious choices. What's going to be the main focus? What's going to be in the foreground versus the background? In the same way, we use insights that are unique to our employees to decide which elements of IC experience we want to accentuate. We can use the lens model to adjust and fine-tune the overall IC experience. Finally, you'll see the employee is placed in the centre of the lens visual, which stands as a clear reminder that, however we choose to approach IC, in our people-first approach, our people are always at the heart of it. We need to invest time and energy to understand what a brilliant IC experience looks and feels like for them.

While we can use the universal themes as a useful starting point when considering what a great IC experience might involve, it's only half the story. We all have individual needs, motivations and preferences which must be considered. Which brings us back to empathy. It is empathy that allows us to build on the theory and science. The science means we can understand what works in general, and empathy then enables us to move to a people-first approach, where we build on the science and ensure IC will actually work for our people. When we apply empathy, the theoretical insights can be transformed into practical, people-first solutions. Empathy ensures that we can design and deliver IC experiences that are not only scientifically sound but are human-centred too. And applying these ideas to practice will unlock a consumer-grade IC experience. For example, we understand the principle of cognitive overload and why we need to avoid it in IC, but it is empathy that enables understanding of the nuances of our employees' experiences. It is empathy that sheds light on what is cognitively overwhelming and why. In later chapters, we'll introduce practical tools to enable you to empathize effectively with your people.

Why this matters: applying the science to People-First IC

Internal communication has always been about more than just sharing information. At its best, it shapes culture, drives behaviour change and builds the right environment in which people do their best work. But in a world of complexity, change and overwhelming noise, intuition alone isn't enough, and neither is expert knowledge of the science. Applying the science of human behaviour, that is the psychology and neuroscience, to internal communication practice gives us a powerful advantage. It allows us to move beyond guesswork and design communication experiences that are not only heard but deeply felt and acted upon.

When we understand the brain's cognitive limits, the emotional drivers of an exceptional experience and the way human beings process and make sense of information, we can design communication that:

- Enhances engagement and builds trust, by respecting cognitive bandwidth and reducing uncertainty.
- Reduces stress and mitigates threat responses, creating psychological safety and emotional resilience.
- Drives real, lasting behaviour change, by aligning with the way human motivation and reward systems work.
- Creates a thriving employee experience, by meeting the deeper needs for meaning, autonomy, connection and belonging.

In short: applying the science turns internal communication from a tactical activity into a strategic lever for organizational success. Science gives us the foundational insights. It helps us understand what tends to work for humans in general. And empathy bridges the gap between theory and reality. It transforms expert knowledge into people-first communication by helping us understand not just what *should* work, but what *will* work for our people, in their real context.

- Science gives us the foundation.
- Empathy makes it human.
- And our people-first approach to IC gives us the methods and tools we need to bring this to life.

But there's an even bigger reason why this matters now. We are entering an era where AI will increasingly take over the process aspects of work (World Economic Forum, 2025), and this will absolutely include communication: drafting emails, segmenting audiences, optimizing channels. If we want to stay relevant and valuable as IC professionals, we must move beyond being great writers or expert channel managers.

We must become IC experience designers, people who understand the messy, beautiful complexity of what it means to be human at work. It's this combination of being informed by science, led by empathy and adopting a people-first approach that will define the most impactful IC professionals. When we combine all three, we don't just communicate better, we create better workplaces and elevate IC from a tactical function to a powerful driver of employee experience, engagement and cultural transformation.

The people-first approach – turning theory into practice

In this chapter, we have explored the science behind effective internal communication. We've unpacked why understanding human behaviour is critical if we want to communicate in ways that truly resonate. And we've shown why empathy must sit alongside expertise to move from 'expert-led' to 'people-first' communication. But how do we turn these insights into action?

In later the chapters of the book, we'll introduce practical tools, frameworks and methods to help you apply a people-first approach to internal communication and move from knowing what matters to knowing how to make it happen. At the heart of every great IC experience is the end user – our people. That's why we don't just apply psychological principles; we go beyond them, using human-centred design to ensure every solution is rooted in *real* employee needs.

And the beauty of our people-first approach is that we have done the heavy lifting for you. The methodology we share with you weaves together everything we've explored in this chapter:

- The science of how people process, respond to and act on communication.
- What makes a great experience.
- The empathy needed to truly stand in the shoes of your people.
- The human-centred design methods that bring it all to life were signposted in a practical way.

By following the people-first approach and using the tools we'll introduce, you'll be working in a way that's already grounded in the latest neuroscience, psychology and experience design thinking, without having to become a behavioural scientist yourself. You'll design and create communication experiences that are more engaging, more intuitive, more human and ultimately, more effective.

Let's take a brief look at how our approach has the science and empathy foundations baked into the tools and methods we will share with you.

- *Empathy at the heart*: Throughout our people-first approach are the tools to enable you to use empathy, not as a buzzword but as a discipline. Tools like empathy maps and personas will help you truly understand and design for the lived experiences, motivations and emotions of your people, and not just what you *assume* they need.

- *Avoiding cognitive overload*: The approach and tools we'll share are designed to enable you to prioritize your activity and work on what really matters to your people. This helps to avoid overwhelm by prioritizing simplicity and clarity to protect cognitive capacity, rather than overloading it.

- *Belonging and connection*: Co-creation activities, which are many within the methods we share, naturally promote feelings of belonging by inviting people into the process rather than designing solutions for them, without their voice.

- *Emotion-driven design*: You'll see how storytelling tools, experience mapping and journey design help you build communications that engage emotional centres of the brain, making the IC experience more memorable, meaningful and impactful.

- *Supporting autonomy and choice*: Through the design sprint methods and co-creation activities, you'll learn how to build communication solutions that offer employees more voice, more flexibility and more influence. This, in turn, strengthens intrinsic motivation and engagement.

- *Uncovering meaning*: The tools will also help you to understand what truly matters to your people, rather than making assumptions. This means your IC solutions will connect with the values your people hold, their aspirations and lived realities, making them feel personally meaningful and relevant.

- *Building trust and psychological safety*: Every tool and approach, from problem framing to solution prototyping, is designed to involve your people early, listen deeply and respond transparently. All of which are key drivers of organizational trust and emotional safety.

In short, the methods we share as part of our people-first approach are not just a toolkit. They provide a way of working that embeds the science of communication and experience, the power of empathy and the best of human-centred design into every step.

By following the people-first approach, you'll be:

- Working with, not against, how the human brain and heart operate.
- Moving beyond broadcast communications to real engagement.
- Future-proofing your skills in a world where AI will replace much of the process of IC but never replace human connection.

Table 3.1 provides a summary of how the theory and concepts we have shared within this chapter are integrated into our people-first IC approach.

TABLE 3.1 From science to practice: how the people-first approach brings it to life

Human principle	What the science tells us	How the people-first approach to IC embeds it
Empathy	Deep understanding of needs, emotions, motivations drives better engagement and relevance.	Empathy maps and personas help you stand in your people's shoes and design communication around their real experiences.
Emotion-driven engagement	Emotional resonance makes communication more memorable and action-inspiring.	Storytelling frameworks, experience mapping and journey design focus on creating emotional, meaningful experiences.
Cognitive capacity	Overload reduces attention, memory and trust. Simplicity and fluency are key.	Tools like design sprints, problem framing and prioritization help you simplify, align and reduce cognitive load.
Autonomy and choice	Giving people voice, influence and choice increases engagement and intrinsic motivation.	Co-creation workshops and prototyping allow employees to contribute, shape and influence their IC experience.
Trust and psychological safety	Trust grows when people are listened to, understood and involved early.	Discovery activities (e.g. experience mapping, empathy interviews) surface real needs early and guide transparent design.
Meaning and purpose	Purpose and meaning drive connection, motivation and resilience.	People-first tools help you uncover what matters most to your people, enabling the design of IC experiences that feel personally meaningful and relevant.
Belonging and connection	Humans thrive when they feel connected and included.	Human-centred design methods foster inclusion, capture diverse voices and create shared ownership of outcomes.

From science to practice: how the people-first approach brings it to life

We've explored the science of internal communication and why it gives us a powerful foundation. But it's empathy that makes that science actionable, relevant and truly human. The best IC isn't just informed by theory; it's designed for people, with people and around what they really need to thrive at work.

Understanding cognitive load helps us simplify. Understanding emotion helps us connect. Understanding human motivation helps us build communications that empower and energize. But when we bring empathy into the picture, we stop guessing and we start designing experiences that feel personal, intuitive and meaningful.

And we have emphasized why you should care – you'll future-proof your skills in the era of AI, elevate the role of internal communication and most importantly, create workplaces where people feel heard, valued, connected and empowered to thrive. As we move into the next chapter of the book, we'll look at future-proofing your skills and explore what this means against a backdrop of AI, which is disrupting workplaces beyond anything we have seen in our lifetime. In subsequent chapters, we'll equip you with the practical tools and methods to bring people-first IC to life. This means you'll be able to design and deliver communication experiences your people will feel, remember and act on. Because great communication isn't just delivered, it's experienced.

CHAPTER IN SUMMARY

- **Internal communication is human at its core**: It's about what people need to think, feel and do to engage, connect and thrive at work.

- **Psychology and neuroscience give us a strong foundation**, showing how people process information, respond to emotion and experience motivation.

- **Empathy is the bridge** between theory and lived experience. It ensures we design IC around what actually matters to our people.

- **Great IC experiences feel intuitive, personal and emotionally engaging**, much like the best consumer experiences.

- **The future of IC lies in becoming experience designers**, blending behavioural science with empathy and human-centred design.

- **Our people-first approach bakes these ideas into practical tools and methods**, enabling you to deliver communication that informs, inspires and elevates the employee experience.

References

Achor, S (2011) *The Happiness Advantage: The seven principles of positive psychology that fuel success and performance at work*, Random House Group Publishing, London

Ajzen, I (1991) The theory of planned behavior, *Organizational Behavior and Human*, 50 (2), 179–211

Baron-Cohen, S (2011) *The Science of Evil: On empathy and the origins of cruelty*, Basic Books, New York

Baumeister, R F and Leary, M R (1995) The need to belong: Desire for interpersonal attachments as a fundamental human motivation, *Psychological Bulletin*, 117 (3), 497–529

BetterUp (2020) The value of belonging at work: New frontiers for inclusion, BetterUp, https://grow.betterup.com/resources/the-value-of-belonging-at-work-the-business-case-for-investing-in-workplace-inclusion#:~:text=Findings%20 from%20our%20latest%20groundbreaking,what%20makes%20 belonging%20so%20important%3F (archived at https://perma.cc/55JA-L5SW)

Bridger, E and Gannaway, B (2024) *Employee Experience by Design: How to create an effective EX for competitive advantage*, 2nd ed, Kogan Page, London

Brown, T (2009) *Change by Design: How design thinking creates new alternatives for business and society*, Harvard Business Press, Cambridge

Dweck, C S (2006) *Mindset: The new psychology of success*, Random House, New York

Edelman Trust Institute (2024) *2024 Edelman Trust Barometer: Innovation in peril.* [pdf] Edelman, www.edelman.com/sites/g/files/aatuss191/files/2024-02/2024%20Edelman%20Trust%20Barometer%20Global%20Report_FINAL. pdf (archived at https://perma.cc/U3QV-FV3Q)

Edmondson, A C (2019) *The Fearless Organization: Creating psychological safety in the workplace for learning, innovation, and growth*, Wiley, Hoboken, NJ

Frankl, V E (2004) *Man's Search for Meaning*, Rider, London (Original work published in 1946)

Fredrickson, B L (2001) The role of positive emotions in positive psychology: The broaden-and-build theory of positive emotions, *American Psychologist*, 56 (3), 218–26

Goleman, D (2006) *Social Intelligence: The new science of human relationships*, Bantam Books, New York

Hamilton, D R (2017) *The Five Side Effects of Kindness: This book will make you feel better, be happier & live longer*, Hay House UK Ltd, London

Irvine, W B (2013) *The Meaning of Life*, Oxford University Press, Oxford

Kalbach, J (2020) *The Jobs to Be Done Playbook: Align your markets, organization, and strategy around customer needs*, O'Reilly Media, Sebastopol, CA

Lemon, K N and Verhoef, P C (2016) Understanding customer experience throughout the customer journey, *Journal of Marketing*, 80 (6), 69–96

Neumeier, M (2005) *The Brand Gap: How to bridge the distance between business strategy and design*, New Riders, Berkeley, CA

Pink, D (2009) *Drive: The surprising truth about what motivates us*, Canongate, Edinburgh

Rock, D (2008) SCARF: A brain-based model for collaborating with and influencing others, *NeuroLeadership Journal*, 1 (1), 1–9

Ryan, R M and Deci, E L (2000) Intrinsic and extrinsic motivations: Classic definitions and new directions, *Contemporary Educational Psychology*, 25 (1), 54–67

Wilson, T D (2002) *Strangers to Ourselves: Discovering the adaptive unconscious*, Belknap Press of Harvard University Press, Cambridge, MA

World Economic Forum (2025) *The Future of Jobs Report 2025*, World Economic Forum, Geneva, reports.weforum.org/docs/WEF_Future_of_Jobs_Report_2025.pdf (archived at https://perma.cc/6V5W-HL8J)

Zak, P (2017) The neuroscience of trust, *Harvard Business Review*

Zaki, J (2019) *The War for Kindness: Building empathy in a fractured world*, Crown Publishing Group, New York

04

Reimagining your role for the people-first future of IC

A profession at a crossroads

We've explored the evolution of our profession and shown how, for more than a century, internal communicators have responded to the changing demands of the day. From the welfare-minded pioneers of the Victorian era and the message-focused industrial editors of the mid-20th century, to the multi-channel digital experts of today; our roles have constantly been reimagined and retooled. And now we stand at the edge of another transformation. But this one is different. Today's shift isn't evolutionary, it's revolutionary.

Right now we are experiencing a convergence of powerful political, economic, social and technological forces that are shaking the very foundations of work. First, employee expectations are rising, with people demanding greater flexibility, more meaning, genuine transparency and fairness from their employers. Second, AI is rapidly acquiring many of the skills we've traditionally been celebrated for – writing, summarizing, editing, planning. And finally we have reached a point where traditional approaches to internal communication no longer work. We struggle to capture and maintain the attention of employees, change programmes fail, engagement levels remain stubbornly low and the level of noise constantly increases. Add to that a world that is increasingly volatile, uncertain, complex and ambiguous (VUCA) and you have the perfect storm.

Battered by these winds of change, the identity of our profession is once again in flux. What are we here to do? What's the role of the communicator in the age of AI with increasing employee expectations at work? Is more content the answer? Do we really need more channels? Who owns employee engagement? How does IC fit with employee experience? What is internal communication anyway?

No longer is it enough to craft a killer message or manage an integrated campaign. These skills remain important but they are no longer what defines our value. Today, internal communicators are being called on to do something much more profound: to shape meaningful experiences, build human connection and quite literally 'make sense' in the messy, unpredictable reality of modern work.

In short, we're being asked to shift from expert to enabler. From information engineer to experience designer. From message crafter to meaning-maker. This is not a crisis though; it's the start of a new and exciting era for our profession. It's an invitation for us to reimagine our roles and refocus on the human aspects of work. It's an opportunity to let go of narrow definitions of our worth and step into something bigger and bolder than what came before. Indeed, it's nothing short of a professional revolution.

But to seize this opportunity, we need to first look in the mirror. Many of the skills and capabilities we've spent years building, developing and fine-tuning are now being automated or augmented by AI. The machines are already able to generate first-class copy, adapt tone of voice, recommend actions and personalize messages at scale. What AI can't do, however, is deeply understand context, sense emotions, earn trust, or navigate the nuances of culture. It doesn't and can't know what it feels like to work in your organization or to juggle the many conflicting priorities of modern life.

And here lies the big opportunity for internal communicators.

The future of IC belongs to those practitioners who can do what AI can't do – those who can empathize, connect, listen, inspire, co-create and sense-make. To succeed in this brave new world, we must double down on our humanity, not distance ourselves from it.

In earlier chapters, we explored what it means to adopt a genuinely 'people-first' approach to IC. We traced the evolution of IC through the three ages: process-led, expert-led and people-first. We explored the science behind designing communication experiences that resonate, based on empathy and a deep understanding of human nature.

This chapter brings those threads together. We're going to explore what this means for you, the communicator navigating this inflection point. We'll explore the human strengths, core skills and technical capabilities you need to not just survive but thrive in the age of AI, and how you can begin to develop them right now. We'll look at existing competency frameworks and explore where they still serve us and where they fall short. We'll introduce six distinct human strengths that we believe will define the people-first communicator of the future. And we'll explore how to cultivate them in yourself and your team. We'll also examine how to partner, rather than compete, with AI and why this partnership is key to being more human, not less.

Ultimately, this is a call to reimagine your role, recalibrate your skill set and redefine your professional identity. This is about future-proofing your career too, by shifting the focus to the areas AI can't touch, at least not yet. Because what got us here won't get us there. But if we embrace this shift and lean into the deeply human qualities that machines can't replicate, we won't just survive this transformation, we'll lead it.

What got us here won't get us there

In the two decades since this millennium began, internal communication has come of age. Once seen as a low-level, tactical function, focused on newsletters, posters and cascade packs, it's now increasingly recognized as a strategic discipline. Much of this transformation has been shaped and enabled by professional bodies and thought leaders through competency frameworks and professional development that help define, develop and evaluate internal communication expertise.

These frameworks, a number of which we have helped shape, have provided much-needed structure to a historically under-defined and in the eyes of many senior stakeholders, 'fluffy' profession. They have undoubtedly raised the professional bar, encouraged new entrants to carve out a career in IC, supported career progression and bolstered the case for IC to be recognized by the C-suite. But as we step into the new world of work, shaped by AI, complexity and consumer-grade expectations, we must ask an uncomfortable but necessary question: are the skills and competencies that once made us successful still fit for purpose?

Mapping the landscape

Let's begin by taking a look at some of the competency frameworks that have emerged since the early 2000s. A quarter of a century ago, IC legend Bill Quirke published the first edition of his seminal book, *Making the Connections* (2000). One of the first works to focus on the evolving role of the internal communicator, its publication coincided with a shift towards a more structured and professional practice. With the technological transformation gathering pace, IC professionals were being forced to evolve from the 'organizational post office' to technical specialists and, increasingly, leadership advisors. His 'roles ladder' captured the five different types of role communicators were being asked to fulfil (listed here from bottom rung to top):

- Distributor – focus on sending stuff out.
- Crafter and drafter – focus on writing, designing, briefing and event planning.
- Technical advisor – focus on channels, technology, messaging and targeting.
- Consultant – focus on planning, prioritization, coordination and facilitating thinking.
- Coach – focus on strategy planning, strategic alignment, objective setting and advising clients.

Quirke highlighted that IC practitioners were typically required to work with clients in one of three ways: shaping strategy, planning and managing programmes, or execution. He stressed practitioners needed to operate at all three levels and move up and down the roles ladder at will.

In practice, that meant that a senior-level IC specialist had to not only provide expert advice and coaching to senior leaders but also be able to roll up their sleeves and draft copy or distribute messages. Whatever step on the roles ladder you were at, Quirke argued, you had to possess the skills of the steps 'beneath' the level you were at.

This model was compelling back then and has remained relevant since, but the rise of AI forces us to rethink the nature of our roles today and in the future. Gen AI can craft and draft, personalize and distribute content, and it knows the answers to all of the technical questions we could ask. And very soon, agentic AI will do even more, acting as an IC assistant. That's a threat if you're competing with AI to get a foothold on the first few rungs of the roles ladder, but a blessing if you can ask it to hold the ladder steady while you climb!

Interest in professional skills continued throughout the 2000s. In 2003, the authors were both part of a collaborative, cross-industry task force established to create the first-ever competency framework for IC. Built with representation from a range of international professional bodies, the 'Inter-Comm Matrix' identified the knowledge, skills and experience needed to succeed as an internal communicator at any stage in your career. The first of its kind, the Inter-Comm Matrix was both groundbreaking and influential. It provided a single, unified view and delivered much-needed guidance for IC pros.

However, for all its strengths, the Inter-Comm Matrix failed to acknowledge the messy reality of a career in IC. It implied progress was a simple linear route from new entrant to mature professional. Like Quirke's roles ladder, it was interpreted as a tool to get you from A to B in a straight line.

The first decade of the 21st century saw the emergence of new specialist roles, the creation of ever more sophisticated corporate IC functions and a genuine diversity as people moved into the field from elsewhere. The authors are a good example of this richness, with Emma coming from an academic background with a strong focus on psychology and Lee shifting from a broader corporate communication and PR role during the early part of his career. There was a growing recognition that a different kind of professional framework was needed, one that could be 'flexed' to take account of the different entry points, career routes, types of role and style of practitioner that now existed.

Enter Competent Communicators

In 2007, Liam Fitzpatrick and Sue Dewhurst, two original members of the Inter-Comm working party, published a new competency framework (Fitzpatrick and Dewhurst, 2007). They understood that the world of IC was evolving at a rapid pace and undertook extensive research to uncover 12 competencies for IC.

For each of these competencies, they identified three levels of performance, basic, intermediate and advanced, together with associated behaviours. The addition of behaviour was transformative as it shifted the focus from what a person needs to know and do, to how an individual approaches their role. Importantly, the precise mix of competencies required to operate effectively depended on the role. For example, a communication leader needed a different mix to an events specialist. This wasn't a one-size-fits-all framework, but was designed to be flexed to suit specific circumstances, addressing the key weakness of the Inter-Comm Matrix.

We love that their framework captured both technical and human-centred skills. The importance of emotional intelligence, empathy, relationship building, active listening and adaptability – skills that are even more vital today.

TABLE 4.1 Competent Communicators: 12 competencies for IC

Building effective relationships	Developing and maintaining relationships that inspire trust and respect. Building a network and being able to influence others to make things happen.
Business focus	Having a clear understanding of the business issues and using communication to help solve organizational problems and achieve organizational objectives.
Consulting and coaching	Recommending appropriate solutions to customers; helping others to make informed decisions; building people's communication competence.
Craft (writing and design)	Using and developing the right mix of practical communication abilities (e.g. writing and design management) to hold the confidence of peers and colleagues.
Cross-functional awareness	Understanding the different contributions from other disciplines and working with colleagues from across the organization to achieve better results.
Developing other communicators	Helping other communicators build their communication competence and develop their careers.
Innovation and creativity	Looking for new ways of working, exploring best practice and delivering original and imaginative approaches to communication problems.
Listening	Conducting research and managing mechanisms for gathering feedback and employee reactions.
Making it happen	Turning plans into successfully implemented actions.
Planning	Planning communication programmes and operations, evaluating results.
Specialist	Having specific subject-matter expertise in a specialist area.
Vision and standards	Defining or applying a consistent approach to communication and maintaining professional and ethical standards.

IABC Global Standard and Career Roadmap

In 2011, the International Association of Business Communicators (IABC) initiated a major global initiative to define career paths and related competencies across the communication profession (IABC, 2013; Cropley, 2013). This work culminated with the publication of the Global Standard for the Communication Profession. It aimed to create a unified framework that would guide communication professionals of all types – whether focused internally or externally – across various industries and regions.

The IABC Global Standard is built around six core principles:

- Ethics: Adhering to the highest standards of professional behaviour, including honesty, integrity and respect for cultural values.
- Consistency: Ensuring a coherent and unified message across all communication channels and audiences.
- Context: Understanding the internal and external environments in which the organization operates.
- Analysis: Conducting thorough research and evaluation to inform communication strategies.
- Strategy: Developing and implementing communication plans that align with organizational goals.
- Engagement: Fostering meaningful interactions with stakeholders to build relationships and support organizational objectives.

Complementing the Global Standard, the IABC Career Roadmap outlined four career milestones that represent the progression of a communication professional's development: foundation, generalist/specialist, strategic advisor and business leader.

However, once again, the approach assumes a linear career journey focused largely on technical and analytical skills.

IOIC PROFESSION MAP

More recently, the UK's Institute of Internal Communication (IoIC) has established a new benchmark for the skills, knowledge and behaviours needed to excel in IC.

The IoIC Profession Map Framework was first published in 2016 and has been regularly updated since then (IoIC, 2016, updated 2023). It helps individuals articulate the role of IC within organizations, map their skills and knowledge, identify gaps and create personal development plans. It captures six professional practice areas and outlines, for each, what we need to know (knowledge) and do (skills).

The profession map includes not just the technical aspects of IC, but also some of the human-centred elements of it. Importantly, it emphasizes the need for practitioners to foster a sense of connection, purpose and informed engagement with employees, recognizing that these human-centred skills are integral to the role of internal communicators.

FIGURE 4.1 The IoIC profession map

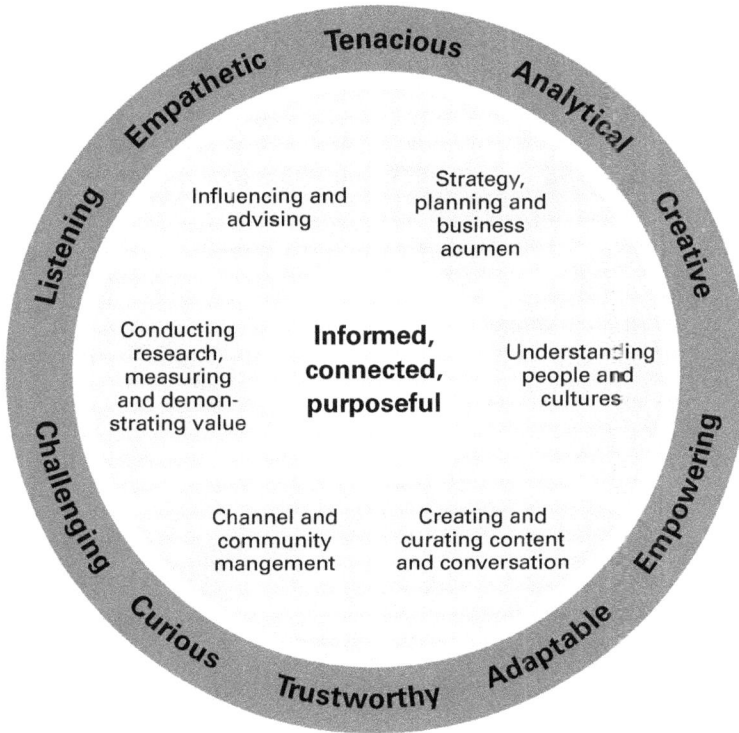

A shift of emphasis

These frameworks have provided a solid foundation for the evolving communication profession, but feel very much 'of their time'. They were built for a world where the core challenge was scaling communication and ensuring employees had the information they needed to do their job. The communicator's job was to take expert knowledge and distribute it efficiently and clearly. In that context, technical skill and functional expertise were paramount.

The changing needs of employees, rapid advancement of technology, particularly AI, and the increasing emphasis on human-centred approaches demands a change of emphasis. The challenge has shifted from distribution to connection. We are dealing with increasingly complex, highly distributed workforces, hyper-personalized expectations, growing trust gaps, accelerating change and cultural fragmentation.

Internal communicators must move from being experts in communication output to enablers of communication experience. This means reframing our expertise from the knowledge we hold, to the trust we build and the insight we generate. It means prioritizing the human strengths of empathy, sense-making, influence and co-creation.

We need to stop seeing our value in 'what we do' and start recognizing it in *how* we design and deliver a brilliant communication experience. This doesn't mean discarding the technical skills but embracing the fact that we now have an agile and expert partner in AI to help with all of this. Our role now is to turn up the focus on the human side of the job. We need to integrate and prioritize human-centric competencies to ensure that IC remains effective and relevant in today's workplace. These human strengths are moving from support act to headliner.

AI is already transforming IC

We've built our careers on our ability to write well, plan and execute campaigns, craft compelling messages and manage an ever-growing array of channels. These were the skills and knowledge that made us trusted experts in our organizations, and rightly so. Until now, these capabilities were in short supply and high demand.

But the world has shifted on its axis, and it is continuing to change at lightning speed. AI is reshaping every industry and profession, including ours. The rise of AI is not just a technological disruption; it's a redefinition of what it means to be a professional in IC.

We asked Monique Zytnik, global communication leader, author of *Internal Communication in the Age of Artificial Intelligence* and IABC EMENA Region Chair for 2024/25, to share her thoughts on what all this means in the context of our professional skill set. Her article captures just how profound a shift this is.

REAL-WORLD EXAMPLE
The future skills internal communicators need in the age of AI agents

BY MONIQUE ZYTNIK

Introduction

In early 2024, working with large language models (LLMs) like ChatGPT and Gemini was like managing an intern. These tools needed careful guidance, explicit instructions and constant supervision. Significant time needed to be invested. Additionally, hallucinations were frequent, and referencing reliable sources was still hit-and-miss.

Fast forward to mid-2025, and the picture has changed significantly. These tools have evolved into capable digital assistants. They help us execute communication tasks faster and with greater accuracy. But while productivity is improving, and according to a Danish working paper released in May 2025, slowly at 3 per cent, our profession is facing something deeper: transformation.

Artificial intelligence (AI) is not just a tool for doing the same work faster. It has the potential to significantly reshape how we fulfil the role of internal communication itself. From how we collaborate with leaders to how we engage employees, the boundaries of our profession are expanding. And with that expansion comes a critical question: What new skills must we develop to stay relevant and lead with impact?

The shifting landscape

Let's begin with what's already changed. Imagine being asked to write an article about a workplace well-being initiative. In the past, you may have interviewed key stakeholders, researched the topic and drafted content over several hours. Today, with the help of tools like Claude or ChatGPT, you can generate a research-backed draft in seconds. Pre-set the tone, structure and target audience, and you'll get a version ready to review. If your audience personas are integrated into the LLM, you can even customize the content for different employee groups instantly.

The challenge is, if we can quickly do these tasks with AI, then so can others. If your HR business partner can generate a well-written all-staff email using an AI tool, what unique value do you bring as a communicator? AI has enabled people who can't draw to bring their artistic visions to life, people to become fashion designers without knowing how to design clothes, and so much more including models to model using their digital twin, without being there.

Communication is no different.

That's where our strategic mindset becomes essential. While AI may be able to draft emails and create communication strategies, it can lack contextual judgement. It might not understand your organizational culture, change sensitivities or the sequencing of key messages. It can't sit with a leader, challenge assumptions or navigate internal politics.

As AI continues to evolve, communicators must reposition themselves. Our value is not in the tasks we complete but in the outcomes we enable.

The rise of agentic AI

The next significant shift is already underway: agentic AI. These systems don't just respond to prompts. They can initiate tasks, collaborate with other AI agents and manage interconnected workflows. This is a leap beyond tools like ChatGPT, which rely on direct human input.

Agentic AI systems are being deployed by companies like Amazon, which is using them to manage logistics, and by professional services firms like Deloitte and EY to streamline operations and enhance productivity. These platforms can act autonomously, completing tasks that once required multiple human interactions.

What does this mean for us? It means we're no longer just working with AI tools; we're potentially going to be operating in hybrid teams made up of people and AI agents. This requires a new set of competencies: not just knowing how to prompt effectively, but understanding how to delegate, monitor and evaluate work done by AI counterparts.

Seven future-ready communication skills

To remain relevant and valuable in this emerging environment, internal communicators must develop a range of new capabilities and enhance existing ones. Here are my top seven:

1. *Deep audience understanding*

We need to move beyond traditional segmentation and develop a more multidimensional view of our audiences. This includes behaviour, culture, language, engagement history and channel preferences. AI can help uncover these insights at scale and enable advanced segmentation based on factors like engagement levels or responsiveness to communication. Marketing customer relationship management (CRM) platforms like Klaviyo use AI segmentation based on several different data points to assess how engaged customers are and where they are on their purchase journey to allow for more nuanced messaging and communication flows.

This opens the door to designing communication journeys that are not only data-driven but dynamic, responsive and more effective.

2. *Relationship building across functions*

Internal communication doesn't operate in isolation. We need to strengthen partnerships with HR, IT, legal, DEI and operations. As our scope broadens, new roles like 'Employee Experience Director' or 'Workplace Culture Partner' may emerge, requiring us to operate with greater influence and integration.

3. Designing communication experiences

We need to shift thinking from 'What content do I want to share?' to 'What experience do I want our people to have?' How can we streamline the experience so they aren't overloaded by content? What is the information flow within this experience? How do the individual messages fit together to tell our desired narrative? This becomes increasingly important following the University of Nottingham's research in 2024, showing a direct link between information overload and burnout/stress in the workplace. Too much untailored, irrelevant content without clear communication channel use does harm to our people.

4. Strategic counsel and crisis leadership

Our role as advisors becomes even more critical in an AI-influenced world. Leaders may rely on AI-generated plans, but communicators are needed to question, contextualize and guide decision-making. We are the voice of conscience, context and clarity. We are there to challenge, whereas AI is designed to please. For example, in April 2025, OpenAI rolled back GPT because the update was overly flattering or agreeable, but disingenuous, often described as sycophantic. To get a balanced view, a CEO would need to specifically ask their LLM to challenge them.

5. Narrative and storytelling alignment

AI can generate words, but it can't weave a story that aligns with a company's strategic direction, values and long-term narrative. That's our job.

6. Tech and data fluency

We don't need to be data scientists, but we do need to understand how AI works, how data flows and how communication technologies are evolving so we can reimagine how we work. Collaborating with IT and using data dashboards to inform decisions should be a normal part of our role. Understanding data and data visualization tools also helps us spot trends, for example, in sentiment analysis of our enterprise social networks such as Slack or Microsoft's Viva Engage.

7. Legal nous

AI governance, making sure we have the right guardrails in place, and are following laws, adds another layer of complexity. I wouldn't say this is a skill, but rather an understanding we need to invest time in. For example, the European AI Act is still fresh from 2024 and evolving.

Working in hybrid teams

Hybrid teams are no longer just about working remotely or in-office. They now include AI agents as active contributors. These agents will handle everything from scheduling meetings and preparing recaps to drafting emails and analysing feedback data.

Our role is to coordinate, interpret and optimize their outputs. We must also ensure ethical considerations are respected, especially in areas like employee data, tone of voice and accessibility.

As Richard Socher, CEO of You.com, noted, 'An AI agent that does 80% of the workflows of 80% of digitized jobs might be around the corner in about three years' (2024). That's a massive disruption to how we work and an even bigger opportunity to lead the change.

Regional perspectives and a shared future

Different regions are moving at different speeds. European communicators may focus more on data governance, privacy, multilingual content and navigating regulatory frameworks. In other regions, the focus may be on scale, speed and adoption of new platforms.

But by 2030, a shared professional standard will likely emerge. The internal communicator of the future will be strategic, tech-savvy, emotionally intelligent and a trusted ethical guide who can connect communication to business outcomes.

Our core purpose remains

Despite all this change, our fundamental role remains the same: to connect people, build trust, support culture and align employees with the organization's goals, and to communicate at scale with our employees from CEO to front line, for business success.

AI doesn't take this away. It expands what's possible. It enables us to scale personalization, deepen engagement and measure impact like never before.

The path may be different, but the purpose remains.

Monique's piece touches on the incredible pace of change and some of the ways AI will impact our roles. Like us, she sees this as an opportunity more than a threat – a chance to reinforce our core purpose and extend our impact.

New AI tools are entering the market almost daily, enabling highly effective communication with minimal 'expert' intervention. For example, at the time of writing, Google's Notebook LM is enabling webinars or video content to be turned into bite-sized podcasts, complete with AI hosts pulling out and chatting through the key themes. A few years ago, to produce and deliver podcasts like this would have taken considerable time, effort, resources and critically, expertise. Now this happens as a push of a button. According to McKinsey (2023), up to 30 per cent of the typical employee's time is now potentially automatable through AI, and in IC, this could be significantly higher. Looking ahead, it's hard to imagine IC roles will remain as they are today.

Alarmed? You shouldn't be – we believe this technological shift will liberate us.

The gift of letting go

Once we stop defining ourselves purely by our outputs, the newsletter we created, the PowerPoint deck we built, the update we edited, we open ourselves up to a far more meaningful and lasting contribution. If AI can draft a pin-sharp message in seconds, then our value can't rely on us being the fastest writer in the business. If AI can plan content calendars using predictive analytics, our value can't lie in logistics and 'air traffic control'. And if AI can measure and report on channel engagement in real time, then our value can't be in counting clicks.

So where does our value lie? We believe that answer lies in what AI cannot do:

- Understanding the mood of a workforce after a tough restructure.
- Facilitating a conversation between a nervous manager and a disengaged team.
- Spotting the invisible dynamics that derail a change initiative.
- Unearthing a human story that makes people feel seen, inspired and connected.
- Knowing employees at a deep level.

These are the irreplaceable human acts of communication. And they are what will define our future. One of the compelling arguments for the shift to People-First IC is the recognition that, in the age of AI, expertise is no longer scarce. Until now, our professional identity has been shaped by being the communication expert in the room. But this expertise no longer has the currency it once did. As the AI age gathers pace, the expert-led approach to IC will become increasingly obsolete. Instead, we must recalibrate our roles around the human parts of the job, for example, co-creation, curiosity, facilitation empathy, adaptability and trust.

This is a big shift and one that mirrors broader organizational changes. As hierarchies flatten, agility increases and employee expectations shift, we're going to see declining demand for many experts. And an increasing demand for people who can build trust across silos, connect leaders with employees, sense and respond to cultural undercurrents and critically co-design brilliant IC experiences, not just cascade content.

From producer to partner

This shift is already underway. At London's Heathrow Airport, teams are integrating generative AI into operational workflows, using it to enhance communication, streamline safety briefings and improve HR content delivery (Capgemini Research Institute, 2024, p 23). This shift allows communicators to focus more on experience design and human-centred engagement.

Instead of spending hours crafting copy, AI-empowered teams are able to invest time in empathy interviews with front-line colleagues, co-creating onboarding materials and training people managers to have better conversations with their teams.

Similarly, at accountancy firm KPMG, internal teams are being equipped with AI prompt engineering and content prototyping skills to accelerate communication workflows and enhance audience engagement. In parallel, KPMG is advancing AI governance through its Trusted AI framework – empowering professionals to ensure ethical, inclusive and transparent use of generative AI across the organization (KPMG, 2025).

In both examples, AI isn't a threat. It's an assistant, a powerful support tool that expands human creativity, insight and strategic influence.

The paradox is that as we integrate AI into our daily work, it gives us the much-needed time and space to become more human. It's not an either/or decision; to stay relevant, we must refocus on the aspects of communication that cannot be automated and partner with AI to streamline those that can. We must evolve from expert practitioners to AI-enabled human experience leaders.

We asked Liam FitzPatrick, one of the architects of the Competent Communicators framework, for his thoughts on this topic. Liam specializes in the development of communication teams and processes and is co-author of two landmark handbooks on professional practice. Here he discusses how technology is empowering internal communicators with rich intelligence and freeing them up to focus on their role as trusted advisors and guides.

REAL-WORLD EXAMPLE
Structuring your employee intelligence operation

BY LIAM FITZPATRICK

Increasingly, technology makes it easier to reflect on employee sentiment. It has always been the communicator's role to run an internal intelligence operation; listening, analysing and explaining, so with the development of AI and other tools, there's space to focus on the higher value part of the process – helping leaders make better communications decisions.

In every branch of communications practice, acting as a bridge between an organization and its audiences is a vital capability. The skilled professional knows their organization and its plans well enough to explain them. And they understand stakeholders or audiences so they can anticipate their response, frame relevant messages and advise the organization on reactions.

We're good at it because most of us are driven by a combination of empathy and a desire to try out new approaches – be that messaging, channels or strategies to deliver for our organizations.

Which is why I've always used the analogy of running an intelligence operation – the process of bringing together information gathering, analysis and reporting. Although part of the process can be done routinely or even automated, it takes human curiosity and empathy to deliver deep value, helping leaders make better decisions.

Without those attributes, the holy grail of communications practice – mutual understanding and support – remains elusive.

Historically though, the whole value chain from listening to advising has been a challenge for many communicators. With limited tools available, a practitioner's sources and methods have often been poor. The annual survey was sometimes as useful as a cracked rear-view mirror on a motorway and gathering opinions could be a time-consuming and expensive task.

In particular, the data from surveys isn't always deeply analysed. Apart from applying benchmarks from similar organizations (which can be disappointing), many employee studies can limit themselves to creating indices of engagement or motivation from an aggregation of responses to a few questions. The time-consuming work of manually coding open-ended comments doesn't always produce useful information, and the results are rarely cross-referenced with the wealth of information that exists about what employees are actually doing or how the organization is performing.

No matter how intrigued or motivated the communicator, few of us have had the time to keep looking for answers that are now available in moments. The advent of more sophisticated technology brings a wealth of opportunities.

Surveying has become simpler and can be done more quickly without relying on catch-all annual census questionnaires. Reviewing the sentiment of online comments can be automated and there's a stronger prospect of cross-referencing data with the things that matter to the organization or to customers.

Once, it took an army of statisticians to align information about attrition, performance, customer experience, recruitment, benefits take-up, engagement with communications or internal media use. Now, leaders are excited by the possibilities of bringing information together to spot underlying patterns.

However, research from organizations like Gartner is sounding a note of caution about the role of AI in HR and workforce processes. Communicators will recognize immediately why – it takes people to really understand people. This is where our empathic antennae come into play.

Communicators are adept at making time to seek out regular colleagues and have conversations with them about what they are hearing and understanding. Short conversations in the coffee queue, the car park or after all-hands meetings tell us a lot about what is really happening. Such connections are a defence against kidding ourselves that people are reading our content, understanding our messages or agreeing with everything the boss is saying. Without it, we risk relying on the cold data tables and the tendency to hear what we want to hear from survey results alone.

Now, combining personal networking with smarter data tools offers a combination of speed, depth and human interpretation. The communicator who understands the audience is better placed to ask questions of the available data and make sense of the outputs from automated listening. If you know the people, you understand the picture that the data is painting.

Well-trained automated agents, under the guidance of experienced practitioners, should now be able to shortcut the analysis or fusion stage of the intelligence operation. The marriage of personal insight with facts and evidence better supports strategies that drive change.

Leaders have always expected their communications teams to bring creative and human-centred ideas, but they are also learning that it is possible to have evidence-based conversations about what has been treated as a soft subject in the past. There's more demand (and more opportunity) for advisors who can be trusted.

And for many of us, the advisory part of the job is perhaps the most enjoyable bit!

When Sue Dewhurst and I asked several hundred communicators about their skills some years ago, we were struck by the importance of the soft, personal qualities over craft skills. While the ability to deliver well-written copy or to shape messages was important, our surveying highlighted the emphasis that practitioners placed on relationships, on insight based on experience, on data and on the ability to coach and advise.

There was an acknowledgement that strong delivery capability mattered but that being proficient with the pen, the camera or the keyboard only took us so far. Developing plans, debating channel choices or preparing a leader to present with confidence and authenticity has always drawn on human traits and competencies.

As the employee communications profession tries to understand the benefits of artificial intelligence, it seems that it has potential to bolster and support the things which practitioners and their internal 'customers' get most from. Better tech-assisted insight gathering and analysis makes space to explore with real managers of real humans how awareness, understanding, support and behaviour change can be delivered.

This then deepens the opportunity for the professional advisor to develop their skills as a counsellor and guide. Helping colleagues shape their messaging to achieve outcomes has always been what excites many of us and is what we I-supported leaders have learnt to expect; used intelligently, AI can help us carve out the time and the insight that we know really makes the difference.

Introducing the People-First IC Capability Model: a prototype for a changing profession

Over the past decade, a range of frameworks have helped us understand what effective internal communication looks like. But as the world of work evolves and AI automates many traditional tasks, a new question emerges: what makes internal communication truly *human* and irreplaceable? The value of IC is no longer rooted in delivery and execution. Many of the traditional technical skills featured in legacy frameworks we've shared here are increasingly being automated. All of this means it's time to redefine what makes IC professionals indispensable. We're calling this the **People-First IC Capability Model,** but consider it a working title and a living prototype. In true experience design fashion, we're building this in real time, getting curious, testing our assumptions, listening to feedback and iterating as we go.

This model is a reflection of the journey so far and the future we want to shape together. It builds on the best of what's already out there while reframing what's needed for the future. It aims to bring together human strengths and future-facing skills in a model that's as dynamic and adaptable as the communicators it serves. This is what we believe People-First IC looks like in practice: collaborative, emergent and experience-driven. We're sharing this early version openly because we believe internal communication is evolving and we want you to help lead that change. What follows is a working prototype, shaped by ongoing learning, experimentation and dialogue across our community.

How we got here

To build this model, we looked at three powerful sources of insight:

1. THE BEST OF TODAY: THE IOIC PROFESSION MAP

We started with the IoIC's trusted Profession Map, which is still the gold standard for internal comms capabilities. It continues to be a solid foundation for technical skills like planning, writing and stakeholder engagement. But we also recognized a need to go further, especially in a world shaped by AI, changing employee expectations and the growing need for experience design.

2. THE PEOPLE-FIRST FUTURE: EX ARCHETYPES AND DESIGN PRACTICE

We also turned to our own employee experience-focused research, particularly the EX Archetypes framework (The EX Space, 2023), to explore what it means to be an experience designer, not just a communicator. This helped us understand the strengths and skills that matter most when you're co-creating moments that shape how people feel at work.

3. EXTERNAL SIGNALS: WHAT THE FUTURE DEMANDS

Finally, we analysed the World Economic Forum's Future of Jobs Report (World Economic Forum, 2025) and Microsoft's Work Trend Index (Microsoft, 2024). These reports show a consistent trend: in a tech-saturated world, human strengths – like creativity, empathy and social influence – are more important than ever.

When we analysed these inputs we came up with a prototype for the People-First IC Capability Model which is built around three distinct layers.

FIGURE 4.2 The People-First IC Capability Model

STRATEGIC SKILLS	SUPERPOWERS	KEY CAPABILITIES
Human-centred design	Empathy	Creating and curating content
Behavioural science	Curiosity	Strategy and planning
Systems thinking	Resilience	Programme delivery
Facilitation and coaching	Creativity	Channel and community
Stakeholder engagement	Influence	management
AI-augmented practice	Courage	Measurement and reporting

IC strengths – what we're calling our 'superpowers'

In the context of internal communication and increasingly, the future of work, we can think of strengths as the enduring, energizing human qualities that shape how we show up and succeed. Unlike technical skills, which can be trained and sometimes automated, strengths are rooted in human psychology. They reflect our natural preferences, emotional tendencies and ways of engaging with the world. Yet while they may feel innate, they are not fixed. As the field of positive psychology has shown, strengths can be nurtured and developed over time through self-awareness, intentional action and supportive environments.

Psychologist Martin Seligman, one of the founders of positive psychology, defines strengths as 'pre-existing capacities for particular ways of behaving, thinking, or feeling that are authentic and energizing to the user, and enable optimal functioning, development and performance' (Linley, 2008, cited in Seligman, 2002).

This perspective positions strengths not as static traits but as dynamic capabilities. In an age of AI, it is precisely these human strengths, such as empathy and curiosity, that will differentiate internal communicators and elevate our impact. These are our 'superpowers'; they are qualities AI cannot replicate but which we can refine, strengthen and bring to the fore.

We have outlined in Table 4.2 what we believe the People-First IC superpowers are.

TABLE 4.2 The six IC superpowers

Strength/ superpower	Description
Empathy	Deep emotional and cognitive understanding of others. Involves deep listening and includes trust-building and emotional intelligence.
Curiosity	The drive to learn, explore, question and challenge assumptions. Fuels creativity and insight.
Resilience	Flexibility, endurance and optimism in the face of uncertainty and change.
Creativity	The ability to generate fresh ideas, reframe problems and design original solutions.
Influence	Building credibility and relationships to shape decisions, perceptions and behaviours.
Courage	Speaking truth to power, challenging norms, and acting with integrity and purpose.

TABLE 4.3 Strategic skills/learnt capabilities

Skill	Description
Human-centred design	Designing communication *with* people, not just *for* them. Includes tools like personas, journey maps and rapid prototyping.
Behavioural science	Using psychology to understand decision-making and shape behaviour. Includes nudging, habit formation and motivation theory.
Systems thinking	Seeing connections, feedback loops and power dynamics across the organization. Helps IC pros work with complexity and influence culture.
Facilitation and coaching	Creating space for dialogue, learning and co-creation. Enabling others rather than broadcasting to them.
Stakeholder engagement	Building trust, credibility and shared ownership with leaders, peers and influencers.
AI-augmented practice	Using AI tools ethically and effectively to enhance communication. Includes prompt engineering, tool fluency and human review.

STRATEGIC SKILLS – OUR LEARNT CAPABILITIES

If human strengths are what define us, strategic skills are how we bring those strengths to life in the work we do. These are the methods, mindsets and applied abilities that allow internal communicators to design experiences, shape behaviour and work systemically within complex organizations.

In traditional IC capability models and frameworks, these skills might have been seen as 'advanced' or 'specialist'. They certainly wouldn't have been at the top of the list of skills needed for IC, if in fact, they even featured at all! But in the People-First IC world, they are **foundational** to design and deliver what we need. They enable IC professionals to step into new roles as facilitators of co-creation, designers of IC moments that matter and advisors in shaping the overall employee experience.

FOUNDATIONAL CAPABILITIES – STILL MATTER, LESS DEFINING

The skills in this layer have traditionally been seen as the 'core competencies' of internal communication: writing, planning, channel management and reporting. And of course they still matter, but their strategic value is changing.

Thanks to rapid advancements in generative AI and automation, these once-differentiating areas of expertise are now increasingly:

- automatable by AI tools
- assisted via co-pilot agents
- expected, rather than exceptional.

That's why we no longer see these as defining strengths of the profession. Instead, we view them as 'foundational capabilities', which are still necessary for delivery but not sufficient for leadership or influence.

They are the 'hygiene factors' of IC; we need them to operate, but they are no longer what sets us apart. The real value now lies in the strategic layer above and in the human strengths that AI can't replicate.

TABLE 4.4 Foundational capabilities

Skill	Description
Creating and curating content	Writing, editing, message development. AI can assist, but humans add emotional nuance and context.
Strategy and planning	Structuring communication journeys. AI can sequence and automate; IC adds strategy and intent.
Programme delivery	Turning plans into action. AI can develop plans, but humans need to coordinate activity and involve others.
Channel and community management	Coordinating message flow across platforms. AI helps optimize; IC ensures relevance.
Measurement and reporting	Interpreting performance data. AI shows patterns; humans surface meaning and act on it and demonstrate ROI.

Each layer reinforces the others. Strengths give IC its human edge. Skills turn strengths into action. Technical tools support scale but no longer define value.

DIAGNOSTIC: YOUR PEOPLE-FIRST IC CAPABILITY SELF-ASSESSMENT

Use this self-assessment as a reflection tool for personal development or team growth.

1. Strengths check – reflect on what energizes you.

Rate each on a scale from 1 (rarely shows up) to 5 (a core strength):

- Empathy: ___
- Curiosity: ___
- Resilience: ___
- Creativity: ___
- Influence: ___
- Courage: ___

Reflection:

- Which feel most natural?
- Which could you develop further?
- Which would you like to grow?

2. Strategic skills inventory – audit your capabilities.

Rate your comfort and confidence (1 = low, 5 = high):

- Human-centred design: ___
- Behavioural science: ___
- Systems thinking: ___
- Facilitation and coaching: ___
- Stakeholder engagement: ___
- AI-augmented practice: ___

Reflection:

- What are your strongest tools?
- What's missing from your toolkit?

3. Foundational capabilities review – reflect on your evolving role.

Which technical skills do you still perform regularly?

- Content creation?
- Campaign planning ?
- Channel orchestration?
- Community management?
- Measurement and reporting?
- Anything else?

Reflection:

- Which tasks could AI support or automate?
- Where can you refocus your time?

Use your answers to map out:

- strengths to lean into
- skills to build
- tasks to reimagine or delegate.

You can revisit this tool quarterly or with your team as part of professional development planning.

Developing your IC superpowers

Understanding which human strengths will define the future of internal communication is one thing. Developing them is another.

Unlike technical skills, which can often be acquired through a well-chosen training course, qualification or textbook, the six superpowers are more dynamic. They're behavioural, contextual and deeply human. We all possess these strengths to a greater or lesser extent, but they require reflection, experimentation and above all, bucketloads of practice to become real superpowers.

The good news? You don't need a big training budget or CPD programme to start developing them. You just need intention, curiosity and a willingness to shift your mindset from 'what do I need to deliver?' to 'how do I want to show up?'

Here's how to get started in seven steps.

1. Cultivate a growth mindset

Personal and professional development starts with mindset. The communicators who will thrive in the future aren't those with the most polished writing skills or the deepest channel knowledge. They're the ones who are open to learning, unlearning and relearning.

Ask yourself:

- Where do I default to 'expert mode' instead of curiosity?
- What human qualities do I most admire in others – and how can I develop them in myself?
- When was the last time I tried something new, risky or outside my comfort zone?

Keep a journal. Make reflection part of your daily or weekly practice. Get feedback, not just from colleagues on your work, but from your family and friends, on your presence.

2. Start by looking in the mirror

Many of the human strengths begin with self-awareness: knowing your own biases, triggers, energy and how others experience you.

Try:

- **360 feedback:** Use tools like the Johari Window or ask for informal feedback on how well you listen, facilitate or build trust.
- **Self-assessment:** Rate yourself across the six strengths. Where do you feel strongest? Where is your biggest stretch?
- **Coaching or mentoring:** Find someone who can reflect your blind spots and encourage deeper self-awareness.

You can't lead others in culture or connection if you haven't done the inner work first.

3. Build through practice, not theory

You don't learn to facilitate by reading a textbook. You learn by rolling up your sleeves and having a go. Each of these six human strengths can be built and deepened through practice, reflection and intentional experience.

They're not fixed traits, they're muscles you can grow over time. Here's how.

EMPATHY

What it is: Deep understanding of others' emotions, needs and perspectives, foundational for trust, connection and psychological safety.

How to build it:

- Shadow employees in different roles to see work through their eyes.
- Use tools like *empathy maps* and *personas* to reflect on real experiences.
- In feedback sessions, ask: *'How did that message make you feel?'*

CURIOSITY

What it is: A mindset of learning, questioning and exploring. Curiosity fuels insight and innovation.

How to build it:

- Host 'curiosity conversations' with people in other teams.
- Try a new technique: journey mapping, rapid ideation, AI prompting.
- Replace 'I know' with 'I wonder' in your approach to problems.

RESILIENCE

What it is: The ability to adapt, stay grounded and recover in the face of change or challenge.

How to build it:

- Reflect on how you've bounced back from past project setbacks.
- Develop rituals for self-care and boundaries during intense delivery phases.
- View feedback not as critique, but as insight for growth.

CREATIVITY

What it is: The capacity to see new connections, reframe challenges and generate meaningful ideas.

How to build it:

- Rewrite a policy as a story.
- Run a 'bad ideas first' brainstorm to unlock new directions.
- Remix old campaigns into new formats, think cross-channel and cross-functional.

INFLUENCE

What it is: The power to shape decisions, perceptions and behaviours through relationships, credibility and insight.

How to build it:

- Run a 1:1 with a sceptical stakeholder to understand their goals.
- Use *insight-led storytelling* to shift mindsets at senior levels.
- Show, not tell, your value by co-creating with others.

COURAGE

What it is: The strength to speak up, challenge outdated thinking and act with integrity, even when it's uncomfortable.

How to build it:

- Say the hard thing, kindly, in your next project review.
- Share a new idea or experiment even if it's imperfect.
- Push back when asked to 'just send a message' that doesn't align with purpose.

4. Experiment and reflect in safe spaces

Skills improve when we have room to try, fail and learn from our mistakes. Create or seek out environments that support this kind of development.
Ideas include:

- **Peer circles or learning cohorts:** Partner with a few friendly colleagues to reflect on your communication experiments and insights.
- **Safe-to-fail pilots:** Introduce a new approach (e.g. empathy interviews or AI-assisted copy generation) with one team or on one project, test and learn.
- **Feedback loops:** After facilitating a session or presenting a narrative, ask for direct feedback on how you landed and how you could improve.

Treat your work as a *lab*, not a performance.

5. Beg, borrow and steal from elsewhere

Many of the human strengths communicators now need are more deeply developed in other functions and disciplines:

- Design thinking for empathy, journey mapping and iteration.
- Systems thinking for seeing patterns and dynamics in culture.

- Facilitation and coaching for enabling dialogue and trust.
- Storytelling and narrative craft for shaping meaning and belief.
- Behavioural science for influence grounded in human psychology.

Seek out colleagues with expertise in these areas; you're sure to find pockets of expertise and passionate individuals in other parts of the organization, like HR, marketing, customer experience and ops. Identify and partner with other functions to develop a joint capability and learn from each other.

6. Model the shift for others

The best way to embed new strengths isn't to talk about them, it's to live them.

Model:

- curiosity over certainty
- co-creation over control
- conversation over cascade
- questions over answers.

Invite others to join you on the journey towards being people-first. Run an experiment with your team. Start an 'AI Friday' test-and-learn group. Introduce storytelling exercises into leadership comms. The more we practise, the more we change.

7. Commit to lifelong learning

This isn't about achieving perfection in all these areas. It's about becoming more intentional in using your inherent strengths, noticing where you're strong, where you're stretching and how you're showing up in the moments that matter.

The best communicators of the future won't be defined by how many frameworks they've memorized or how many channels they manage. They'll be known for how they made people feel, how well they listened and how bravely they connected humans in a world increasingly driven by machines.

That starts now, with one new behaviour, one experiment, one courageous conversation at a time.

From messages to moments: thinking
like an experience designer

Traditional 'expert-led' IC is focused on outputs: crafting and delivering messages, managing channels, measuring clicks and views – it's communication done to employees. In contrast, People-First IC is focused on outcomes: shaping IC key moments and the overall experience. It recognizes that people don't remember the message in an email or poster; they remember how communication made them feel.

People-First IC deliberately shifts the emphasis from technical skills to human-centred skills. It recognizes that the core skills our profession has been built on are increasingly part of the AI capability. Rather than trying to compete with AI, we need to refocus on the skills and strengths that are uniquely human and at the same time, learn how to partner with AI to get the most out of it.

As well as developing and refining the six 'superpowers', making the leap to People-First IC first requires a shift to start thinking and operating as experience designers. This is a way of thinking that prioritizes the overall experience of employees at work and it means:

- Empathizing deeply with employees.
- Designing communication from their perspective.
- Focusing on what people need to feel and do, not just think and know.
- Understanding communication as a series of moments, not just messages.
- Seeing employees not just as workers, human resources or audiences, but as people with individual wants, needs, expectations, goals and emotions.

It's a mindset focused on creating a workplace where people feel valued and appreciated, empowered with autonomy and trust to do their best work, supported with development opportunities to grow and connect with a sense of belonging and purpose. It about creating a world of work where people matter.

An EX designer mindset means thinking about every stage of the employee journey, from recruitment to retirement and intentionally designing the *communication experiences* that guide that journey, working hand in hand with the people involved.

Reframing internal communication as a critical employee experience is transformational. It means hosting a leadership Q&A, which makes people feel heard, delivering a change comms campaign that reduces fear and enabling a line manager to have a conversation that sparks a sense of belonging.

An experience isn't just what happens, but how it makes the individual feel. It means focusing on hearts as well as heads, on emotions as well as information – not just what we need employees to know and do but how we want them to feel too.

Making this shift positions internal communication as an enabler of employee experience, moving practitioners towards the more human aspects of the profession. This empowers us to add more value by unlocking not just understanding but engagement, productivity and a host of other valuable organizational outcomes.

An EX designer mindset doesn't just deliver benefits for the organization though, it elevates the experience of each and every employee, ensuring a more enjoyable, satisfying and enriching experience. Given we spend around a third of our lives working, that's an equally important outcome. We'll cover the IC experience toolkit in the coming chapters, but adopting an experience mindset is how we orient ourselves.

Recalibrate and rise!

The old playbook has served us well. It brought our profession out of the shadows and into strategic conversations. We've undoubtedly come a long way since that dedicated group of industrial editors sat down in 1945 to form the first professional body for internal communicators.

But it's becoming ever clearer that the skills and competencies that have got us here are no longer fit for purpose. A new playbook is needed, one that positions internal communication as a catalyst for human experience.

This isn't about abandoning what you know. It's about amplifying it through new ways of being, thinking and operating. It's about how we do what we do, not what we deliver.

AI is undoubtedly a game-changer, but far from seeing this as an extinction-level event, we believe there is a bright future of IC. However we must acknowledge the direction of travel, embrace the change and recalibrate our roles around our deeply human strengths.

We believe making the leap to People-First IC will not only future-proof our careers but will open up a new realm of opportunity for internal communicators.

Make no mistake, this is a pivotal moment for our profession. Powerful forces are reshaping how work gets done, what roles are valued and what it means to be human at work. Internal communication must evolve once again. But this time, the shift is not about new channels or metrics. It's about identity. It's about what we choose to value, prioritize and bring to our work.

The future of internal communication isn't about expertise or having all the answers. It's about asking better questions, showing up more humanly and designing IC experiences that help others do the same.

Now is the time to recalibrate and rise. Your people-first future starts today.

CHAPTER IN SUMMARY

- **The IC profession is at a turning point**: Driven by rising employee expectations, technological disruption (especially AI) and the failure of traditional approaches to engage, influence and inspire.

- **To survive, IC professionals must evolve**: From message distribution to experience design – shifting from expert to enabler, and from content creation to human connection and meaning-making.

- **AI is rapidly automating many core technical IC tasks**: Making human qualities like empathy, creativity and trust-building more valuable than ever.

- **Legacy competency frameworks helped raise the professional bar**: But were built for a different era and now need updating.

- **The People-First IC Capability Model comprises three layers**: Human strengths (or superpowers), strategic skills and foundational capabilities.

- **Internal communicators must adopt an experience designer mindset**: Focusing on moments that matter, emotional impact and the entire employee journey.

- **Partnering with AI is a vital skill**: Enabling IC pros to focus more on strategic influence, creativity, co-creation and advisory work.

- **It's time to recalibrate your role**: Embrace change and step into a more human, impactful and future-proof space as an internal communicator.

References

Capgemini Research Institute (2024) *Harnessing the Value of Generative AI*, 2nd edn, Capgemini Research Institute, London

Cropley, A (2013) Establishing the global standard: A framework for the future of communication, IABC, thecsce.com/global-standard (archived at https://perma.cc/Z6G3-NA86)

FitzPatrick, L and Dewhurst, S (2007) *The IC Space: Internal communication competency framework*, Melcrum Publishing, London

Institute of Internal Communication (IoIC) (2016, updated 2023) *IoIC Profession Map: Skills, knowledge and behaviours for internal communicators*, Institute of Internal Communication, Milton Keynes

International Association of Business Communicators (IABC) (2013) *The Global Standard of the Communication Profession*, IABC, San Francisco, www.iabc.com/professional-development/global-standard (archived at https://perma.cc/VN6D-TS4P)

KPMG (2025) Trusted AI framework: A strategic approach to designing, building, deploying and using AI responsibly, KPMG, kpmg.com/xx/en/what-we-do/services/ai/trusted-ai-framework.html (archived at https://perma.cc/LY47-7MHR)

Linley, P A (2008) *Average to A+: Realising strengths in yourself and others*, CAPP Press, Coventry

McKinsey Global Institute (2023) Generative AI and the future of work in America, McKinsey & Company, www.mckinsey.com/mgi/our-research/generative-ai-and-the-future-of-work-in-america (archived at https://perma.cc/4LW6-PJBV)

Microsoft (2024) Work trend index: 2024 annual report – the AI-Employee Alliance, www.microsoft.com/en-us/worklab/work-trend-index (archived at https://perma.cc/88X5-4644)

Quirke, B (2000) *Making the Connections: Using internal communication to turn strategy into action*, Gower, Aldershot

Seligman, M E P (2002) *Authentic Happiness: Using the new positive psychology to realize your potential for lasting fulfilment*, Free Press, New York

Socher, R (2024) AI agents will soon do 80% of office work, *Business Insider*, www.businessinsider.com/former-salesforce-exec-richard-socher-says-agi-still-years-away-2024-3 (archived at https://perma.cc/NGX7-XM8D)

The EX Space (2023) EX archetypes: Understanding the different approaches to employee experience, The EX Space, www.theexspace.com/course/ex-practitioner-archetypes (archived at https://perma.cc/L5XE-FX6T)

World Economic Forum (2025) *The Future of Jobs Report 2025*, World Economic Forum Geneva, https://www.weforum.org/publications/the-future-of-jobs-report-2025 (archived at https://perma.cc/CK3L-45M4)

Zytnik, M (2024) *Internal Communication in the Age of Artificial Intelligence*, Business Expert Press, New York

05

Introducing the People-First Internal Communication framework

Welcome to your People-First Internal Communication (IC) framework; your definitive guide to enable you to design and deliver internal communication experiences that really make a difference. From here on, we're going to shift gears, moving from the 'why' of People-First IC to the how. In this section of the book, we'll walk you through the People-First IC framework and share practical tools to help you bring it to life in your own organization. We want to help you move from thinking to doing; in previous chapters, we have shared some big ideas and new ways of working with you. Now it's time to put it all into practice.

The framework and tools included here, and subsequent chapters, are tried and tested and will allow you to navigate the complexities of taking a people-first approach to IC with ease and confidence. The guidance will be your roadmap to success in the evolving landscape of IC. Packed with practical steps, tools and templates, you'll discover a comprehensive, yet accessible framework, built on the latest thinking. Whether you're relaunching your vision and values, improving employee voice or enhancing workplace culture, you'll find everything you need to design and deliver impactful, People-First IC.

The tools you'll work through will help you to understand how to design and deliver IC that puts your people first and how to take actionable insights to build the IC 'moments that matter' for your people. In summary, you'll have everything you need to design and action IC that is not only right for your organization and but critically, is right for your people.

How to use the tools: applying 'tailoring' to designing IC experiences

When designing IC experiences, the concept of tailoring is helpful. You're no doubt familiar with the concept of tailoring with respect to menswear, adjusting and working on men's clothing in order to achieve the right fit and look for the individual. This concept was then applied to the field of project management (Project Management Institute (PMI), 2017) and is now established practice. Within the context of project management, tailoring is used to apply the right amount of structure and governance without impacting the success of the project. And within the world of Agile (Highsmith, 2002), tailoring is simply using tools, methods and approaches to fit your specific context and environment. In summary, tailoring is about making the tools work for you and rather than letting them dictate how you should work!

We love this pragmatic approach of 'as much as necessary, as little as possible' and highly recommend keeping this in mind as you work through the tools we've included here. It's not always necessary, or correct, to follow every step and use every tool. The idea is to just make it work for you. By customizing your approach, you can adopt our People-First IC approach to its full potential without it becoming a bureaucratic burden. Remember one size will never fit all, and that each aspect of the IC experience you're working on will need to work for your context and of course, the people you're designing for.

Introducing the foundations of our people-first approach

Our approach pulls from different disciplines, but the beauty is that the science and disciplines are baked into the approach. This means you can have confidence that the framework is based on the latest science and thinking, and is evidence-based. Concepts from design thinking, service design, product design, agile guidance and positive psychology are all used and complement each other to create a holistic approach to IC problem-solving and innovation.

Here's a quick summary of each.

Design thinking

Tim Brown (2009), CEO of IDEO, popularized design thinking in the mid to late 2000s as a human-centred approach to innovation and problem-solving grounded in empathy, creativity and iteration. In summary:

- Design thinking is a human-centred approach used to identify and solve problems by focusing on empathy, creativity and iteration.
- It advocates taking the time to genuinely understand user needs, way before any solutions are considered.
- At the heart of design thinking is a creative, human-centred approach to problem-solving.

Service design

Service design emerged in the early 1990s at the intersection of design thinking, operations management and marketing, as a way to apply human-centred design principles to the creation and improvement of services rather than physical products (Stickdorn et al, 2018). In summary:

- Service design builds on the principles of design thinking and applies them specifically to the design and improvement of services.
- The tools used in service design go a little deeper than those used in design thinking, encouraging understanding of the 'behind the scenes' experience.
- The approach looks at the holistic service experience, and then helps the designer to come up with ways to meet the needs of the end user.

Agile

Agile emerged in the early 2000s as a response to the limitations of traditional, linear project management methods. Most notable was the publication of the Agile Manifesto in 2002 (Highsmith, 2002), which was created by a group of software developers seeking more flexible, collaborative and adaptive ways of working. In summary:

- Agile is an iterative approach to project management and product development that encourages flexibility, collaboration and continuous improvement.

- It involves breaking down projects into smaller, manageable tasks (sprints), prioritizing iteration to deliver value.
- Agile teams work in cross-functional and self-organizing units, which supports them to work together, respond quickly to changes and deliver high-quality results efficiently.

Positive psychology

Positive psychology emerged in the late 1990s as a formal discipline within psychology, led by Martin Seligman (2011) and others. The aim was to increase the focus on what makes life worth living and how to thrive, rather than just focus on diagnosing and treating mental illness. In summary:

- Positive psychology is a strength-based approach that focuses on that which helps people to thrive and lead fulfilling lives.
- It focuses on promoting well-being and optimal human functioning.
- The tools from this practice work well with the design process, helping to stimulate a 'growth-mindset' creativity and psychological safety.

Product design

Product design has its roots in industrial design and engineering, evolving throughout the 20th century to focus not only on aesthetics and functionality but also on user experience, as companies increasingly recognized the value of creating products that are both desirable and practical.

- Product design involves the creation of solutions that are highly attractive to the end user as well as being realistic to build and produce.
- The approach doesn't just focus on how something looks but emphasizes the way it is used in real life.
- Product design puts the user at the heart of the approach and uses many of the same tools as design thinking and service design.

Introducing the People-First IC Design Loop

Now we're ready to start exploring our People-First IC approach in more depth – we call this the People-First IC Design Loop. The design loop involves five distinct phases, outlined next. The guidance is a lot less linear and a lot

FIGURE 5.1 The People-First IC Design Loop

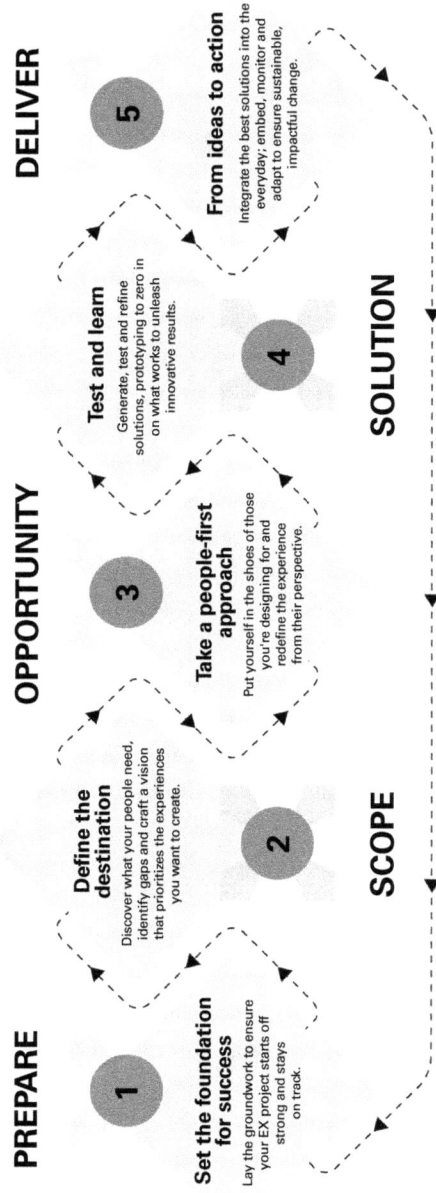

PREPARE

1

Set the foundation for success

Lay the groundwork to ensure your EX project starts off strong and stays on track.

SCOPE

2

Define the destination

Discover what your people need, identify gaps and craft a vision that prioritizes the experiences you want to create.

OPPORTUNITY

3

Take a people-first approach

Put yourself in the shoes of those you're designing for and redefine the experience from their perspective.

SOLUTION

4

Test and learn

Generate, test and refine solutions, prototyping to zero in on what works to unleash innovative results.

DELIVER

5

From ideas to action

Integrate the best solutions into the everyday; embed, monitor and adapt to ensure sustainable, impactful change.

more iterative than the model suggests. However, by sharing it in this structured way, we hope to give you the confidence to get started and make it work for you. One of the most compelling benefits for adopting this approach and way of working, is that it enables you to take a problem that is often ambiguous and complex, and provide a clear and simple way to understand it and solve it. In subsequent chapters, we'll share the tools you can use for each of the steps.

Let's walk through the People-First IC Design Loop step by step.

THE PEOPLE-FIRST IC DESIGN LOOP

1. ***Prepare – set the foundations for success***   Here is where you lay the foundations for your IC project or approach. This will no doubt be familiar territory to IC pros, involving key steps such as making the business case, mapping your stakeholders and putting a project plan in place, for example. The aim of this step isn't to come up with solutions but to ensure your approach is well organized and supported by relevant stakeholders.

2. ***Scope – define the destination***   The scoping phase is all about discovery and really taking the time to explore both the current IC experience (if relevant) and map out the future desired IC experience. The tools here will help you to discover the extent to which IC meets the needs of your people, as well as your organizational context, and understand where it is and isn't delivering. Here you'll get clear on the vision of the IC experience you're aiming for and use that to prioritize where to focus design efforts.

3. ***Opportunity – take a people-first approach***   This is where you'll get up close with the people you're designing for and stand in their shoes. The tools will help you to use empathy to broaden and deepen your understanding of what you're working on. Using insight from the discovery phase, you will revisit and possibly redefine the IC vision and experience you are aiming for. By the end of this stage, you'll have clarity on the problem you're trying to solve or the opportunity you are going for.

4. ***Solution – test and learn***   It is only when you reach this step that you're going to begin considering possible solutions. Here is where you generate ideas, and lots of them, to solve the problem or realize the opportunity you've identified. Your ideas will be turned into rapid small prototypes to test and get feedback. By testing different solutions at a small scale, you

can reject those that don't work, learn about what could work and then develop the solutions you want to take forwards.

5. *Deliver – from ideas to action*   Once again, we're back in familiar territory for IC pros. Here is when we take the successful prototypes we've tested and develop a plan of action to activate them. The big difference is that these solutions are 'people-first', and you'll have evidence to give you confidence in what you are proposing.

REAL-WORLD EXAMPLE
Navigating complexity with simplicity and empathy

BY TAREK KAMIL, FOUNDER AND CEO OF CERKL

A powerful illustration of the People-First framework in action comes from Tarek Kamil. Tarek Kamil is the Founder and CEO of Cerkl, an industry-leading platform revolutionizing internal communications through AI-powered personalization and workforce insights. With a background in technology and a passion for solving complex engagement challenges, Tarek brings a forward-thinking perspective to the future of employee communication.

Tarek's story brings to life how the principles of design thinking and agile, combined with deep empathy for end users, can help untangle systemic challenges and drive practical, people-centred solutions. This case sets the stage for the framework that follows, showing that the tools we're about to introduce don't just sound good in theory, but truly work in the messiness of real life. Over to Tarek:

Information Age? I think not

For as long as I can remember, I've been fascinated with solving things – games, puzzles, chess, algebra. At age 12, I began writing software. The convergence of problem-solving and technology has been a constant in my career.

Fast forward to 2012. While serving on the school board in Madeira, Ohio, I encountered a pervasive issue: parent disengagement. But as I dug deeper, I realized it wasn't apathy – it was overwhelm. Think about that time: the smartphone was five years old, and social media platforms like Facebook, Twitter, Pinterest and YouTube were exploding. The stat that cemented the issue for me? We were creating more content every three hours than in all of human history up to 2003. People were drowning.

When I looked at brands successfully engaging me – Netflix, Amazon, Audible, Spotify – they all had one thing in common: they made me feel like their only customer. Their content cut through the noise and saved me time. That epiphany inspired the creation of Cerkl (pronounced 'circle').

Cerkl's idea was simple: apply the learning and personalization of the most engaging consumer brands to internal communication. Why send the same email to 3,000 people when you can tailor messages to individual interests and continuously learn and adapt over time?

We're not in the Information Age. We're in the Too Much Information Age. For communicators, that's a crisis. We all have finely tuned filters for anything that wastes our time. Think about your own inbox. How many emails do you unsubscribe from daily? How many sit unopened in your mental 'someday' drawer?

Internal communicators who succeed in this environment recognize we've entered the Attention Age. And they know it's time to borrow from the consumer playbook.

A consumer-grade employee communication experience

When I think about what that looks like, here are the must-haves:

1. BE PERSONALIZED

Not 'Dear [First Name]' personalized – I mean truly tailored. Know what I need and want to see, and what I've already seen. If I've read the CEO message on the intranet, why is it the lead story in my newsletter?

2. BE TARGETED

Communicators should be able to segment and target messages using any people data attribute – without relying on IT or manually building spreadsheets.

3. BE CHANNEL-AGNOSTIC

Engagement isn't about which channel you use. It's about whether the message is relevant. Publish once, let employees consume where they prefer. Stop spamming by duplicating content across every internal channel. Instead, earn the right to be in the inbox.

4. LEARN

True engagement comes when you understand what employees care about as humans. Use technology to learn their preferences, so your comms can evolve with them.

5. NOT BE TIMEBOUND

Email is a snapshot. But information needs to live beyond the send date. Say you win a 'Best Place to Work' award in January – why shouldn't a new hire in February see that? AI-driven, personalized newsfeeds make that possible.

6. PROVIDE GRANULAR CONTROL

Internal comms is harder than marketing. You have to deliver 'need-to-know' information, even if it isn't flashy. How do you do that without spamming people? Through relevance and smart delivery.

This is where AI shines: creating personalized experiences that ensure every employee sees what they need to see, when and where it matters. That's a paradigm shift.

The win-win

Employees win because they finally get communication that feels relevant and respectful of their time. But communicators win, too:

- **More engagement**: Content gets more reach and longer shelf life.
- **More time**: No more Outlook formatting marathons or copy-pasting into five platforms.
- **More insight**: Real-time analytics + AI = smarter decisions. Imagine asking, 'Give me three ways to improve click-rates with low-engagement groups' – and getting real answers.

TABLE 5.1 Impact of AI on IC (Cerkl)

	Impact	Why
Internal newsletter open rates	Up 21%	Subject lines are built by AI for the recipient.
Internal newsletter click rates	Up 112%	The content is curated for that individual based on what they still NEED to see and what they WANT to see.
Time spent building newsletters	Down 5 hours/ week	Let AI curate your content for each individual.
Content reach	Up 64%	Because content can be given a shelf life and can be distributed across all of your channels, AI can automatically optimize content reach through smart delivery.

Ultimately, some things sound great on paper but fail in execution (I'm looking at you, open office plans). Being an engineer, I love numbers. When I look across all Cerkl customers globally, here's what we're seeing:

Imagine spending less time doing mundane work (e.g. laying out a newsletter) and spending more time on creating content all while driving reach and engagement. That's the power of a consumer-grade experience inside of your organization and it's the secret brands have been relying on for years.

Getting started

Even with statistics and case studies, I'm often met with looks of bewilderment from internal communications professionals. After a little more digging, I find that it's not because they don't believe the data, it's because they don't know how to start. I get it. Organizations can be daunting – especially when you're trying to implement change. Here are six best practice tips we've seen from our clients as they move from traditional comms to consumer-grade.

STEP 1: FRAME THE PROBLEM IN BUSINESS TERMS

Objective: Make this *their* problem too.

- Avoid 'We send too many emails.' Instead, say:
    - 'Employees are missing critical updates – hurting compliance and engagement.'
    - 'We can't segment by role or region, which causes confusion and wasted time.'
    - 'We have no insight into what's landing, which means we're flying blind.'
- Tie to business KPIs: retention, productivity, safety, compliance, front-line enablement.

STEP 2: BUILD THE BUSINESS CASE

Objective: Secure budget by tying to ROI and risk reduction. Include:

- **Cost of status quo**: Missed messages, redundant tools, wasted employee time.
- **Benchmarks**: 'Top-performing companies personalize communication and reduce turnover by X%.'
- **Tools rationalization**: Replace static intranet add-ons, email tools or survey platforms with a unified system.
- **Expected ROI**: Reduced attrition, fewer helpdesk tickets, improved engagement, faster onboarding, better safety compliance.

STEP 3: PRE-EMPT IT CONCERNS

Objective: Build trust and clear technical hurdles.
Bring answers to:

- **Security**: Is it SOC 2? GDPR compliant? How is data encrypted?
- **Integration**: Can it sync with AD, Workday, etc.?
- **Hosting**: Where is it deployed? (e.g. GCP, AWS, Azure)
- **Authentication**: Does it support SSO/SAML?

STEP 4: MAP AND MOBILIZE STAKEHOLDERS

Objective: Build a cross-functional coalition.

Create an 'Internal Communications Transformation Taskforce'. Give it a name. Make it real.

STEP 5: SELL THE VISION INTERNALLY

Objective: Make people want this change.
Create a five-slide deck:

1 What's broken
2 Who it's affecting
3 What great could look like
4 What we need to get there
5 What success will look like.

TABLE 5.2 Stakeholder matrix

Stakeholder	Why they care	How to involve them
HR	Engagement, retention, onboarding	Co-design employee segments, launch campaigns.
IT	Integration, security, governance	Involve early, address SSO, AD sync, compliance.
Compliance/legal	Risk, accuracy, audit trail	Show platform's approval workflows and audit features.
Exec sponsor	Culture, performance, org alignment	Give them visibility and wins they can share.
Front-line managers	Enablement, productivity	Give them analytics and prebuilt templates.

Include employee quotes (good and bad).

We provide our customers with screenshots of Broadcast's personalization, MyNews feed and real-time analytics. This is where you **move hearts and minds**.

STEP 6: START SMALL, THEN SCALE

Objective: Reduce risk, show quick wins and expand.

- **Pilot with one region, business unit, or comms use case** (e.g. new hire onboarding, safety updates, people manager comms).
- Show data: open rates, click-throughs, reduced email volume, improved segmentation.
- Create a 'Before and After' story to share with other stakeholders.

STEP 7: SECURE LONG-TERM OWNERSHIP AND MOMENTUM

Objective: Prevent this from becoming another 'comms tool graveyard'.

- Appoint a **product owner** for internal comms (yes, even if unofficial).
- Regularly review analytics and employee feedback.
- Embed the tool in HR onboarding, IT provisioning and leadership reporting.

This is not just about buying software – it's about changing behaviour and expectations. The communicator must become:

- a translator (business goals $\rightleftarrows$ comms strategy)
- a connector (pulling in HR, IT, front line)
- a visionary (painting what *could* be)
- a builder (of trust, processes and momentum).

Bottom line

The gains in engagement, time and insight are real. But even with all that, I always come back to one simple question for communicators: *'How would you like to be treated?'*

Start there, and you won't go wrong.

Prepare: set the foundations for success

This stage will feel pretty familiar to IC pros, which is why we haven't provided a stand-alone chapter for this first step. Designing and delivering great IC involves a number of activities and steps to ensure that the process is well-organized and supported by relevant stakeholders. There's already a ton of great content out there to support you here which we don't want or need to replicate. We recommend some further reading if you'd like to explore further at the end of this chapter.

Key considerations within this stage

CREATE YOUR CASE FOR CHANGE

You may be required to articulate a compelling case for change to outline why improving the IC experience is essential for organizational success. Or it might be the case that working through tools outlined in later stages of our People-First IC Design Loop will help you to return to this stage and build your case for change. For example, in the scoping stage, you might gather insights while mapping a specific comms journey, highlighting challenges or pain points in the current IC experience and identifying opportunities for improvement. In doing this, you might uncover insights that will link improvements to broader business objectives, which gives you what you need to build your case for change. The framework and journey are often less linear than they appear, but presenting it in this way enables you to check that you have covered the key steps.

Pull together data and insights from employee engagement surveys, any performance metrics you might have, employee retention figures and any other relevant sources to help you make your case for change. The case needs to be written and presented in the best way to convince key stakeholders, making clear the benefits of investing in IC and addressing potential objections or concerns. Again, there is no one-size-fits-all approach to making a business case and a quick internet search, or a conversation with Gen AI will give you templates and suggestions. But the magic really happens when you apply your specific knowledge of the context you're working in, for example, linking your case to your organization's business objectives and outcomes. Can you make a compelling ROI case? And it's useful to consider what your stakeholders are passionate about and what keeps them awake at night; linking your business case to their agenda can really help.

FIND YOUR WHY AND SET YOUR FOCUS

Ensure you and your stakeholders are clear on why you are designing, or redesigning, the IC experience. Again, it might be that this conversation happens further down the line, when you have some hard evidence from your people to help you make the case for change. This could involve defining clear objectives, outlining aims and how success will be measured. Determine the focus of your project, including which aspects of IC will be addressed, for example, supporting a business transformation programme or modernizing your intranet, and any constraints or limitations that need to be considered.

GATHER RESOURCES AND CREATE A CROSS-FUNCTIONAL TEAM

Map out and identify what resources and expertise you might need to support your IC design. This could include subject matter experts, budget, tech and even external consultants where necessary. Put together a multidisciplinary team and consider how this team could represent different perspectives and areas within your organization. Consider how you can tap into the collective intelligence and insights you have at hand to help add value to the IC experience design process.

CREATE YOUR PROJECT PLAN

Design a project plan to clarify key elements such as the timeline, milestones, deliverables and responsibilities. Allocate resources and put in place communication to ensure that everyone involved knows what they need to do and how they will need to contribute.

STAKEHOLDER MANAGEMENT

Identify those stakeholders who will be impacted by or have influence over the IC experience you're designing. This could include subject matter experts, senior leaders, front-line managers and employees. Map out their roles, interests and level of influence in relation to the IC experience you are working on. Use this thinking to help you understand and prioritize engagement and communication throughout the design process. Develop a stakeholder engagement plan that outlines how you will work with each stakeholder group, communicate updates, gather feedback and address concerns.

Working with AI on the IC process

In Chapter 2, we introduced our People-First IC model and argued that AI can now pick up much of the work that used to consume our time as IC pros – that is, the IC process. It's easy to see how AI can help us with many of the tasks outlined in this foundational stage. And of course, this then frees us up to focus on the human side of IC. This is where we can really add value; steps 2, 3 and 4 of the design loop are where we'll get to focus on the deeply human aspects of IC, but more of that later.

As a quick example AI can help you to:

- Analyse employee data from a comms audit, including free comments, highlighting key themes, pain points and opportunities.
- Draft a case for change in the right tone of voice.
- Analyse stakeholder data, create stakeholder maps and suggest an approach and comms.
- Draft project plans, Gantt charts and milestones.
- Summarize strategy documents and pull out key points for consideration.

And used in the right way, AI can free up your time to allow you to focus on areas such as:

- building trust with stakeholders
- asking the right questions and listening deeply
- challenging assumptions and navigate internal politics with empathy and insight.

Working in partnership with AI on any of these tasks can produce a better result. For example, AI can give you a best practice business case, but it can't know that your CEO is passionate about sustainability, and a business case that links your IC work to a sustainability agenda might be the hook that secures buy-in. AI can give you a well-structured stakeholder map, but it won't know what you know; that is, one department head is under significant political pressure, or that another is quietly influential despite their 'lower' org chart position.

AI can help us to move quickly to put the foundations in place, for example, a business case that can be developed in minutes rather than hours or even days! However the human side is still absolutely critical; your judgement, emotional intelligence and understanding of your people and culture are key. Remember, AI is the tool, but you're in charge, you're the designer. In summary, not only does AI free up our time to focus on the people side of IC, but we can also get a superior outcome when we collaborate with AI. Next is an example of focusing on an intranet refresh to bring this to life.

TABLE 5.3 Stakeholder matrix

AI-only approach	Human + AI people-first approach
AI quickly drafts a business case for an intranet redesign. It references best practices, notes that the current system is outdated and estimates cost savings based on industry averages.	You ask AI for the same task. Then, using your human insight: • You connect the intranet to a current pain point flagged in your last listening session: front-line teams can't access policies easily. • You know the COO is under pressure to improve productivity, so you include a stat on how search failures waste employee time. • You phrase the opening in your CEO's own words from the last town hall to hook her attention.
The business case is logical, polished and technically sound.	The business case is emotionally resonant, politically aligned, and more likely to land with decision makers.
It's a business case.	It's your organisation's business case.

Introducing the People-First IC Maturity Path

On the surface, our people-first approach to IC might feel very familiar. Let's be honest, IC pros *are* in the business of understanding people and building connection. But here's the challenge: it's very often the case that IC is focused on our expertise, fundamentally being 'expert-led', which dictates what communication goes out. We need to move into the people-first space and focus on what our people are truly experiencing.

We've developed the **People-First IC Maturity Path** to help you reflect on where your practice is today and what you might need to focus on to move towards a people-first approach. This is based on the original Employee Experience Maturity Path, developed by Emma and Belinda Gannaway (Bridger and Gannaway, 2024), which maps how organizations evolve their employee experience (EX) practice, from isolated fixes to fully integrated, people-centred strategies. It's rooted in human-centred design, collaboration and continuous improvement.

But here's the powerful insight: everything that makes for a better employee experience; being insight-led, inclusive, emotional and iterative, also makes for better internal communication. That's why we've adapted the EX Maturity Path to develop the People-First IC Maturity Path. While the

FIGURE 5.2 The People-First IC Maturity Path

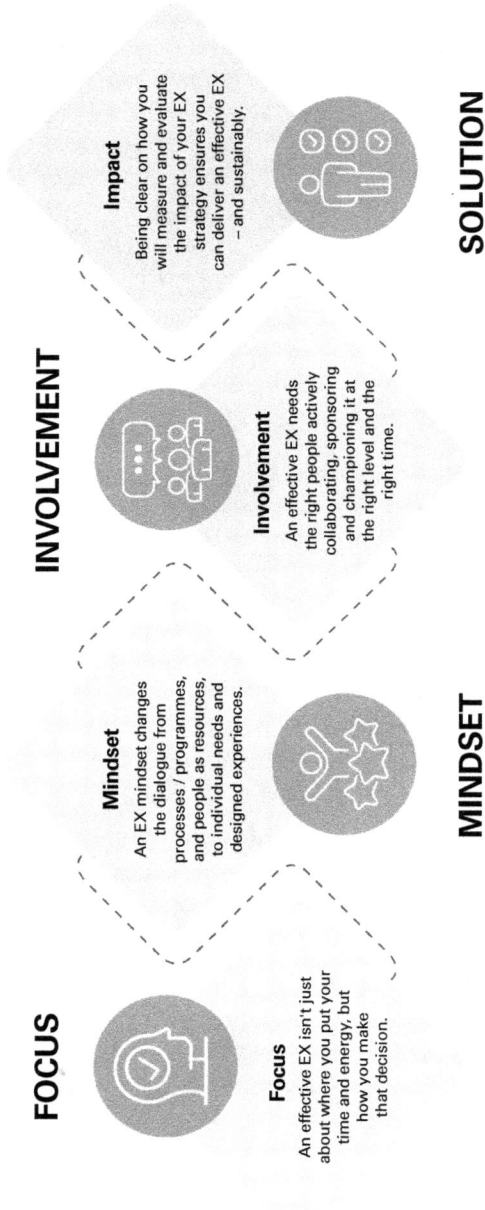

FOCUS

Focus
An effective EX isn't just about where you put your time and energy, but how you make that decision.

MINDSET

Mindset
An EX mindset changes the dialogue from processes / programmes, and people as resources, to individual needs and designed experiences.

INVOLVEMENT

Involvement
An effective EX needs the right people actively collaborating, sponsoring and championing it at the right level and the right time.

SOLUTION

Impact
Being clear on how you will measure and evaluate the impact of your EX strategy ensures you can deliver an effective EX – and sustainably.

EX model looks at how organizations design overall employee experiences, the IC version focuses specifically on how communication professionals design communication as an experience. In short, moving from broadcasting information to co-creating meaningful moments with employees.

Like the original EX model, this adapted maturity path is built on four core pillars:

- **Focus** – what are we working on and why?
- **Mindset** – how do we think about IC and the people we're designing for?
- **Involvement** – who's shaping communication experiences?
- **Impact** – how do we measure success and demonstrate value?

In the original model, there are three stages – forming, performing and transforming – to describe how maturity evolves. These stages aren't about being 'good' or 'bad' – they reflect how embedded people-first thinking is in your practice and how intentionally your work is designed with employees in mind. When applied to IC this might involve:

- **Forming** is where many teams start. IC activity is often reactive, driven by requests from leaders or quick fixes. There's passion and effort, but limited insight or collaboration.
- **Performing** describes a more strategic stage. IC is aligned to business goals, communication quality improves, and some collaboration and user-centred design is emerging.
- **Transforming** represents a fully people-first approach. Communication is insight-led, co-created with employees and focused on delivering meaningful experiences that support both people and performance.

Let's take '**Focus**' as an example to see how this plays out. In the EX model, low maturity means EX activity is reactive, opportunistic and driven by others (like HR). As maturity grows, activity aligns to business strategy and is informed by deep employee insights.

In the IC version, that becomes:

- **Forming:** We're reactive – fixing inbox overload or publishing business updates.
- **Performing:** We're more strategic – aligning IC with business goals and considering the 'think/feel/do' for employees.
- **Transforming:** We prioritize based on human insight, designing communications that deliver meaningful employee experiences.

This isn't just semantic; it's a shift in how we see our role moving towards being experience designers.

Why it's useful

The *People-First IC Maturity Path* is a practical reflection tool. It's not about scoring you or your team or labelling your work, it's about helping you:

- *Make the invisible visible*

  Shine a light on the patterns, habits and assumptions shaping your IC practice today.

- *Shift from activity to insight*

  Ask deeper questions about who you're designing for and whether your work is creating real value for them.

- *Identify where to focus next*

  Spot the strengths and gaps in your current approach and choose your next step with intention.

- *Facilitate better conversations*

  Use the model to engage leaders, stakeholders and your own team in defining what 'good' looks like in your organization.

This model recognizes that we're all at different stages. Some IC teams are just starting to explore people-first thinking. Others are already applying people-first approaches to complex challenges. Wherever you are now, this path can help you grow your impact, step by step, conversation by conversation.

Let's explore the maturity path in more detail.

FOCUS – WHAT ARE WE WORKING ON AND WHY?

TABLE 5.4 Maturity path: focus

Forming	Performing	Transforming
Our IC efforts are largely reactive. We focus on fixing visible problems (e.g. email overload, outdated intranet) or responding to senior leader requests.	We're increasingly strategic. We align IC with broader business goals and invest in facilitating behaviour change.	Our IC strategy is grounded in human insight and aligned to organizational purpose. We prioritize work that delivers meaningful experiences for employees.

MINDSET – HOW DO WE THINK ABOUT INTERNAL COMMUNICATION AND THE PEOPLE WE'RE DESIGNING FOR?

TABLE 5.5 Maturity path: mindset

Forming	Performing	Transforming
We see IC as messaging. Our role is to deliver the right information to the right people. We focus on efficiency and accuracy.	We start to think in terms of audiences and engagement. We value emotional tone and experience design.	We see IC as an experience. We consider emotion motivation and meaning. We design communications around people's needs – not just business objectives.

INVOLVEMENT – WHO'S INVOLVED IN SHAPING THE COMMUNICATION EXPERIENCE?

TABLE 5.6 Maturity path: involvement

Forming	Performing	Transforming
IC is led by the IC team, often in isolation. We give advice.	We collaborate more widely, with HR, IT, leaders and sometimes employees on key projects.	Employees are co-creators. We regularly involve people from across the business to design, test and shape communication experiences. Leaders are coached and supported to play active roles.

IMPACT – HOW DO WE MEASURE SUCCESS AND DEMONSTRATE VALUE?

TABLE 5.7 Maturity path: impact

Forming	Performing	Transforming
We track outputs – email open rates, town hall attendance, intranet visits.	We begin measuring outcomes – like understanding, trust and behaviour change.	We evaluate impact at multiple levels – employee experience, engagement and business performance. We use insights to continuously improve

BRINGING IT TO LIFE

So, how do you actually use the *People-First IC Maturity Path*? This model is designed to help you reflect and take action no matter where you are on your journey.

You can use it to:

- **Benchmark your current practice:** Where are you today across each of the four pillars?
- **Spot strengths and gaps:** What are you doing well? Where might you be stuck?
- **Shape your growth path:** What does moving forward look like in practical terms?
- **Spark deeper conversations:** Use it as a shared language with leaders, collaborators and your team.

It's not a one-size-fits-all roadmap. Your culture, your context and your people are unique. But what is universal is this: great internal communication doesn't just happen *to* people, it happens *with* them.

This is a tool for reflection, not judgement. A starting point for growth, not a checklist for compliance. The *People-First IC Maturity Path* is more than a diagnostic; it's a mindset shift. A way to step back from the noise of daily delivery and ask: are we designing communication that truly serves our people? It's not about being perfect. It's about being intentional in how you listen, how you design and how you lead. This model offers a way to grow your IC practice with purpose. To embed people-first thinking into your day-to-day work. And to become a communication team that's not just delivering messages, but shaping experiences.

Stepping into people-first practice

In this chapter, we moved from theory into practice, outlining our people-first IC design loop and the five stages involved. Moving from 'expert-led' IC to 'People-First IC' is something that starts with intention and an honest appraisal of where your practice currently is right now. You can use the people-first maturity path to help you understand where you are at on your journey.

We also introduced the first stage of the framework where you'll put in place some of the foundations to provide clarity and alignment. This first stage will no doubt feel familiar to most IC pros; it's our safe space, where we've been operating for years. However, there is a game-changing opportunity here to work with AI on these tasks, to free up your time to focus on the 'human factors' and in doing so you'll find that the outputs will be all the better for it. Remember, you bring the EQ and strategic and cultural context, and AI brings the best practice and sheer speed to pull together documents that in previous times took hours or even days. AI can help us move faster so we can focus and go much deeper than ever before.

In the following chapters, we're going to share the tools and templates to help you quickly adopt and use a people-first approach in your IC work. This is your opportunity to move into a new IC era of being people-first. Let's get started!

CHAPTER IN SUMMARY

- **Introduction of the People-First IC Design Loop:** The chapter marks the transition from theory to practice, offering a comprehensive framework and practical tools to deliver impactful, People-First Internal Communication.

- **Tailoring IC experiences:** Here we emphasized adapting tools and methods to fit your unique context rather than rigidly following prescribed steps. Flexibility and pragmatism are key.

- **Foundational disciplines integrated:** The framework is informed by design thinking, service design, agile, product design and positive psychology, creating a multi-disciplinary, evidence-based approach.

- **The People-First Design Loop:** We introduced our five-stage process:

  1 Prepare – Lay strong foundations (e.g. stakeholder mapping, case for change).

  2 Scope – Understand the current IC experience and envision future goals.

  3 Opportunity – Use empathy to deeply understand employee needs.

  4 Solution – Generate and prototype ideas for testing.

  5 Deliver – Implement and scale validated people-first solutions.

- **The Role of AI in the Design Loop:** We explored how AI can handle technical and repetitive tasks (like drafting business cases or summarizing data), freeing up IC pros to focus on strategic, emotional and human-centred work.

- **People-First IC Maturity Path:** We shared a reflective tool adapted from EX design, helping teams assess and evolve their IC practices across four pillars: Focus, Mindset, Involvement and Impact.

Further reading

Exploring Internal Communication by Kevin Ruck. An academically grounded and CIPR-endorsed book that brings together theory and practice, now widely used in university and professional training.

Internal Communication Strategy: Design, Develop and Transform Your Organizational Communication by Rachel Miller. A modern, practical guide grounded in real IC practice. Rachel Miller brings decades of front-line experience into an accessible strategy framework with tools, templates and case studies.

Making the Connections: Strategies for Effective Internal Communication by Bill Quirke. A classic in the field, this book helped elevate IC to a strategic business discipline and is still cited in corporate communication strategies.

Successful Employee Communications by Sue Dewhurst and Liam FitzPatrick. This hands-on guide focuses on delivering comms that actually work, based on years of practitioner insight. It's especially helpful for developing campaigns and measuring impact.

The Wiley Handbook of Strategic Internal Communication edited by Betteke van Ruler and Dejan Vercic. An academic heavyweight with contributions from global scholars and practitioners. It offers an advanced, research-based perspective on IC as a strategic function.

References

Bridger, E and Gannaway, B (2024) *Employee Experience by Design: How to create an effective EX for competitive advantage*, 2nd ed, Kogan Page, London

Brown, T (2009) *Change by Design: How design thinking creates new alternatives for business and society*, Harvard Business Press, Boston

Highsmith, J (2002) *Agile Software Development Ecosystems*, Addison-Wesley, Boston

Project Management Institute (PMI) (2017) *A Guide to the Project Management Body of Knowledge (PMBOK® Guide)*, 6th ed, Project Management Institute, Newtown Square, PA

Seligman, M E P (2011) *Flourish: A Visionary new understanding of happiness and well-being*, Free Press, New York

Stickdorn, M, Lawrence, A, Hormess, M and Schneider, J (2018) *This is Service Design Doing: Applying service design thinking in the real world*, O'Reilly Media, Sebastopol, CA

06

Scoping strategy with a people-first lens

In my experience, internal communication (IC) pros are fixers and doers; we are responsive, resourceful and love to make a difference. The problem is that we often become the victim of our own success; the bigger the difference we make, the more everyone wants our services. Because we care deeply about the work we do, the answer is nearly always yes, until we're spread too thin. A senior director needs a message sending out asap – no problem! A new product launch we just heard about needs a full campaign – sure thing! I'm sure this resonates with many of you.

And IC is never 'done'; no matter how many hours in the day, no matter how big the team is or how large the budget, there is always more to do. We will never reach a place where we can declare that IC is perfect and our job here is done. The downside is that the IC remit can quickly become overwhelming, with competing demands from powerful stakeholders, even when we have a carefully developed strategy and plan. Somewhere in the midst of this we can lose sight of why we're doing what we do and if we're even doing the right thing at all. We've never met an IC pro who wasn't constantly busy, but we've met many who, over time, have questioned the impact they have.

This is why the scoping space matters; we need to slow down in order to speed up. As IC pros, we have a deep 'expert-led' instinct to jump straight to solutions and demonstrate our value by delivering at pace. But our People-First IC approach asks you to be intentional with your curiosity, something we believe is an unrealized strength of many IC pros. In this chapter, we zoom out to reframe the scoping phase as a strategic design decision. We make the case for moving from an expert-led to a people-first mindset – one that aligns with business goals but is rooted in the lived experience of our people.

We'll explore how to redefine IC strategy through the lens of experience, using tools like the 'Levels of Experience' model and the 'Life-Spiral' – first developed and shared by Emma and Belinda in their book *Employee Experience by Design* (2024). These tools enable us to take a broader, more holistic view of communication. This chapter sets the foundation for everything that follows, helping you build a strategy that doesn't just look good on paper but genuinely works for your people. This is the first step in moving from an expert-led approach to a genuinely people-first approach. The way forwards starts with understanding, not doing.

Scope: define the destination

The scoping phase, which is step 2 in our People-First IC Design Loop, is all about discovery and really taking the time to explore both the current IC experience (if relevant) and map out the future desired IC experience. But, crucially, from the perspectives of the people we are designing for. This presents an opportunity to move beyond simply responding to requests from stakeholders and solving problems from our 'expert-led' lens, and get really clear on what we are trying to solve through the lens of our people. The scoping stage takes inspiration from the British Design Council's 'double-diamond' framework, which begins with 'discovery'. This is all about taking the time to deeply understand the problem we are working on: 'This diamond helps people understand, rather than simply assume, what the problem is. It involves speaking to and spending time with people who are affected by the issues' (Design Council, 2019).

The tools we share here, and in the next chapter, will help you to do just this and discover the extent to which IC meets the needs of your people, as well as your organization, and understand where it is and isn't delivering. The tools will help you to get clear on the IC experience you want and use the insights you surface to prioritize where to focus. This means you can move away from trying to do it all and avoid jumping straight to solutions. However, just to be clear, taking a people-first approach in no way means ignoring strategic alignment. IC efforts should be aligned to organizational goals to ensure they make a meaningful contribution to the business.

Moving from an expert-led approach to a people-first approach

It's often the case that when we introduce our people-first approach to comms teams, they push back, arguing that they already do this! Some of the typical objections we hear are:

- We always start with the insights – we've run some focus groups!
- We ask what we want people to think, feel and do. This means we are strategic, not reactive.
- We challenge our stakeholders' assumptions with best practice and our expertise.

In Chapter 2, we explored the evolution of IC from process-led, to expert-led to people-first, outlining what this journey looks like. The ideas and theory are useful but nothing beats bringing it to life with a simple case study, which we've outlined here.

REAL-WORLD EXAMPLE
Human-centred listening as the foundation of strategy

BY HOWARD KRAIS, FOUNDER OF TRUE COMMUNICATIONS

Before we dive into the people-first approach further, it's worth spotlighting one of the most fundamental shifts in this way of working: authentic listening. This story, from the team at True Communications, brings listening to life, not just as a step in a process but as a leadership mindset and an organizational superpower. Their journey, which culminated in the publication of Leading the Listening Organization, *offers compelling proof that strategy grounded in listening is far more likely to land, and last. Over to Howard Krais, one of the founders of True Communications:*

Why listening is at the heart of people-centred internal communication

Being people-centred was a founding principle when I set up True Communications with my co-founder Ann-Marie Blake in early 2023. After many years of working in major global organizations, I was asking myself why, even though we were producing ever more high-quality, creative and comprehensive communications, they weren't supporting a sea-change in performance or engagement; and why change was not landing as expected?

I realized that while we were focusing on making leaders look good, on cascade processes and on improving channels – the things that might have been important to us sitting close to leadership in the centre – these were not necessarily the things that were important to our colleagues. So how did we know what was important and how could we know if we were making a difference?

Starting to listen

At an event in Copenhagen in 2018, run by the International Association of Business Communicators (IABC), I had the opportunity to start a conversation about this. I asked the question whether internal communicators were listening enough, and if not, then what could we do about it.

Coming out of the event, together with Mike Pounsford and Dr Kevin Ruck, we decided there might be some interesting work that we could do together to understand this topic of listening to employees.

What followed over the next few years, including through the pandemic, were surveys, articles, presentations and the publication of four reports. Then in December 2023, our book *Leading the Listening Organisation* was published, the first book to focus on why and how organizations listen to their employees.

At this point, I should offer a definition of listening. For me, listening means 'understanding the perspective of others and responding appropriately'. In other words, it is not enough to ask people what they think, you need to do something (and be seen to do something) with that information.

At its heart is a realization that, as individuals, from an early age, we expect or even demand to be listened to when we have something to say. When we are properly listened to, when someone takes us seriously and responds appropriately to what we say, we feel good, we feel valued and well-disposed to the person who has listened to us. On the other hand, when we sense the other person hasn't listened (and we can always tell), we feel the opposite – frustrated, undervalued and disappointed.

It is no different when you consider organizations. When we believe that the organization is really interested in what we think, then we feel good. If we believe that the organization is just going through the motions, then we will likely stop taking an interest in what the organization wants to say to us.

Why listen?

When we listen to employees, we can understand why processes or systems might not be working as they should and get a good idea of how they could work better; we can understand the questions and concerns that get in the way of employees understanding or accepting change, and we can encourage diverse voices to share ideas to support innovation.

Effective listening helps leaders make better business decisions; it supports better risk mitigation and leads to more successful implementation of change.

The listening leader

Being prepared and able to listen to employees is a foundation for people-centred internal communications. However, it is not just the communicator who needs to be prepared to listen. Our research made it clear that listening is a leader's responsibility. It is leaders who create the climate within a workplace and the leader who demonstrates the behaviours that are valued. How a leader listens tells employees whether their views matter or not.

The question is how many leaders listen? I've been fortunate to work with some exceptional leaders who understand the benefits of listening to their people. It is not always like that. Our research found that while 73 per cent of organizations said they took what their employees said seriously, only 42 per cent admitted to responding promptly to feedback. Given the earlier definition of responding appropriately, these figures suggest that only two in five organizations can be called listening organizations.

As a listening leader, when you listen, you will make better decisions. You will feel more confident that you are bringing your team with you, and you will build trust and engagement. As a communicator, when we get this right, we can demonstrate that a people-centred approach to internal communications pays big dividends.

Supporting line managers

Our work demonstrated the importance of managers listening at all levels. While the research confirmed that it is senior leader listening that is of most importance in generating strong outcomes, the role line managers play is also relevant.

Listening at a line manager level works best when it is embedded into regular team meetings. This is reliant on managers adopting an open-minded approach to listening to suggestions and ideas, as well as the organization having effective processes for responding. This also relies on organizations helping line managers to feel confident and enabled to listen.

The role of a line manager or supervisor seems to continuously evolve with more expected of people appointed into these critical roles. Unfortunately, our research showed that listening is rarely part of leadership or management training. This provides an opportunity for communicators and HR professionals to add value to the ways we help people managers take a people-centred approach.

How should we listen?

When we did our research, businesses told us that the top method of listening was the big organization-wide, typically annual, survey. Of course, when a survey leads to real change then it can be a great tool; however, this is often not the case and surveys can become examples of the pretence of listening. Sometimes more effort appears to be put into cleansing the data or obtaining a high response rate rather than delivering transparent improvement following the survey.

These days we hear the term 'survey fatigue' often. For me, this doesn't mean we're tired of doing too many surveys, rather that we are fed up with being asked to complete another survey where we know little is going to happen as a result.

There are many ways to listen other than surveys. The book details over 20. We found that focus groups and interviews were underused and there were great opportunities to listen better online, for example, places like Viva Engage (or even Glassdoor) where employees feel more comfortable sharing views and comments but where both communicators and leaders might not be present.

Getting emotional

There is one other aspect that ties listening with people-centred internal communications. That is the understanding that, as individuals, we are driven as much by our emotions as we are by a logical argument, if not more so.

As our understanding of neuroscience improves, we know that when we receive information, it doesn't go straight to our rational brain. Instead, it first passes through the limbic system – the part of the brain responsible for emotion, motivation and memory. Only after that emotional filter does the information reach the prefrontal cortex, where logical reasoning happens. In simple terms, this means we feel before we think. With listening also delivering an emotional response, when the organization listens, it demonstrates it is taking a people-centred approach.

What does this mean for communicators?

Setting out measurable listening objectives, supported by a listening strategy, enables the communicator to lay out clearly how listening can directly support achievement of an organization's goals. Linking listening to business objectives avoids listening being seen as a 'tick box' exercise. Once a leadership group starts to recognize how listening can help them, they will be more likely to invest in the right tools and processes as well as give more of their own time to being involved.

Therefore, it is incumbent on communicators to enable people to have the space and time to make sense of key business issues – and to listen to what they have to say. Creating a climate where people feel able to ask their questions, raise their concerns and share their ideas is a critical part of a people-centred approach.

Communicators should now be putting listening at the heart of their strategies and plans. This is not only to better demonstrate the real business value we deliver but also to reap the rewards that come from tapping into the ideas, the passion and the expertise that our employees have.

Being seen to listen, which includes responding appropriately, will be one of the best ways that you can demonstrate a commitment to a people-first approach to internal communications.

Expert-led vs people-first: a tale of two approaches

Picture this familiar scene: we got a call from a client asking for help. Their recent annual survey had indicated that just 42 per cent of employees said that they understood the company strategy. The team had been tasked by the executive committee to take action to address this. The problem was that the exec had already made assumptions about the problem and possible solutions:

- 'People haven't read the strategy; we need more visibility. Let's get a campaign out ASAP.'
- '*Awareness* is the issue, our people don't understand our strategy because they haven't seen it.'
- 'We just need more communication; we need a full campaign involving mailers, intranet micro-site, CEO video and posters.'

The IC team were confident that the exec were having a knee-jerk reaction to the survey findings and wanted to address the symptom rather than the cause. They came to us to help them take a different approach and convince the exec this was the right thing to do. Of course, we recommended going through an 'IC design-sprint' taking our people-first approach. This took some convincing; the team were still very firmly in the expert-led space and had sought our help to undertake some more traditional research elements, such as a survey and some focus groups. What they initially wanted to do was:

- Conduct a channel audit, reviewing clicks and opens to digital channels.
- Review existing comms relating to strategy communication such as mailers, newsletters and CEO updates.

- Review the content itself – was it on brand and in the right tone of voice? Was it accessible and easy to read and understand?
- Run a few focus groups to confirm themes arising from this initial research.

These insights were intended to help them develop and refine the solution they had already come up with – a 'strategy made simple' campaign, involving:

- new visuals
- bite-sized 'exec' video explainers
- a simplified 'strategy on a page'
- refreshed slide decks
- a new intranet micro-site with an animated strategy explainer video
- a regular strategy podcast
- employee stories to bring the strategy to life.

At first glance, this looks like a solid response. But the fundamental issue is that the problem was still being viewed through an 'expert-lens' rather than a 'people-first lens'. The insights they wanted to gather were focusing on the message and content and the way the communication reached people. And the insight process itself was seen as a task to complete to help inform and shape the ideas the team already had. The IC team had already landed on what they believed the solutions should be. However, their approach was missing ways to gather insights about the IC experience itself. Their approach wouldn't have explored what great strategy communication looks and feels like for people. The insights wouldn't have shed light on the context employees are in when they engage with the communication, or how it makes them feel. The approach to gathering insights wouldn t have truly enabled the team to stand in the shoes of the people they were designing for. Their approach might have addressed the symptom, but it wouldn't have gone deeper to address the cause. The bottom line is that their approach would have produced a seemingly credible campaign but would likely have fallen short of any meaningful behaviour change.

Initially, the team were resistant to running an IC design sprint; we get it! They questioned what our approach would offer in addition to their preferred approach. However, we were able to convince them to keep an open mind and get curious about new ways of working; sharing success stories from other client projects really helped us to make the case. Rather than asking, 'What do we need to say and do differently to help land the strategy comms?' we asked, 'What's the *current experience* of strategy communication for your people – and what *could* it be?'

We started by mapping some current 'strategy comms' experiences with a range of employee groups, ensuring different perspectives were captured including:

- front-line employees, both online, offline, office based and remote workers
- managers with responsibility for delivering comms and engaging their teams in conversations about the company strategy
- senior leaders and the exec
- subject matter experts who were involved in the strategy comms experience.

And we ensured the key demographics were covered such as tenure, job role and level.

We asked questions such as:

- When and where do people encounter strategy messaging?
- We asked not just have you seen this but what does it mean to you?
- How do these comms and touchpoints make you feel?
- Who delivers them?
- What happens next?

We also explored the desired future experience, asking if it was as good as it could be, what would be happening and how would they feel? And then we asked people to identify the 'moments that matter' – that is, what really makes the difference to you? We asked what might make strategy communication more personal, relevant, inspiring and meaningful to you?

These workshops gathered deep insights involving stories, tensions and emotions, not just statistics and reactions. And the insights from this initial scoping phase were enlightening. In summary, we discovered that there was no emotional attachment to the strategy – people just didn't care about it. Yes they had seen it, and they understood it, but no one could explain why it mattered and specifically answer why it mattered to them. The way it was communicated and the language used made it feel corporate, abstract and disconnected from the day-to-day reality of working in the organization. And the specific channels the team had spent time and energy on were not valued; the town halls felt transactional, too 'show and tell', the CEO video largely forgotten and the slide decks rarely viewed. Managers also felt they lacked the tools and direction to translate the big picture into meaningful actions and engage their teams in the strategy. And the current experience felt like a one-off campaign rather than an ongoing conversation.

It became clear very quickly that the assumptions made at the outset were flawed; this was not about raising awareness or helping people to better understand the strategy. The underlying cause was that people needed to care about and connect with the company strategy. And the answer definitely did not involve the IC team creating more noise.

Starting from this place enabled the team to get to the heart of the experience and gather insights to inform what comes next, avoiding a knee-jerk reaction to keep the exec happy. When the insights were shared with the exec, it helped to challenge their assumptions but without confrontation. This wasn't the world according to the comms team; this was direct feedback from their people and therefore it was hard to argue with! The team could demonstrate that the problem was clearly understood, and the subsequent response felt way more credible. And the insights enabled the move from a vague, top-down 'ask' from the exec into a robust evidence-based approach.

In summary: This is the value of scoping done well, it's an intentional design decision. But we recognize that IC teams will be at different stages of maturity in their approach. The tools we share here and in subsequent chapters are practical, and they can be used in any way that works for you, no matter where you are on your journey. They are there to help you to truly understand the problem you are trying to solve or the opportunity you have identified. Getting clear on what you are trying to achieve is the foundation of creating a brilliant IC experience. The purpose of the scoping stage is simple, to get clear on where you are today and where you want to get to.

TABLE 6.1 Expert-led versus people-first: overview

	Expert-led	People-first
Insight depth	Surface-level	Deep and contextual
Problem framing	'They don't get it'	'They can't connect it to what matters and why'
Solution ownership	Led by IC team	Co-created with employees and managers
Speed	Fast to start, slow to land	Slower to start, fast to gain traction
Outcome	Activity	Impact

Reframing your IC strategy with a people-first lens

The scoping stage of our 'People-First IC Design Loop' is where we take the time to get super-clear on the problem we're aiming to solve and the direction we want to travel in. The tools we'll share here will help to overcome assumptions and bias, prioritize what really matters and set the direction before diving into delivery. Scoping helps to ensure we are taking a more strategic approach, which is why this is a good time to talk about IC strategy.

Traditional comms strategies haven't really changed in the last 20 years or so and with good reason. They are built using our expert lens and aligned to business goals. They begin by asking what the organization wants to achieve and then consider how IC can contribute to the business strategy. A decent IC strategy will set out our purpose and objectives, and likely involve variations on the following:

- Engage our people in bringing our vision, values, objectives and brand to life and help create the culture to make it happen.
- Deliver effective communication solutions to help the business achieve its goals.
- Provide clarity of our objectives to our people and stakeholders to facilitate delivery of results.
- Create an understanding among our leadership of what excellence in communication looks like and how it can be delivered.
- Deliver a suite of 'best in class communication processes and systems' designed to measurably improve communication.
- Develop an effective communications team.

Then follows a 12-month plan to outline what we'll do to deliver these objectives. Typically, this includes our channel strategy and content plan, as ways to get key messages out, such as 'all-hands', town-halls, newsletters, the intranet and more. Then we have the standalone comms campaigns to deliver specific objectives; for example, to launch a new product, a health and safety campaign, a new approach to performance management or the roll-out of a new operating procedure. There will likely be some focus on employee voice to ensure we listen to our people as well. And hopefully, some efforts to support effective line manager communication, given we recognize that this is where much of the real work of comms happens.

So far so good – this all make sense. And of course we can't lose sight of the need to align our work with organizational goals. But we believe we are missing a huge opportunity here and it's time to evolve our strategy from being expert-led to people-first. Rather than asking questions like:

- What do we need to communicate?
- How can our communication contribute to delivering our company strategy?

We need to flip this and ask:

- What is the experience of communication like for our people and how can we shape it to help them succeed and contribute to our organizational success?

This is a subtle but meaningful shift, focusing our IC strategy on experience rather than just the outputs of comms. This is an evolution not a revolution, it is absolutely not about throwing out everything you know. This is about developing a strategy and plan that not only aligns with your organizational strategy but works for your people too. Let's take a closer look:

Internal communication strategy on a page: expert-led vs people-first

Table 6.2 outlines the differences between an expert-led IC strategy and a people-first, 'experience-led' approach. The goal isn't to replace the expert-led approach but to evolve it, so IC aligns with business goals, while also improving the lived experience of communication for employees.

TABLE 6.2 Expert-led versus people-first: strategy elements

Strategy element	Expert-led approach	People-first approach
Purpose	Support business goals through comms campaigns and channels.	Design brilliant communication experiences that work for our people and support our organization goals too.
Objectives	Engage employees with vision, values and objectives. Improve clarity, consistency and reach.	Improve the communication experience across employee journeys and moments that matter.

(continued)

TABLE 6.2 (Continued)

Strategy element	Expert-led approach	People-first approach
Focus	Message clarity, content quality, cadence and channel management.	Employee journeys, emotional tone, timing, trust and relevance.
Insight	Review channel stats, conduct surveys and run occasional focus groups.	Map communication experiences, co-create with employees, and identify pain points and moments that matter.
Tactics	Deliver campaigns (e.g. transformation, values), manage newsletters, town halls and intranet.	Design comms around employee life cycle touchpoints (e.g. onboarding, becoming a manager, exits). Collaborate with HR and managers to embed communication into real experiences.
Success measures	Email opens, campaign reach, leader satisfaction, channel audits.	Employee feedback on their experience, trust, engagement and how comms support real work and well-being.

The traditional IC strategy model works, but it needs updating. It's built around organizational goals and while we mustn't lose sight of this, it's simply not enough anymore. We need to switch it up to incorporate the IC experience too. We need a people-first communication strategy that still aligns with business objectives but is also designed around the actual lived experiences of employees.

IC levels of experience: a thinking tool to help develop your people-first strategy

To help you make this shift there are two tools to get you started. First up, let's explore the 'Levels of Experience' model and how we can make this work for IC pros. This model was first published in Emma and Belinda's book *Employee Experience by Design*. In the original iteration, they argued that it is helpful to consider the difference between what they call the 'umbrella experience' and 'nested journeys'. Their Levels of Experience model helps to illustrate this.

FIGURE 6.1 Levels of Experience model

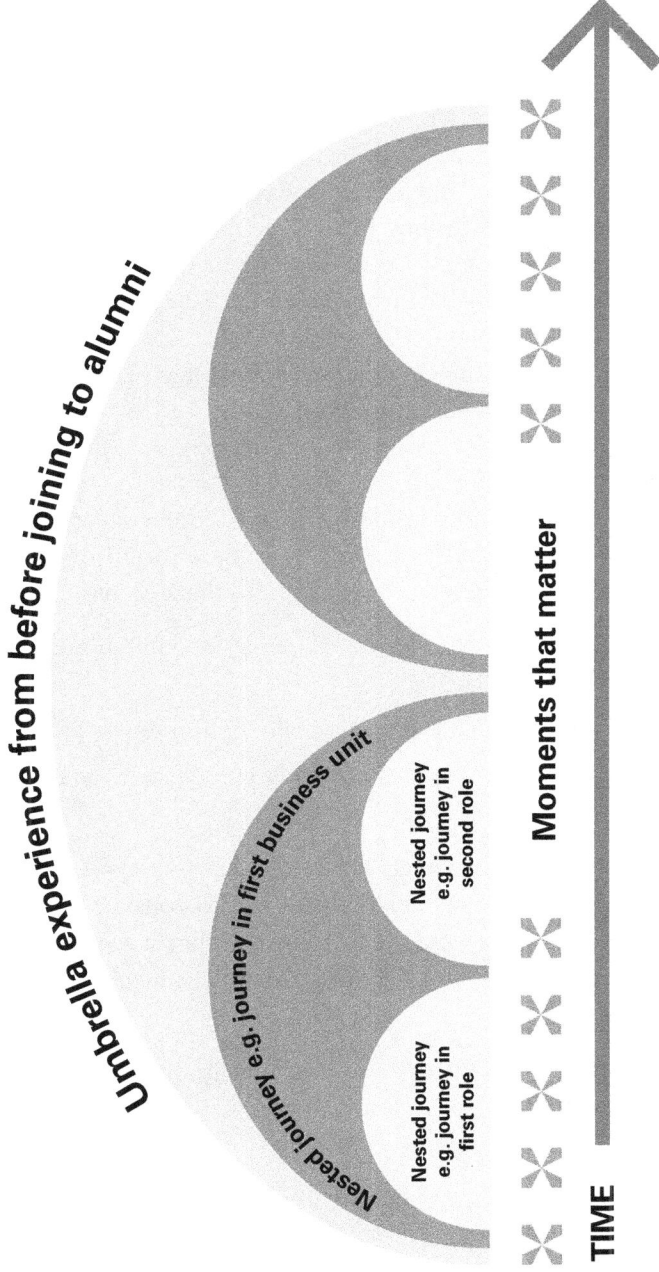

Umbrella experience from before joining to alumni

Nested journey e.g. journey in first business unit

Nested journey e.g. journey in first role

Nested journey e.g. journey in second role

Moments that matter

TIME

SOURCE Bridger and Gannaway

The umbrella experience refers to the overall, end-to-end experience employees have with the organization, which begins before they even join on day one and extends after they exit the company. Underneath the umbrella experience are nested journeys, which might include experiences that last months or years, such as the employee journey on a graduate scheme or in their first business unit. And there are shorter nested journeys, such as the experience someone has on day one with the company or the experience someone has returning to work after a leave of absence. And along the way, there will be moments that matter to the employee, such as their first promotion or taking maternity or paternity leave. The purpose of this model is to enable practitioners to consider the different types and levels of experience employees have and how they might impact each other.

The model can be easily applied to an IC context and help us consider a more experience-driven strategy and approach. Instead of structuring IC strategy purely around business goals and outputs, we can map our strategy to different levels of experience.

First up, we might want to consider the overall 'umbrella' communication experience employees have during their time with an organization, from pre-boarding to exit. Here we might want to think about:

- The tone, consistency, quality and transparency of communication across the employee lifecycle.
- Our communication culture: is it open or closed? Top-down or involving?
- The degree to which communication feels human or aligns with our values, behaviours or brand.

We can think of this as the strategic landscape that underpins and shapes our entire comms approach. We might also want to consider nested journeys, which are related to specific IC experiences that happen within the broader umbrella experience. For example, they might involve longer-term communication journeys such as:

- the communication experience of someone on a graduate scheme or as a first time manager
- internal comms during a restructure
- the communication experience during onboarding and first 100 days in a company.

Or they might be shorter-term or event-based communication experiences:

- comms experience related to the annual survey process
- comms around return from parental leave
- communication around annual goals, or pay reviews, etc.

Each nested journey is a thread in the broader IC experience and each one shapes how an employee feels about working in our organization.

And finally, we must pay attention to moments that matter, which are those emotionally significant communication moments and might involve:

- how someone is welcomed on day one and who communicates with them
- how news of an organizational change is delivered
- how recognition or feedback is shared
- how mistakes are communicated and responded to.

These moments can have a disproportionate impact on the overall comms experience, which is why we need to pay attention to them. Let's work through an example to illustrate real-life application.

Let's say your organization is undergoing a transformation programme involving a new strategy, some structural changes, productivity measures and the roll-out of new tech. It's big, business-critical and likely to stretch over two years. In previous 'expert-led' approaches, the focus might be on considering what we want people to think, feel and do and then crafting a plan which focuses on messaging and channels. The Levels of Experience model is a useful 'thinking tool' to help intentionally design a communication approach as a lived experience. This takes into account how this might feel for our people and what elements of that transformation really matter to them.

For example, the 'umbrella experience' considers the overall communication landscape, the context and the culture. How does this support (or not) the comms experience we want to deliver for the transformation programme?

The consideration of 'nested journeys' help us to think about specific comms experiences as part of this change. We could go deeper here and use experience or journey mapping tools to gather insights from the perspectives of the people we are designing for. The purpose of the Levels of Experience model is to simply help us consider what these different nested journeys might be, and think about how they might differ depending on role, team or personal impact, for example, a line manager asked to communicate the change or a front-line employee in an impacted business unit. Further exploration of these nested journeys, using an experience or journey mapping tool will uncover pain points or opportunities to help inform our final solutions. For example, we might discover that line managers are nervous about being asked questions they can't answer or that they don't actually agree with the changes being made. Or we might find impacted employees find town halls impersonal and vague and are cynical about the changes.

We then need to pay attention to the 'moments that matter', which we'll explore in more detail later in this chapter. In summary, though these can have a significant impact on the communication experience, carrying emotional weight. These moments matter because they stick – people may not remember the facts or the detail about the change, but they will remember how they were spoken to, how their concerns were handled and whether they felt respected. These moments are where communication becomes emotional, human and real. And they shape the legacy of the change.

Why this model matters for IC

Paying attention to the different levels of communication experience enables us to reframe our approach, to think beyond campaigns and channels and move to an intentional communication approach which puts people front and centre. Internal communication doesn't happen in isolation. Every message, channel and interaction contributes to a broader experience of what communication feels like in your organization. The Levels of Experience model is a thinking tool to enable us to better understand the different layers of the communication experience, zooming out to see the big picture and zooming in to identify the moments that matter most. All of which contributes to a superior communication experience for our people and will ultimately have a positive impact on business outcomes.

The employee life-spiral model

You're no doubt familiar with the concept of the employee life cycle. It is typically presented as a circular visual depicting key touchpoints employees encounter during their time with an organization: from recruitment and onboarding, to reward and performance, and even exit. The life cycle is often presented through this 'expert lens', in that these are the key touchpoints the experts manage for their people. In their book *Employee*

Experience by Design, Emma and Belinda flipped this model to make it people-first, calling it the 'life-spiral' and used it as a thinking and conversation tool.

The life-spiral

The spiral represents the overarching employee experience from excitement before joining, to leaving and becoming an alumnus. The life-spiral makes the employee and their experience the focal point – it's a small, but significant shift that really changes how people think and talk about employee experience. In addition, the spiral is not linear, it gives room to the idea of internal mobility and people rejoining the organization, for example. In doing so, it encourages us to move away from thinking about careers as one-way ladders which, again, opens up a different dialogue and more innovative ways of addressing problems and opportunities. In summary, the life-spiral helps us look at employee journeys from the employee's point of view – dynamic, emotional and nonlinear.

You might be asking, 'What has this got to do with IC?' The fact is that IC is present throughout every area of the life-spiral, even though this may not be immediately obvious. Employees don't understand, or often even

FIGURE 6.2 The life-spiral

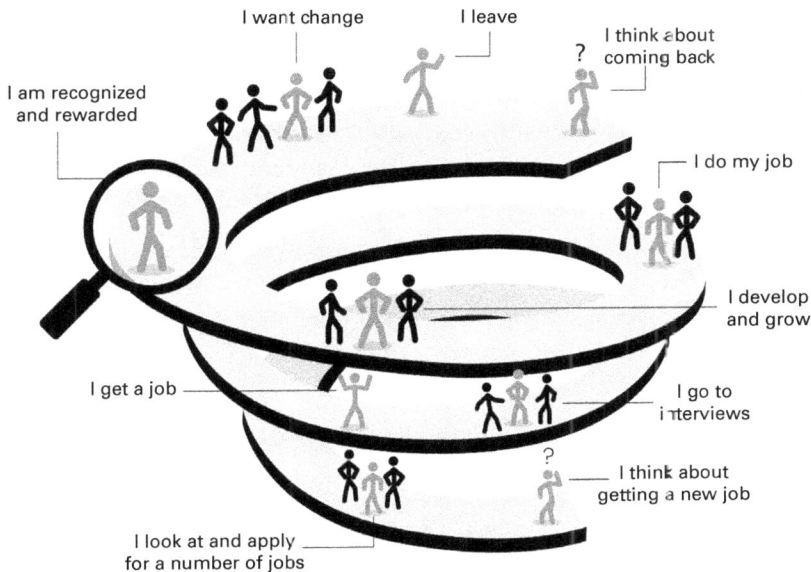

SOURCE Bridger and Gannaway

care, what we deem to be 'IC' or not as the case may be. As IC pros, we have a clear and defined view of what we mean by IC and our strategies, plans and channels support this. But our people probably don't see it this way; they're not IC experts after all. Every conversation, update, message, comms touch-point or even silence, contributes to their lived experience of communication at work; they experience communication as part of the bigger picture.

We can use the employee life-spiral model to help us think broader and take a people-first approach. It can help us to shift from our narrow focus on those IC touchpoints we traditionally own, which are often channel-based, to consider those IC touchpoints that actually matter to our people. In our experience, many of these will sit outside the traditional IC remit, but they are rich opportunities to use IC to improve the overall employee experience, which then contributes to engagement.

A good example of this is to look at what happens to employees between accepting an offer of employment and actually starting with the company. This is a critical time and an opportunity to make a great first impression, but we find that it is often a broken experience. We have worked with many clients to help them improve this experience (and the subsequent onboarding experience), and we have found that IC teams are rarely, if ever, involved with this. But they should be, and IC can offer huge value to improve this experience. It's often the case that once an offer of employment is accepted, the communication is either non-existent or just not very good.

We worked with a social care company who were growing quickly but struggling to translate recruitment into 'day one' starters. The nature of their work meant there was a prolonged period of checks that needed to happen before new recruits could actually start. And in the absence of communication from the company, many were assuming something had gone wrong and taking jobs elsewhere. In short, the comms experience was severely lacking, but until we mapped the current experience with new recruits, this wasn't obvious. As soon as we got the IC team involved, they were able to turn this around quickly and significantly improve the numbers starting, both improving the experience for employees but also contributing to the business strategy and bottom line.

Let's take a look at another example.

Communicating a new parental leave policy

The HR team approach you asking for help to communicate their refreshed maternity, paternity and shared parental leave policies. On paper, they look great; they're progressive, people-focused and aligned with the company's values. You work with the team to put a plan together which involves:

- CEO updates in monthly briefings.
- Features in the internal newsletter with a clear summary and a quote from HR.
- Managers are given talking points for their regular team briefings and encouraged to talk it through in team meetings.
- The policy is uploaded to the intranet with a new 'Family Matters' section.

You conduct a quick pulse check and proudly share the stats that people have read and understood the new policies and there is overall support for them too. So far, so good. But let's fast forward 12 months and meet Priya.

Priya has recently returned to work after taking nine months of maternity leave. She's proud of her company's values, and she remembers seeing something about the updated parental leave policy before she left. But her experience of communication around this important life moment is, at best, underwhelming:

- Before her leave, no one followed up with her after she informed her manager. She got a formal letter from HR, which felt very corporate and cold, but no human conversation.
- During her leave, she felt largely invisible. No team updates, no check-ins and no context on what was changing while she was away.
- On her return, she was in the dark about how it would work and what to expect.
- Her manager seemed uncomfortable discussing her return to work, making her feel anxious about how it would play out.

On paper, the refreshed policy looked great, but the reality was far from it. The IC team had done a great job of communicating the policy, but Priya's communication experience was confusing, isolating and poor. What she didn't need was a great quote from her CEO endorsing the policy. What she did need was someone to check in with her. What she didn't need was a mention of the new policy in her team brief. What she did need was an ongoing conversation with her manager and emotional support. You get the idea.

So what might have been different if the team had used a people-first approach instead? Instead of than jumping straight to drafting the CEO script and building the intranet pages, they would have started by mapping the current experience and asked: 'What does communication feel like today for someone going on, and returning from, parental leave?'

Mapping the journey, they would have understood the perspectives from their people with lived experience, as well as manager's perspectives and that of the teams that owned the delivery of the policy. They would have unearthed insights to understand that communication was absent, confusing and inconsistent, and better understood how it made people feel.

They would have defined the desired future experience asking 'What should this IC experience feel like if we get it right?'

And they would have worked this through from different perspectives including EDI, HR, line managers and recent parents to define what a great IC experience could involve. They would have understood that people need to feel supported, both managers and employees, that the practical steps were really clear and that returning to work needs to feel human rather than transactional.

Identifying the moments that matter would have surfaced where communication can make the biggest difference:

- The first conversation with their manager.
- The 'what happens next' after telling HR.
- How they're communicated with while on leave – for example, in the UK, this needs to be reasonable and appropriate, but what does this mean to people? Spoiler alert, it likely means different things to different people, and this needs to be mapped out.
- The tone and content of the return-to-work communication.
- The welcome-back approach from their team.

These are the moments that defined the success (or not) of the refreshed policy, and the IC team hadn't been involved in any of them before. These insights would have enabled the team to develop a range of ideas that they could prototype and test to understand if they worked in a real-life setting. And when they landed on ideas that worked, they could be confident in scaling them across the company.

In this scenario, Priya's manager was given support at the moment of need to help him better support Priya. The entire comms journey was mapped as a full sequence to ensure Priya was kept in the loop all the way through the journey. After telling HR her news, it triggered a whole sequence of human comms and touchpoints to help her feel listened to. She received regular comms while she was off and a personal note from her manager a few weeks before her official return, offering flexibility and support. Her team had a 'welcome back lunch', and they'd been prepped with a few talking points to make her feel at home. In summary, a very different overall experience for Priya, and IC made a big contribution to improving how it felt.

Communicating around 'the edges'

As IC pros, we spend much of our time designing and delivering big comms campaigns and keeping our channels going to deliver our strategy. The problem with this approach? So much of the communication that happens in organizations takes place outside of this formal system, it happens around the edges. For example:

- in the gaps between the formal IC campaigns and channels
- in the informal moments that shape how people feel
- in the small details we assume are 'owned by someone else'.

In summary, the traditional IC approach looks at:

- what we manage
- channels
- campaigns
- formal comms
- content
- what we say and how we say it.

In contrast, using the life-spiral as a thinking tool helps us to consider:

- the overall IC experience
- communication 'moments that matter'
- emotions involved
- informal human communication
- how it feels.

You might already know this and possibly be thinking, 'If only we had the bandwidth to get involved in this way.' Thinking about IC in this way can feel overwhelming and unwieldy; it can feel too big – just where do you start? And we're not saying that IC pros need to be involved in every single touchpoint across the employee life cycle; clearly that would be unrealistic. We'll continue to emphasize throughout this book that one of the most compelling benefits for adopting this approach is that it enables you to take a problem that is often ambiguous and complex and provide a clear and simple way to understand it and solve it.

And of course, when you add AI into the mix, we have way more bandwidth than in previous times. Take our example of Priya, returning to work after maternity leave. AI can't replace a thoughtful conversation with her manager, but it *can* ensure that conversation happens in the first place. For instance:

- **Personalized communication journeys** can be triggered automatically when someone notifies HR of parental leave. These can include timely check-ins, return-to-work guidance and reminders tailored to the employee's stage in the journey.

- **AI-driven nudges** can support managers with suggested messages, inclusive language tips and checklists at key points. This helps them lead with empathy, even if it's their first time supporting someone through parental leave.

- **Smart intranet content** can show relevant resources based on where someone is in their leave or return journey, ensuring that practical information and emotional support are easy to find.

- **Real-time sentiment tracking** through AI-enabled feedback tools means the IC team can move from measuring clicks to truly understanding how people feel and act quickly if something's not landing well.

In summary, the life-spiral model, and applying the thinking and tools of our people-first approach, will help you to unearth and work on communication that really matters to your people.

How to use it the life-spiral tool in IC

You can use the life-spiral as a 'thinking' tool to help you move towards considering IC as an experience. While scoping your IC strategy or project, use the life cycle to:

- Make a shift to put the emphasis on the IC experience, ensuring comms are intentionally designed around what it feels like for our people, not just what we might need to communicate.

- Introduce People-First IC to stakeholders who are probably new to this approach.
- Discover data and insight gaps by exploring what is and isn't already known about different parts of the IC experience.
- Take a holistic view of the whole IC experience to discuss and prioritize which communication experiences need most attention or will make the biggest difference.

The life-spiral will help you to consider the employee experience from the perspective of your people.

Using the Life-Spiral IC SWOT to prioritize communication efforts

The Life-Spiral IC SWOT is a simple but powerful tool that helps IC pros take a more strategic, experience-led approach to their work. By blending a traditional SWOT analysis (strengths, weaknesses, opportunities, threats) with the employee life cycle this tool helps IC teams identify where communication is working well, where it's falling short and where there's potential to improve the employee experience through better communication.

Rather than relying solely on campaign calendars or ad hoc requests, the Life-Spiral IC SWOT encourages a more intentional focus: aligning IC priorities with the moments that matter most in the employee journey. It can surface blind spots, highlight risks and point to quick wins, ensuring that IC activity is rooted in the real needs of employees, not just organizational demands.

Typically run as a collaborative workshop, it's most effective when you bring together people from IC, HR or people teams and key business stakeholders. Participants map out communication experiences across each stage of the employee lifecycle, reflecting on what's working, what's not and where IC can make a real difference. The result is a shared understanding of priorities, framed by what employees actually experience, not just what the business wants to say.

LIFE-SPIRAL WORKSHOP STEPS

1 **Set the context**
   Explain the purpose: to explore the communication experience across the employee journey and prioritize where IC can have the biggest impact.

2 Start with strengths

Ask: *Where are we getting communication right across the life-spiral?*

Anchor in data where possible. Place them on the relevant points of the spiral.

3 Then explore weaknesses

Ask: *Where do we fall short? What do people say we don't do well?*

Capture pain points, gaps or inconsistent experiences.

4 Explore opportunities and threats

For each area of the spiral, ask:

o *What's the opportunity to use IC to improve or amplify this experience?*

o *What's the risk if we don't improve it – for our people or the organization?*

5 Prioritize

As a group, agree what's:

o Now – urgent and high impact.

o Near – important, but not immediate.

o Far – keep on the radar, but not a current priority.

6 Wrap up with alignment and next steps

Summarize the areas of focus, highlight any insights gaps to follow up and agree what to take into strategy development or design work.

This approach is particularly valuable when:

- refreshing or refocusing your IC strategy

- tackling specific challenges like onboarding, change or retention

- building alignment across teams and stakeholders

- embedding a people-first mindset into comms planning.

Ultimately, internal communication shapes how people feel about their work, their team and the organization itself. Tools like the Life-Spiral IC SWOT help IC teams move beyond messaging and channels, towards designing meaningful, experience-driven communication across the entire employee life cycle.

Evolving your IC strategy: a quick summary

In this section, we have made the case for taking a people-first approach to your IC strategy and shared some tools to help you evolve your approach. Here's how you might get started using the tools we have shared so far.

1 Consider people's experience, as well as business requirements.

   o What are the moments and journeys that matter most to your people?

   o How do we want them to *feel* about communication?

2 Then align with business goals.

   o How can IC help achieve strategic objectives *through* the IC experience?

   o How can a brilliant IC experience contribute towards business strategy and goals?

3 Map communication across the levels of experience.

   o Umbrella – What's the overall comms experience like?

   o Journeys – Which employee journeys do we need to focus on? Where can IC add the most value?

   o Moments – What are the IC moments that matter?

4 Use the life-spiral to understand where IC can have the biggest impact.

   o Identify neglected/broken moments (onboarding, exits, becoming a new parent).

   o Integrate comms that bring vision/values to life within those touchpoints.

   o Partner with other teams to co-own these moments.

5 Design with employees, not just for them.

   o In the following chapters, we'll introduce you to a range of tools to help you take a people-first approach e.g. empathy mapping.

And be assured with this approach:

• You're still aligning to business strategy and goals.

• You're still delivering campaigns and using channels.

• But you're also thinking about and intentionally designing the IC experience.

• You're starting to think like an experience designer.

• You're taking a people-first approach by considering their IC experience.

Scoping as a strategic discipline

The scoping phase isn't just about discovery; it's a mindset shift. In this chapter, we explored how to move from being expert responders to strategic designers of the internal communication experience.

By zooming out and reframing your strategy through a people-first lens, we open up space to align more intentionally with both organizational goals and the needs of our people. Tools like the Levels of Experience and the Life-Spiral help us see IC not as a set of tasks or channels, but as a meaningful experience that shapes how people feel about their work every day.

Now that we've laid the strategic groundwork, the next step is to get practical. In the next chapter, we'll introduce a set of tools to help you map and understand IC experiences, from current pain points to aspirational futures, so you can start shaping communication that truly makes a difference.

CHAPTER IN SUMMARY

- Internal communicators are often stretched thin. The scoping phase helps us pause, reflect and ensure we're working on the right things, not just the loudest things.

- The scoping stage is a strategic design decision, it's not just about gathering insights, it's about deeply understanding the problem from the perspective of your people.

- Moving from an *expert-led* to a *people-first* approach means shifting focus from message and channel to experience and emotion.

- Tools like the Levels of Experience model and the Life-Spiral help IC pros take a broader, more strategic view of communication – from isolated campaigns to holistic employee experiences.

- Effective scoping means mapping communication across:

  o the umbrella experience (end-to-end employee comms culture)

  o nested journeys (e.g. onboarding, parental leave, transformations)

  o moments that matter (emotionally significant touchpoints).

- The Life-Spiral IC SWOT is a practical tool to help IC teams identify strengths, gaps and opportunities across the employee life cycle – ensuring effort is focused where it will make the biggest impact.

- AI can help bring People-First IC to life, by enabling personalized journeys, supporting managers at key moments, adapting content contextually and tracking real-time sentiment.

- Scoping well means fewer campaigns, better outcomes and IC that's felt, remembered and makes a difference.

References

Bridger, E and Gannaway, B (2024) *Employee Experience by Design: How to create an effective EX for competitive advantage*, 2nd ed, Kogan Page, London

Design Council (2019) The Double Diamond: A universally accepted depiction of the design process, www.designcouncil.org.uk/our-work/skills-learning/tools-frameworks/framework-for-innovation-design-councils-evolved-double-diamond (archived at https://perma.cc/FK2R-LWEJ)

07

Tools for scoping and mapping the internal communication experience

Having reframed scoping as a strategic act rooted in experience, in this chapter, we zoom in and explore the tools that bring people-first scoping to life. From journey mapping and moments that matter to visioning tools and service design blueprints, this chapter is packed with practical methods to help you deeply understand the current internal communication (IC) experience and imagine what it could be.

Whether you're working on a transformation programme, launching new values, refreshing your digital comms approach or rethinking line-manager communication, the tools in this chapter will help you map what's really going on and where you want to get to. You'll be able to spot pain points, prioritize what matters and begin to design communication experiences that are more human, more effective and more aligned to the reality of work today.

As a reminder, the scoping phase is all about discovery and spending time exploring the current IC experience (if relevant) and mapping out the future desired IC experience, but crucially from the perspectives of the people we are designing for. And the tools we share here will help you to do this.

Mapping the IC experience: today and in the future

In the scoping phase of the People-First IC approach, we're trying to understand the problem from the perspective of the people who experience it. Journeys are a universal way of thinking about different elements of the IC experience with a greater degree of granularity. And they are a great tool to use within the scoping phase of our People-First Design Loop, providing insights on the current experience and the desired future experience from the perspectives of the people you are designing for. Journey maps are a visual representation of an experience from the point of view of an individual or groups. They are one of the most widely used employee experience (EX) tools, to visualize, analyse and then improve the EX. Journey maps aren't just a nice-to-have, they're an essential part of any people-first approach. The British Design Council argues that good design starts with understanding the problem from the user's point of view. Journey maps help us do just that, capturing the lived reality of communication and pointing to where IC can have the greatest impact. 'Design is not just about making things look better – it's about making things work better. That starts with understanding people's needs' (British Design Council, 2019).

IDEO popularized journey mapping as part of human-centred design. They frame it as a way to *empathize* with people's real experiences and uncover pain points that aren't visible from organizational data alone. And yet they are rarely used as a tool in IC, which is a missed opportunity.

Journey maps can be used to capture or identify:

- Steps taken – the things employees do either inside or outside of the organization in pursuit of a particular goal.
- Touchpoints – interactions employees have with the organization, including its tools, systems and people.
- Pain points – steps or touchpoints that don't work and have a detrimental impact.
- Moments that matter – emotionally charged moments in the journey that have a disproportionate impact on the experience.

Journey mapping typically starts with identifying the steps someone goes through, then looking at each step from different angles, for example, what is someone thinking, feeling and doing at each step? This might draw on quantitative data from surveys, qualitative data from observation, participation (i.e. going through the process yourself), interviews or group discussions in workshops. The result is a rich picture of an experience represented on a map. This can be visualized in different ways, from simple lines and text to infographics and even an artistic style.

We often use the terms journey map and experience map interchangeably, with good reason. A journey refers to a sequential IC experience that happens over time, highlighting the clear steps people might go through. For example, you might be mapping the comms journey for the roll-out of a change programme and there will be clear milestones involved. An IC experience, however, might not follow a neat sequence but mapping the experience is still useful, for example, mapping the comms experience of line managers. The point is not to get bogged down with the terminology; the idea of mapping comms journeys or experiences is useful to help take a people-first approach to our comms design.

How to use experience or journey maps for IC

Journey or experience maps are simple, easy-to-use tools that can be used in different ways to help you take a people-first approach to IC. First, you can use them to understand the IC experiences of different groups or personas. In doing this, you can understand the big picture view, spot patterns, highlight recurring themes and pain points. This approach really helps in strategic planning, as it reveals where communication consistently supports (or undermines) the experience.

You can also zoom in and focus on a single persona or a specific moment in the journey. This brings to life the lived experience that sits behind the data. It's a powerful way to unearth insights, emotions and real opportunities to improve how IC lands.

Comparing journey maps from different perspectives can reveal inconsistencies in the internal communication experience. These differences often highlight systemic gaps, siloed practices or cultural nuances that may be invisible from the centre.

Journey maps can also be used to visualize the desired or 'future state' experience, what the experience could look like if communication were redesigned with real employee needs in mind. A future map is helpful for stakeholder buy-in and to bring the case for change to life.

Example journey map

Let's take the example of the Return to Office (RTO) transition, which is a highly relevant, emotionally charged and an insight-rich scenario for mapping current-state internal communication experiences. We worked with a client that was transitioning from 100 per cent remote working to a minimum of a three days in the office. They had rolled out these changes to business-critical departments first and wanted to learn from this experience before a full-company roll-out. Figure 7.1 is an example of a current state IC journey map for employees who had been through the experience.

FIGURE 7.1 Example journey map

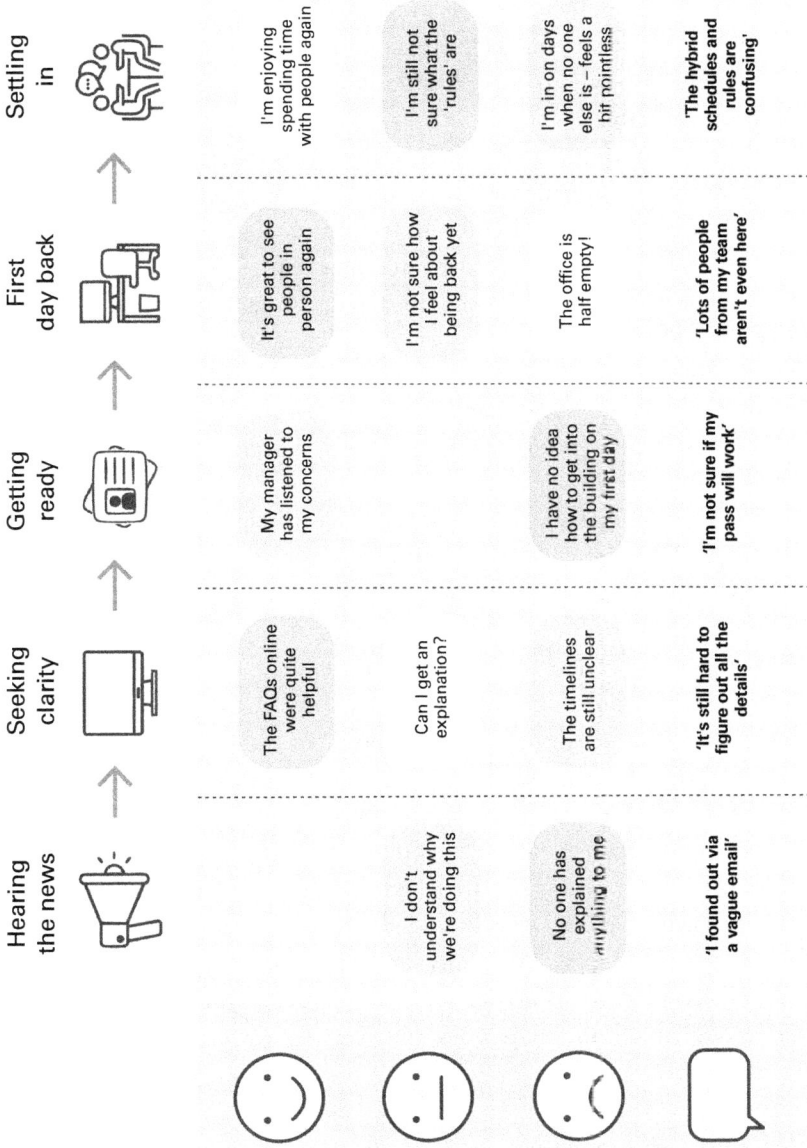

	Hearing the news	Seeking clarity	Getting ready	First day back	Settling in
🙂		The FAQs online were quite helpful	My manager has listened to my concerns	It's great to see people in person again	I'm enjoying spending time with people again
😐	I don't understand why we're doing this	Can I get an explanation?		I'm not sure how I feel about being back yet	I'm still not sure what the 'rules' are
🙁	No one has explained anything to me	The timelines are still unclear	I have no idea how to get into the building on my first day	The office is half empty!	I'm in on days when no one else is – feels a bit pointless
💬	'I found out via a vague email'	'It's still hard to figure out all the details'	'I'm not sure if my pass will work'	'Lots of people from my team aren't even here'	'The hybrid schedules and rules are confusing'

Using an experience/journey-mapping tool for IC

Journey mapping is a powerful way to explore and improve the IC experience by viewing it through the eyes of the people living it. At its core, a journey map tells the story of an employee's IC experience. Whatever the focus, journey mapping helps you understand not just the surface-level actions but also what people are thinking, feeling and doing at every stage of the experience.

What makes journey mapping so effective is that it brings together diverse perspectives. This creates a shared view of what's really going on and often unlocks new energy and commitment to change. When done well, it's as much a team-building and trust-building exercise as it is a research method.

Journey mapping works well both in person and online. Virtual tools like Miro and Mural can be used to create a digital whiteboard, while a physical room with space for a 'swim lane' style map works best in real life. Regardless of format, the process is about listening without judgement, creating psychological safety and giving people the space to speak honestly about their IC experiences.

The process starts with employees identifying the key steps and touchpoints of the journey or experience. Typically, these are labelled across the 'X' axis at the top of the map. From there, the group captures what they were thinking, feeling and doing at each stage, often using colour-coded notes or visuals. These insights are placed along a timeline or flow, bringing the journey to life visually. As the map builds, the group reflects on each stage, asks clarifying questions and looks for patterns or pain points.

One powerful feature of journey mapping is that it invites a sense of co-ownership. It's not about employees reporting issues to leaders; it's about everyone learning together. Depending on your goals and how complex the experience is, journey mapping can take anywhere from 45 minutes to several hours. Simpler sessions might focus on a single journey with one group of employees. More advanced mapping exercises might compare experiences across different employee groups or personas. The important thing is to make the map work for you, it's a tool to explore, not a rigid framework.

IC moments that matter

Moments that matter aren't a design tool as such but a way of identifying critical points in a journey. They are highly emotionally charged moments with a disproportionate impact on experience and engagement, either positive or negative. Gallup define moments that matter in the following way: 'Moments that matter are key interactions and events that significantly influence an employee's experience and perception of the organisation' (Gallup, 2021).

Gallup talks about moments that matter as emotional high points in the employee journey and emphasizes their role in building trust and long-term engagement. Their work connects these moments to outcomes like productivity, retention and brand loyalty. Chui et al (2021) talk about moments that matter as inflection points in the employee experience: 'Moments that matter are emotionally charged moments that define the relationship between the employee and the organisation.'

They argue that these moments should be mapped and then intentionally designed. They recommend identifying moments that matter using employee listening, journey maps and ethnographic research.

In their book *Employee Experience by Design*, Emma and Belinda (2024) describe the way moments that matter are uncovered during the journey mapping process and include:

- Specific moments – such as a first day at work, or meeting a team for the first time.

- Ongoing moments – such as regular team briefs with a manager.

- Created moments – such as a leadership event.

- Broken moments – everyday or routine moments (such as looking for information on the intranet, or sharing feedback) that escalate into something more significant if the experience is not frictionless.

What we think matters as IC pros isn't always what actually matters to employees. For example, you might put significant time and resource into crafting a polished CEO video message to launch a new values campaign. But when you map the employee experience, you might discover that what really stuck with people was a conversation with their colleagues as part of a team-briefing session. Or you may be proud of a well-branded intranet news story about a new well-being initiative, only to learn through journey mapping that the real moment that mattered was when someone tried to access mental health support and couldn't find the information they needed, leading to confusion, stress or silence. In another example, a comms team might focus on orchestrating a flawless change announcement video and email from the CEO. Only to find that employees were far more impacted by the silence in the days that followed, a broken moment where they expected honest follow-up and a space to ask questions, and didn't get it.

These kinds of insights are often invisible until you walk the experience of those impacted and listen deeply to what they *felt*, not just what they *received*. By identifying these moments, we can shift our focus from producing communication outputs to designing communication experiences that respond to what really matters.

How to prioritize moments that matter

Prioritizing moments that matter are a useful way to break the IC design task into something more manageable. There are different ways to do this. You may choose to vote during the journey mapping stage or use a card sort exercise to rank which moments have the biggest impact on an experience. Alternatively, when a number of moments that matter are failing to deliver the experience, a simple two-by-two grid can help you to identify quick wins.

FIGURE 7.2 Prioritization grid

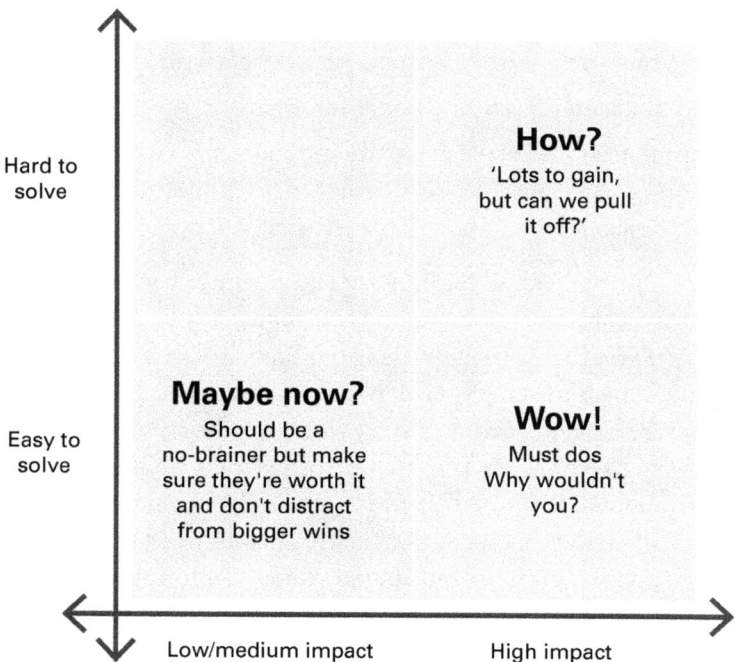

Hard to solve

How?
'Lots to gain, but can we pull it off?'

Maybe now?
Should be a no-brainer but make sure they're worth it and don't distract from bigger wins

Wow!
Must dos
Why wouldn't you?

Easy to solve

Low/medium impact   High impact

PRIORITIZATION GRID

Another way to prioritize moments that matter is to select some criteria and give each a mark out of 10. For example:

- People have a strong emotional response to this moment.
- This moment impacts a large number of people.
- This moment occurs frequently.
- This moment is strongly aligned with our strategic people goals.
- This moment is strongly aligned with our culture and brand values.

Identifying and prioritizing moments that matter within IC is about being intentional. It's a way to design communications that don't just inform but influence how people feel, connect and engage. When we identify moments that matter, we get real clarity on which part of IC makes the biggest difference to people, and we avoid making assumptions about what this might be. When we focus on the moments with the greatest emotional impact, we begin shaping experiences that feel personal, purposeful and human.

Service design blueprint for IC

As you read through this chapter, you might be thinking: 'This is a lot.' And that's totally understandable. We're introducing a range of tools and techniques you may not have come across or used before. But it's important to remember a core principle we outlined earlier in the book, when we introduced the concept of tailoring: *As much as necessary, as little as possible.*

IC experience design isn't about following every step perfectly or even using every single tool. It's about choosing what works for you, your context, your maturity and your goals. There's no gold star for completing the full toolkit; the aim is to create better, more human experiences, not more complexity. The service design blueprint is a great example of this in action. It's a powerful tool that gives you a detailed, systemic view of the IC experience, especially useful when you're looking to improve or redesign a service at scale. But if you're just starting out, you don't need to use this more advanced tool. A simple journey map, combined with moments that matter, is often more than enough to uncover actionable insights and start making meaningful change.

Think of the service design blueprint as a 'build', a tool you can layer in as your practice evolves or when the complexity of the IC problem calls for it.

If your IC experience design journey is a staircase, journey mapping is a solid first step; service blueprints come in when you're ready to build out and look under the surface. So if this feels like a lot, be pragmatic and use the tools that fit, and leave out what doesn't (for now). That's designing with intention and that's what great internal communication design is all about.

A service design blueprint helps us to better understand how a service is provided, which is useful when scoping the IC experience. The service design blueprint was originally developed by Lynn Shostack, a banking executive, who introduced the concept in a 1984 *Harvard Business Review* article. Her goal was to find a way to visualize intangible services in the same way product designers mapped physical product workflows. Shostack described it as a way to map the service delivery process in enough detail to implement it effectively and consistently. In her seminal 1984 *Harvard Business Review* paper, Shostack described the service design blueprint as 'a picture or map that accurately portrays the service system so that the different people involved in providing it can understand and deal with it objectively, regardless of their roles or individual points of view'.

In the following years, the tool has been developed further by leading design organizations like the Nielsen Norman Group, IDEO and the British Design Council, and is now considered a staple of human-centred service design. The Nielsen Norman Group (2017) argue that service blueprints make the invisible visible and help teams see the interconnectedness of user actions, employee workflows and system dependencies.

The blueprint helps us understand not just *what* is happening in a service, but *how* and *why*, by laying bare the systems, processes, people and touchpoints involved, whether visible to the end user or happening behind the scenes. 'When you map the backstage of a service – the support systems, policies, tools and processes – you open up space for better, more human-centred decisions at every level of the organisation' (IDEO via IDEO U, nd).

Working through the steps required to complete the service design blueprint enables better understanding of the problem we are trying to solve and helps define the IC experience we want to create. It helps us to surface what is happening behind the scenes, mapping the systems, including people, processes and enablers that impact a service. Going through the service design blueprint process enables you to map:

- What is happening for the people we are designing for – often called the 'customer actions'.
- The visible interactions, sometimes referred to as 'front-stage interactions', which are those direct interactions between the service and our people.

- The more invisible interactions, sometimes referred to as the backstage interactions, which are the internal processes and actions that happen behind the scenes.
- Physical evidence, which are those tangible elements that our people interact with as part of the service experience.

Using this tool helps us to understand who is responsible for what, as well as the systems and tools that support (or sabotage) the IC experience. The blueprint provides a holistic, more in-depth view of an IC experience. We've illustrated a worked example to bring this tool to life. Once you see it in action, it is a lot simpler and more helpful than it sounds!

Service design blueprint in action: intranet experience

This service design blueprint brings to life the 'find the information I need to do my job' experience, as part of an intranet refresh. It illustrates each stage from the employee's point of view and shows what needs to happen behind the scenes to support that experience.

TABLE 7.1 Service design blueprint in action: intranet experience

Customer action (stage)	Frontstage interactions	Backstage interactions	Third-party services	Physical evidence
I need to find some information	Thinks 'Where do I find this?' and opens intranet	Content strategy aligned with FAQs and tasks	Search index updated	Intranet homepage
I'm looking for this info	Uses search bar or browses menus	Tagged and structured content, maintained metadata	Search engine, content management system (CMS)	Search results page
I have found what I'm looking for	Clicks into a relevant page	Page is up to date, written in plain English	Content review workflows	Intranet content page
I'm doing something with this info and taking action	Follows steps outlined in the content	Process owner ensures info reflects actual process	HRIS, travel booking systems, etc.	Linked forms, tools
I'm returning to this info and also sharing it with a colleague	Returns to content or shares with a colleague	Content stays live and accurate	Analytics tools, email systems	Shared page links, intranet bookmarks

HOW TO USE A SERVICE DESIGN BLUEPRINT

To use a blueprint, start by getting clear on what you're exploring. Are you looking at onboarding communications? Crisis response? Recognition and reward? A comms conference? Choosing a focused area of the IC experience gives your blueprint purpose and clarity.

Next, draw on insights you've already gathered; this might include employee feedback, journey mapping outputs, or observations from working inside the system. These form the foundation of the employee's perspective in the blueprint, often described as *customer actions*. From there, the blueprint builds outwards. You'll layer on the visible interactions (or *front-stage* elements), for example, emails, messages from managers or intranet updates. You'll follow this with the invisible, but essential, back-stage work: the approvals, processes, scheduling, coordination and systems that make these touchpoints possible. You can also include physical evidence, that is the tangible elements employees interact with, like posters, templates or even meeting formats.

What makes a blueprint powerful is that it helps you see not just what's happening but how it's happening, and who's making it happen. This means you can spot gaps, duplications, or blockers in the system and identify any pain points or opportunities.

Above all, keep the employee perspective at the heart of your blueprint. Ask yourself: how does this step or system support or sabotage their experience? And remember the blueprint isn't a static document. It should evolve over time, just like the service it represents. Think of it less as a final product and more as a shared working view that helps your team align, improve and design internal communications that work for your people.

REAL-WORLD EXAMPLE

A people-first approach in action at the University of Leeds with Silicon Reef

BY ALEX GRAVES, CHIEF VISIONARY OFFICER, FOUNDER OF SILICON REEF

The following case study from Silicon Reef, showcasing the work they did with the University of Leeds, brings the people-first approach to life. It shows what it looks like when scoping, listening and co-design tools are used with intention and emotional intelligence, not just to 'fix' a comms channel but to rethink the employee experience from the ground up.

You'll see how Silicon Reef spent time to uncover deep pain points and shape a future-state vision rooted in what people really need. This case also highlights the broader value of People-First IC: it doesn't just create better tools, it fosters trust, connection and culture change. We'll unpack some of these themes in more depth in later chapters, but this is a great example of how you can move from insight to impact and from communication outputs to designed experiences.

Alex Graves is Chief Visionary Officer, founder and seasoned consultant at Microsoft Modern Work Partner, Silicon Reef. Silicon Reef is a leading digital workplace consultancy that specializes in creating intuitive, human-centred solutions using a people-first approach. Alex has over a decade of experience in transforming workplace communication technology through a human-centred design approach. Here he shares the work Silicon Reef conducted with the University of Leeds.

Designing a digital workplace: a people-first case

In a world where artificial intelligence is reshaping the workplace and employee expectations are evolving rapidly, internal communication must undergo a fundamental transformation. It's no longer enough to manage channels, craft messages, or polish visuals. The future of IC lies in designing experiences that are deeply human – experiences that foster trust, belonging and emotional connection.

At Silicon Reef, we've embraced this shift through a people-first approach that places empathy, co-creation and design thinking at the heart of everything we do. Our work with the University of Leeds offers a compelling case study of how this philosophy can be brought to life in a large, complex organization.

The challenge: fragmentation and friction in the employee experience

The University of Leeds, like many higher education institutions, faced a growing disconnect between its internal communication efforts and the lived experiences of its staff. With over 9,000 employees across academic and administrative departments, the internal digital landscape had become fragmented and difficult to navigate. The existing intranet, 'For Staff', was outdated, public-facing and lacked clarity of purpose. Employees described it as 'not the first place I would go to find information' and 'out of date or not relevant to me'.

A 2023 staff survey revealed that only 24 per cent of employees agreed they could easily find the resources they needed to do their jobs, despite 94 per cent saying this was extremely important. The absence of a single source of truth, coupled with inconsistent governance and reactive communication practices created a disjointed experience that hindered engagement and productivity.

The approach: people-first meets design thinking

Our engagement began with a simple but powerful question: What do people at the University of Leeds truly need to feel connected, informed and empowered in their work?

To answer this, we applied a Design Thinking methodology grounded in the people-first model. This meant going beyond assumptions and involving employees directly in the design process. Between April and June 2023, we conducted a comprehensive discovery phase that included:

- a university-wide staff survey with 145 respondents
- eight virtual focus groups with 53 participants
- a technical assessment of existing platforms
- a desk-based review of analytics, strategy documents and engagement data
- an envisioning workshop with key stakeholders to define a shared vision and measurable objectives.

This research uncovered six critical focus areas: Purpose, Communication and Content, Findability and Navigation, Governance, Connection and Culture, and User Experience and Accessibility. These themes became the foundation for a new, human-centred digital workplace strategy.

The solution: a human-centred digital workplace

The outcome of this process was not a single product but a reimagined digital workplace experience. We co-created a platform that brought together communication, collaboration, and culture in one intuitive space. Key features included:

- Personalized dashboards that surfaced relevant news, tools and updates based on role and department.
- Integrated feedback loops that allowed employees to shape future content.
- Microsoft search optimization and navigation that made it easier to find what mattered – without the noise.
- Storytelling spaces where teams could celebrate wins, share learnings and connect across silos.

But more importantly, the platform was designed with emotional resonance in mind. Every interaction was crafted to feel intuitive, respectful and empowering. The tone was conversational, not corporate. The visuals were warm, not sterile. The experience was human, not transactional.

The impact: engagement, empowerment and evolution

Within months of launch, the university saw a measurable increase in employee engagement scores related to communication and digital tools. Feedback from staff highlighted a renewed sense of connection and clarity. Teams reported spending less time searching for information and more time collaborating meaningfully.

But perhaps the most powerful impact was cultural. The project sparked a broader conversation about what it means to design with people, not just for them. It demonstrated that internal communication can be a catalyst for organizational empathy and agility.

Aligning with the people-first principles

This case study exemplifies the core principles outlined in this book:

1. MOVING BEYOND PROCESS FACTORS

Traditional IC often focuses on surface-level outputs – newsletters, announcements and intranet updates. While these are necessary, they are not sufficient. At Leeds, we moved beyond these hygiene factors to explore the emotional and experiential dimensions of communication. We asked: How does this make people feel? Does it reduce friction or add to it? Does it build trust or erode it?

2. PRIORITIZING HUMAN-CENTRED SKILLS

In a world where AI can generate content and automate workflows, the true value of IC professionals lies in their human skills: empathy, curiosity, ethical judgement and the ability to connect. Our team leaned into these strengths – listening deeply, challenging assumptions and co-creating with humility. This culminated in a community of owners who support each other through Viva Engage and quarterly events.

3. DESIGNING EXPERIENCES, NOT JUST COMMUNICATIONS

We treated every communication channel as part of a broader experience. From the moment an employee logged in, to how they navigated content on the intranet, to how they felt after reading a message – every touchpoint was intentionally designed based on our discovery insights. This shift from communication as output to communication as experience was transformative.

4. LAYING THE FOUNDATIONS FOR AI INTEGRATION

To prepare for the integration of AI, as part of our co-created roadmap, we focused on building a robust foundation rooted in thoughtful information architecture, document labelling and streamlined permissions. By creating a clean and well-organized digital environment, we ensured that the university will be able to leverage AI tools effectively while minimizing friction. This strategic groundwork not only set the stage for AI but also reinforced the principles of clarity and accessibility across the digital workplace.

5. REFLECTING ORGANIZATIONAL SHIFTS

The university is undergoing the largest transformational change programme in its history. The digital workplace solution supported this shift by breaking down silos, enabling dynamic collaboration and aligning communication channels with how/where people work. It wasn't just a tool – it was a reflection of a more adaptive, people-powered organization.

LESSONS FOR THE FUTURE OF IC

The project offers several key takeaways for IC professionals navigating the future:

- Start with empathy: Don't assume you know what people need. Ask. Listen. Co-create.
- Design for emotion: People remember how you made them feel, not just what you said.
- Think in systems: Communication doesn't happen in isolation. Design for the whole experience.
- Embrace AI thoughtfully: Lay strong foundations. Aim to use it to enhance, not replace, human connection.
- Be brave: Challenge the status quo. Reimagine what IC can be.

From communication to connection

As technology is evolving to be an extra team member with AI agents becoming more common in the workplace, the role of internal communication is not just to inform with content creation – it needs to inspire, to connect and to humanize the workplace. The people-first model and Design Thinking approach offer a powerful framework for this transformation.

At Silicon Reef, we believe that when you design with people at the centre, you don't just improve communication, you improve culture, performance and well-being, leading you to Work Happy. The University of Leeds case study is proof that this isn't just possible, it's essential.

Moving from the current experience to the future desired IC experience

The tools we have shared so far will help you to really understand the current IC experience, from the perspective of the people you are designing for. In the scoping stage, we also need to get clear on where we want to get to: the desired future IC experience. Remember, this is not about getting into solutions yet; this is about mapping the future desired state and outcomes. How we will get there is still to come. In this next section, we will share some tried and tested tools we have used with IC teams to help them envision the future with the people they are designing IC for.

Future visioning is a critical part of IC experience design. It shifts our mindset from fixing problems to creating possibilities. It draws from the principles of positive psychology, which emphasize flourishing, strengths and what enables people to thrive, rather than just focusing on what is broken and needs fixing. As psychologist Martin Seligman, founder of the positive psychology movement, puts it: 'We need to start focusing on what makes life worth living. It's not enough to cure depression. We need to ask what we want to move towards' (Seligman, 2011).

In a similar vein, experience design thinkers like IDEO often refer to optimistic provocation, which means imagining desirable futures to spark creativity and alignment. They suggest that: 'Designing experiences means projecting into the future. You're not fixing today, you're shaping tomorrow' (IDEO U, nd).

The tools we share enable us to ask what kind of IC experiences we want to create, and why, rather than just focusing on avoiding pain points.

The Best Experience tool – designing towards what good looks like

In the world of IC, we are great at fixing problems, asking what is not working and taking steps to address this. However, there is much to be gained from understanding what good looks like, and this is often overlooked. That's where the Best Experience tool comes in. It's adapted from a strengths-based tool called 'Appreciative Inquiry' originally developed by David Cooperrider in 2005. Cooperrider argues that: 'Human systems move in the direction of the questions they ask' (Cooperrider and Whitney, 2005).

This quote reminds us that if we only ask problem-based questions, we'll keep finding problems and IC design is really about moving towards a desired future. Therefore, if we ask about the 'best of what is', we create energy and insight for what could be. In summary, Appreciative Inquiry is about the search for the best in people, their organizations and the relevant world around them (Whitney and Trosten-Bloom, 2010). Let's just be super clear though, this is absolutely not about ignoring problems but about creating space for hope, creativity and strength-based action, which is what the Best Experience tool is designed to do.

Strictly speaking, the Best Experience tool isn't a future visioning or future state tool; it's not about imagining the ideal from scratch. You can think of it as a bridge between analysing the current state and entering a more 'art of the possible' mindset. By asking people to recall the best of what has already happened, we surface strengths that are grounded in reality. This approach helps shift thinking away from deficit and problems, and towards potential. It is a great tool to get people in the right space for more aspirational, future-focused conversations, which is why we've included it here, as a stepping stone between understanding the present reality and designing for what could be. It's a mindset shifter as much as a diagnostic tool, helping people connect emotionally with what matters to them and then build the confidence to design more of it.

The Best Experience tool was specifically developed by Emma and first published in her book *Employee Engagement* (2014). It's a simple yet powerful activity that invites people to reflect on a time when they experienced great communication and to share what made it work. These personal stories reveal what people truly value, offering IC pros insight into the emotional drivers and behaviours that matter most.

Using the Best Experience tool creates a space for teams to align on what 'great' looks like, bringing focus, energy and purpose to the IC design process. It's especially powerful when paired with other tools like journey mapping and moments that matter because it turns insight into intention. It is a really simple but clever way of unearthing what really matters to people. Sharing and recounting personal stories of great IC experiences enables teams to identify quickly and easily what is important to them and provides IC pros with powerful insights to inform solutions.

You can use this tool in one-to-ones, in workshops, as part of your journey mapping process or as a standalone activity. Just make it work for you.

How to use the Best Experience tool

Start by getting clear on the focus for your best experience conversation. Let's take the example of employee voice. Your latest survey findings show that people don't feel listened to or that they have a voice in your organization. Rather than directly asking why this is the case, using a 'best experience conversation' is a safe way to explore this and unearth powerful insights. Ask people to share a story about a time when they felt genuinely listened to (this might be in or outside of work). You can elaborate further and say a time when they not only felt really listened to, but they felt like they had a voice, when others wanted to hear what they had to say. Ask them to share this story, ask them what made it possible, how it was different from times when they didn't have a voice and how it made them feel.

When all the stories have been shared, ask the group to take a look at the words and stories you have captured and ask them:

- What are their observations of the words and stories captured?
- Are there common themes? And differences?
- What can you do to influence this as a team and create an environment where some of this comes to life?
- So what might need to change?

Why use this tool?

Sharing stories of great times at work enables people to reconnect with what is important to them. This activity also helps to increase empathy by understanding what really matters to others, rather than relying on assumptions. And it's a great way to tap into the personal nature of experience: everyone has a chance to talk about their own experience and what works for them at an individual level.

Before we explore what insights you'll uncover using this tool, let's take a step back and imagine the approach that IC pros might take in the 'expert-led' space to improve employee voice and demonstrate listening. Typically this might involve:

- launching a new listening platform or app
- setting up suggestion boxes or running more surveys
- creating a Teams or Slack channel for feedback
- asking managers to 'listen more' during 1:1s.

This approach is based on assumptions about what employee voice should look like and how to improve it. However, a best experience conversation might surface some more powerful insights such as:

- Those times when people shared their voice, they felt psychologically safe, knowing they wouldn't be judged.
- They felt the other person was genuinely interested in hearing what they had to say, and they made this clear by asking for their thoughts and ideas on a regular basis.
- There was real trust, connection and a relationship with the other person/people they were sharing their voice with.
- The other person reflected back what they had heard, which demonstrated they had listened and understood.

These insights demonstrate the issue might not lie with the ways in which employees can make their voice heard. Adding in further voice channels would not address the root cause. What's needed is to focus possible solutions on how to build more trust, a deeper connection and foster genuine relationships. And critically, how to build psychological safety and demonstrate that employees voices have been heard.

You can, of course, use this tool with any IC experience you want to explore, use AI to help you come up with some questions to ask if you need inspiration and you can also use it to help you analyse the outputs to take forward to the next phase of your IC design.

Future vision mood board

Evidence shows that when we are clear about what we want to achieve, we are much more likely to achieve it. Visioning work is not soft, fluffy or abstract. It's grounded in both neuroscience and positive psychology. When people imagine a compelling future, they're more likely to take intentional steps toward it. From a neuroscience perspective, visioning taps into the 'Reticular Activating System' (RAS), a network of neurons in the brainstem that acts as a filter for attention. When we clearly define a desired outcome or experience, the RAS helps us notice opportunities, ideas and connections that align with that vision – and tune out the noise. Dr Tara Swart (2019), neuroscientist and author, explains that the RAS acts as a 'gatekeeper' for your brain, prioritizing information based on your beliefs and expectations. This means the RAS filters the vast stream of incoming information, directing your attention to what aligns with your goals and priorities. She explains: 'If you repeatedly visualize a desired outcome, your brain, through the RAS, will start noticing opportunities that might otherwise be overlooked.'

In essence, when we visualize the future our brain begins to form new neural pathways that make that outcome more likely. This is known as cognitive priming, activating the same neural networks as if the experience was actually happening. In the context of IC, this means that getting your people involved in imagining the future experience, visually, emotionally and practically, helps create alignment, motivation and forward momentum. It also surfaces ideas and desires that might otherwise remain hidden or unspoken.

This future vision mood board works well as a follow-on from a Best Experience activity. Where Best Experience asks people to reflect on the best of what has been, the future vision mood board invites them to imagine what could be. Used together, they shift the conversation from fixing problems to designing the future, grounded in what matters most.

Involving your people in defining the ideal future IC experience is a powerful way to avoid making assumptions about what good looks like. In this activity, you'll ask the people to create an aspirational vision of the future IC desired experience. It's important to note that this isn't about making promises you can't keep, or changes you can't make, it's about understanding the ideal future experience.

If you are running this activity in person, we highly recommend using an 'art-based' approach and provide art materials, old magazines, etc. to help the group create a future vision mood board or visual of the future desired experience. There's a very good reason for this. When we ask people to write a list for the ideal future IC experience, we tend to find that they operate in analytical, task-focused mode, producing rational, expected answers that reflect what they already know. It's efficient but often limiting. In contrast, asking people to create a mood board, using images, colour, texture and metaphor, bypasses the filters of language and engages the imagination. Design-led organizations like IDEO regularly use collage, sketching and visual prompts in the early stages of problem-solving for exactly this reason. They argue, 'Visualising helps us externalize our thinking so we can reflect, share and improve on it – even if we don't consider ourselves artists' (IDEO, nd).

By giving people permission to work in a different medium, away from words, we open up the kind of creative thinking that drives innovation. The mood board becomes not just a tool for visioning but a catalyst for empathy, energy and new ideas.

Building on the example we used for the best experience conversation, you might ask the group to create a vision of the future where they feel safe to share their voice, where they feel like someone cares about what they have to say and where they feel that they have been understood. You can ask them what is happening, how they feel, what is different to bring their vision to life.

This activity can also be run online. Instead of using art materials, you can search the internet or use AI to find images that best capture what the future could look like. Ask the people you're working with to share their mood boards and talk through them. Ask questions such as, what are the common themes and how does the future vision make you feel? Once again, this activity is a great way to understand the desired future IC experience from the perspective of your people, and it avoids making assumptions about what you and your team believe the future vision should involve.

Future-focused journey maps

You can also use journey or experience mapping to visualize the ideal future experience. You can use a simple map or a more complex map to identify the key touchpoints and moments that matter.

In 'two years' time' or 'can we' statements

Using 'in two years' time' or 'can we' statements is a great way to get the group you are working with to summarize the ideal future experience and state. This tool, while deceptively simple, is very powerful. It taps into future-oriented thinking and collective visioning, all of which are grounded in research from organizational psychology and behavioural science. Inviting people to complete a prompt like 'In two years' time...' or 'Can we...' helps groups articulate a shared vision for the future IC experience in their own words. These prompts help translate abstract aspirations into more grounded, emotionally resonant statements that capture what people hope will be true if meaningful change happens.

Again, this activity is a great build on the previous activities we have shared. Where those tools surface emotional insights and ideals, this activity helps distil these ideas into clear, actionable intent.

We find this works well as a short 'solo and silent' activity to begin with, asking the group to come up with as many statements as possible. You can then ask the group to share and discuss their statements, clustering them into common themes. Below are some examples of 'in two years' time' and 'can we' statements from our employee voice example:

- 'In two years' time... I feel totally comfortable to speak my mind to any level of manager.'
- 'In two years' time... senior leaders are genuinely interested in what I have to say.'
- 'In two years' time... when I share my opinion I am not worried about getting a black mark against my name.'
- 'Can we... build more trust across different levels and teams?'
- 'Can we... find ways to show that something is happening with the feedback I have shared?'

These statements are a great way to complete the scoping phase, given they provide clarity on where the IC experience design is heading. The outputs from these statements are not set in stone. During the next step in the design loop, which focuses on the opportunity, they will be refined, and may even change completely, and that's OK. The people-first approach is dynamic and iterative. But these statements help lay a foundation for shared ambition and practical next steps.

From insights to impact

We have reached the end of the scoping stage of the People-First IC Design Loop. This is where your people-first journey really begins, encouraging the shift from expert-led assumptions to using employee insights to truly understand the problem you are trying to solve. The tools we have shared here, and in the previous chapter, are well used in other parts of organizations, such as marketing, product design, user and customer experience. And while they are gaining popularity within HR and related disciplines, they are not yet common practice in IC. We believe it is time to change this.

The tools will help you to understand the IC experience from the perspective of your people. They will also enable you to prioritize what will really make the difference and have an impact, which will help you move from reactive requests to a strategic approach. These tools don't just help you diagnose problems; they help you design better futures. And they're not about complexity for its own sake; they're about getting clear on what really matters to the people you are designing for.

Scoping will provide you with an evidence-based approach to underpin what happens next. The insights you gather here will help you to push back on poorly scoped requests or 'can you just' demands. And in turn, this will help to build your credibility as a strategic partner who adds serious value by really understanding what is going on in the business.

This approach is not about ripping up the book and starting again, it is an evolution of your practice using a people-first lens. Scoping isn't a one-off task; it's a discipline. Done well, it transforms the role of IC from reactive delivery to proactive experience design. If we take the time to scope well, we can lay the foundations for a more impactful and meaningful IC experience, which is not only right for our people but right for our organizations as well. In the next chapter, we'll move from scoping into opportunity, using the insights gathered to frame the right design challenges, and begin shaping meaningful solutions.

CHAPTER IN SUMMARY

- People-first scoping starts by understanding the internal communication (IC) experience from the employee's point of view, not using assumptions.

- Journey and experience maps are powerful tools to visualize the communication experience, from the perspective of the people you are designing for, helping surface gaps, pain points and emotional touchpoints.

- Moments that matter are emotionally significant events that disproportionately shape experience and perception and should be identified, prioritized and intentionally designed for.

- Service design blueprints provide a deeper, systemic view by mapping front-stage (visible) and backstage (invisible) elements of the IC experience – showing how systems, processes and people interact behind the scenes.

- Future visioning tools like the Best Experience activity, mood boards and 'in two years' time' statements shift focus from problems to possibilities – enabling co-creation of an aspirational vision for IC.

- The goal is not to use every tool, but to apply what fits – *as much as necessary, as little as possible.* That's designing with intention, not overwhelm.

- Done well, these tools help IC shift from reactive delivery to strategic influence – aligning efforts with what people actually need, not just what stakeholders assume.

References

Bridger, E (2014) *Employee Engagement: A practical introduction*, 1st ed, Kogan Page, London

Bridger, E and Gannaway, B (2024) *Employee Experience by Design: How to create an effective EX for competitive advantage*, 2nd ed, Kogan Page, London

British Design Council (2019) The Double Diamond: A universally accepted depiction of the design process, www.designcouncil.org.uk/our-work/skills-learning/tools-frameworks/framework-for-innovation-design-councils-evolved-double-diamond (archived at https://perma.cc/J8CH-YABP)

Chui, M, Chung, R, van Heteren, A and Löffler, M (2021) Redesigning the employee experience: How to win the war for talent, McKinsey & Company, www.mckinsey.com/business-functions/people-and-organizational-performance/our-insights/redesigning-the-employee-experience (archived at https://perma.cc/829C-8XUN)

Cooperrider, D L and Whitney, D (2005) *Appreciative Inquiry: A positive revolution in change*, Berrett-Koehler, San Francisco

Gallup (2021) Designing employee experiences that drive performance, www.gallup.com/workplace/351545/designing-employee-experiences-drive-performance.aspx (archived at https://perma.cc/2FPM-HARA)

IDEO (nd) Journey mapping, www.designkit.org/methods/journey-map.html (archived at https://perma.cc/74D5-XZ5E)

IDEO U (nd) Designing for service, www.ideou.com/products (archived at https://perma.cc/5KSE-9863)

Nielsen Norman Group (2017) Service blueprints: Definition, www.nngroup.com/articles/service-blueprints-definition/ (archived at https://perma.cc/H9MM-UWY7)

Seligman, M E P (2011) *Flourish: a visionary new understanding of happiness and well-being*, Free Press, New York

Shostack, L G (1984) Designing services that deliver, *Harvard Business Review*, 62 (1), 133–39

Swart, T (2019) *The Source: Open your mind, change your life*, Vermilion, London

Whitney, D and Trosten-Bloom, A (2010) *The Power of Appreciative Inquiry: A practical guide to positive change*, 2nd ed, Berrett-Koehler, San Francisco

08

The opportunity space: putting people first

If there's one part of this book that really gets to the heart of everything we're talking about, this is it. So far, we've argued that internal communication (IC) needs to evolve from an expert-led approach focused on delivery, to a people-first practice rooted in empathy. We've challenged the idea that great IC is just about crafting the perfect message or picking the right channel. And this chapter is where the real shift happens; asking you to adopt a mindset that moves from broadcast to belonging, from assumptions to understanding. And providing you with some simple, tried-and-tested tools to bring this to life.

Because here's the thing: most IC pros want to be people-first. We run engagement surveys, build employee personas, focus on employee voice and more. But all too often, these efforts can be surface-level or short-lived because we're time-poor, in constant delivery mode and under pressure to show impact fast. So we default back to what we know and get stuck in expert mode.

But People-First IC asks something more of us. It asks us to slow down, get curious and take the time to really understand the people we're designing for. To see what they see, feel what they feel and design communication that makes sense in their world, not just ours. I often refer back to a conversation I had years ago with Kerrie Hughes, a brilliant customer experience (CX) expert; she said something that really stuck with me:

> I envy people working in internal comms. Your customers are right there, they're your colleagues. In CX, it takes so much time, money and energy to get close to the customer. But you? You have access every day. You have no excuse not to deeply understand them and what matters to them most.

She was right. In IC, our people are our customers, and we really have no excuse not to get closer to them. And here's the good news: there is no one better placed than IC to do this work. No one else sits at the intersection of leadership, culture, strategy and the day-to-day employee experience. No one else has the potential to develop such a rich, nuanced understanding of what it's like to live and work inside the organization.

If we truly commit to this way of working, IC can become one of the most valuable roles in any business. We'll move from tactical support to strategic sense-makers. From being seen as message-pushers to experience designers. From optional to indispensable, which in the era of AI is good news! In this chapter, we'll introduce the practical tools to help you do just that – tools to help you stand in your people's shoes, from empathy maps and personas to ethnographic research and more. These aren't just techniques; they're ways of thinking that will move you from reactive content delivery and channel management to intentional, insight-driven experience design. This isn't about adding more to your plate; it's about transforming your whole approach because the future of IC starts with understanding and empathy, not action.

Introducing the opportunity space

In the scoping space, we shared tools to enable you to explore the IC experience you're working on, to get clear on where you are today and understand where you want to get to. Now we're going to move into the 'opportunity' space. Here is where you'll use empathy to broaden and deepen understanding of the IC experience you're working on. Specifically, the tools here will help you to better understand the experience from the perspective of the people you are designing for. Using insight from the scoping phase, you'll revisit and possibly re-define the IC experience you are working on through your people's eyes. This problem, or opportunity, definition provides the focus to generate ideas around and then develop IC solutions to prototype and test.

We're talking about empathy (again)

People-First IC has empathy at its heart and it runs throughout every part of our approach. But it's in the opportunity space where we really dial up empathy. In Chapter 3, we explored empathy in detail and highlighted how using empathy can help unlock the real problem we need to get to grips with. The tools we'll share in this chapter help us to get up close with the people we are designing for rather than relying on data alone. The tools also help us to overcome our innate cognitive biases, our inbuilt assumptions about what we think is going on and ultimately ensure we come up with a better solution.

One of the push-backs we often hear from IC pros is the inhibitive amount of time and energy required to spend time with the people we are designing for. There is often a desire to jump straight to solutions given. As IC pros, we believe we know what the issue is and know what we need to do to solve it. We get it; in today's fast-paced organizations, there's a need to prove our value and quickly. Why spend precious time gathering insights and empathizing when we know what the solution is? In Chapters 6 and 7, we talked about the need to slow down before we speed up; the same principle holds true here. Using the tools we outline here not only helps us to understand the problem from the perspectives of others, but they also allow us to engage in collective sense-making, which adds value to the end result. This ensures we have more stakeholder alignment around the problem we are trying to solve or the opportunity we want to realize.

Introducing employee personas

To design and deliver compelling IC experiences, you must really understand your people, their needs, their wants and their motivations. And this involves much more than a regular employee survey and a handful of focus groups. You need to uncover detailed insights about your people to help you build a rich picture of who they really are and what is going to work for them. This is where employee personas come in.

Personas were first developed and popularized in the early 1990s by software designer and programmer Alan Cooper. He introduced personas as a practical design tool to help software developers and designers create more user-friendly products by keeping the actual needs, behaviours and goals of users in mind. 'Personas are not real people, but they represent them throughout the design process. They are hypothetical archetypes of actual users. Personas are defined by their goals' (Cooper, 1999).

Cooper observed that many applications were being built with little understanding of the people who would use them. Developers were designing for themselves, not for users. This led to overly complex and frustrating user experiences. To fix this, Cooper introduced the concept of personas: detailed, fictional archetypes based on real user data.

Personas are a 'thinking tool' to help you to take a people-first approach to IC. So, each and every time you're having conversations, running workshops or design sprints, you should be using them. We've been developing and using employee personas for over 20 years, and they are a powerful tool for any experience design work, especially IC.

Sometimes, when we talk to clients about developing and using employee personas, we are met with a very valid challenge: why are we putting people into boxes? At first glance, it's understandable that personas might seem like another way of stereotyping people and 'placing them in a box'. But be assured, this is absolutely not the case. In fact, the opposite is true. Personas give us insights that can help us to genuinely consider things from different perspectives; that's the whole point.

The insights outlined in a decent set of employee personas will challenge assumptions and bias. The clue is in the term 'decent'. Often, we begin developing personas by looking at demographics such as age, tenure, job role, location etc. This is a useful starting point when trying to ensure the data you gather to inform your personas is representative – but this type of data doesn't go far enough. And the problem with relying on demographic data is that you end up with a set of personas that won't give you what you need to step into the shoes of the people you are designing experiences for, which is the whole point of developing and using personas!

For example, taking this approach might give you Figure 8.1.

The challenge with a persona like this is that it doesn't make it easy for us to stand in Bob's shoes. And bias will begin to creep in; we talk about Bob as a 'he' who likes golf. Immediately, we will build a picture of what we think Bob is all about, based on our own assumptions and bias about a Gen X guy, who works in finance and plays golf.

So, we need to move on from this approach to build personas which capture needs, motivations, feelings and behaviours – we call these behavioural personas. And we need to remove, where possible, characteristics that can facilitate implicit bias, such as gender.

Behavioural personas provide far richer insight to help us empathize with the people we are designing IC experiences for. We have to get comfortable with the fact it's not perfect – but it's a huge step in the right direction. And while we are moving quickly towards hyper-personalization with the latest AI tools, we aren't quite there yet.

FIGURE 8.1 Example pen portrait

Pen portrait

'Bob'
Senior manager

Length of service

Prefers face-to-face

Likes playing golf

15
years

→ Bob is a senior manager who has been with the company for 15 years.

→ He works in finance and likes playing golf.

→ He is Gen X and happy to stay with the company until retirement.

→ He is reliable and does what is required to get the job done – no more, no less.

→ He prefers face-to-face communication and email, and rarely uses Viva engage.

→ He is interested in hearing about company updates and the numbers.

To develop a robust set of employee personas takes more than a quick workshop or brainstorm. You need to analyse a lot of data; some of which you might have, such as survey findings, but most of which you'll probably need to go out and collect, to avoid making assumptions about what is going on for your people.

We've found it's often the case that the demographic data is way less relevant than we might expect; for example, look at the example persona (Figures 8.2 and 8.3). This is a fictional example, but a persona that often comes up! We find that actually people like this are everywhere in organizations; it isn't an age thing, a gender thing or even a job role thing. But in this example, tenure is relevant; the 'I'll believe it when I see it' persona has been around a long time! You might not find this is the case in your organization; in fact, you might not have this persona at all! The whole point is don't make assumptions.

FIGURE 8.2 Example behavioural persona A

'I believe it when I see it!'

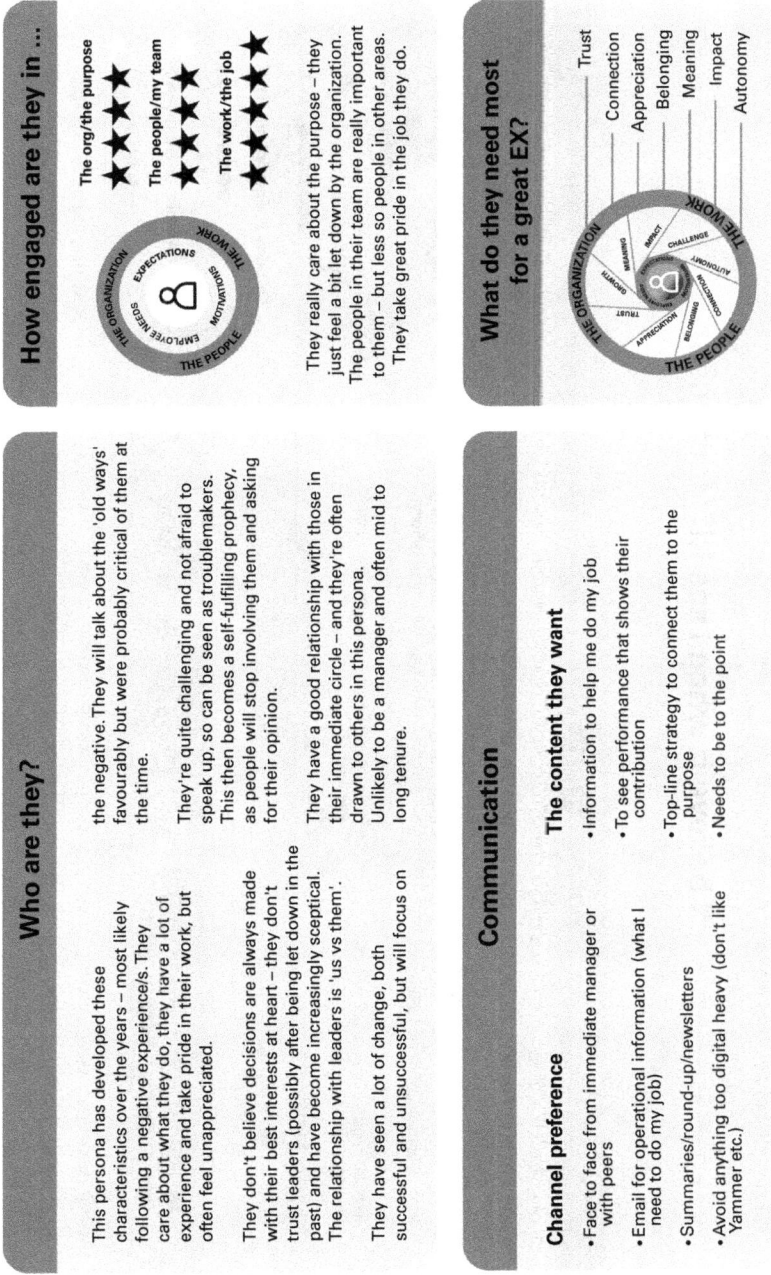

Who are they?

This persona has developed these characteristics over the years – most likely following a negative experience/s. They care about what they do, they have a lot of experience and take pride in their work, but often feel unappreciated.

They don't believe decisions are always made with their best interests at heart – they don't trust leaders (possibly after being let down in the past) and have become increasingly sceptical. The relationship with leaders is 'us vs them'.

They have seen a lot of change, both successful and unsuccessful, but will focus on

the negative. They will talk about the 'old ways' favourably but were probably critical of them at the time.

They're quite challenging and not afraid to speak up, so can be seen as troublemakers. This then becomes a self-fulfilling prophecy, as people will stop involving them and asking for their opinion.

They have a good relationship with those in their immediate circle – and they're often drawn to others in this persona. Unlikely to be a manager and often mid to long tenure.

How engaged are they in ...

The org/the purpose
★★★

The people/my team
★★★

The work/the job
★★★★

They really care about the purpose – they just feel a bit let down by the organization. The people in their team are really important to them – but less so people in other areas. They take great pride in the job they do.

Communication

Channel preference

- Face to face from immediate manager or with peers
- Email for operational information (what I need to do my job)
- Summaries/round-up/newsletters
- Avoid anything too digital heavy (don't like Yammer etc.)

The content they want

- Information to help me do my job
- To see performance that shows their contribution
- Top-line strategy to connect them to the purpose
- Needs to be to the point

What do they need most for a great EX?

Trust
Connection
Appreciation
Belonging
Meaning
Impact
Autonomy

FIGURE 8.3 Example behavioural persona A (continued)

'I believe it when I see it!' (continued)

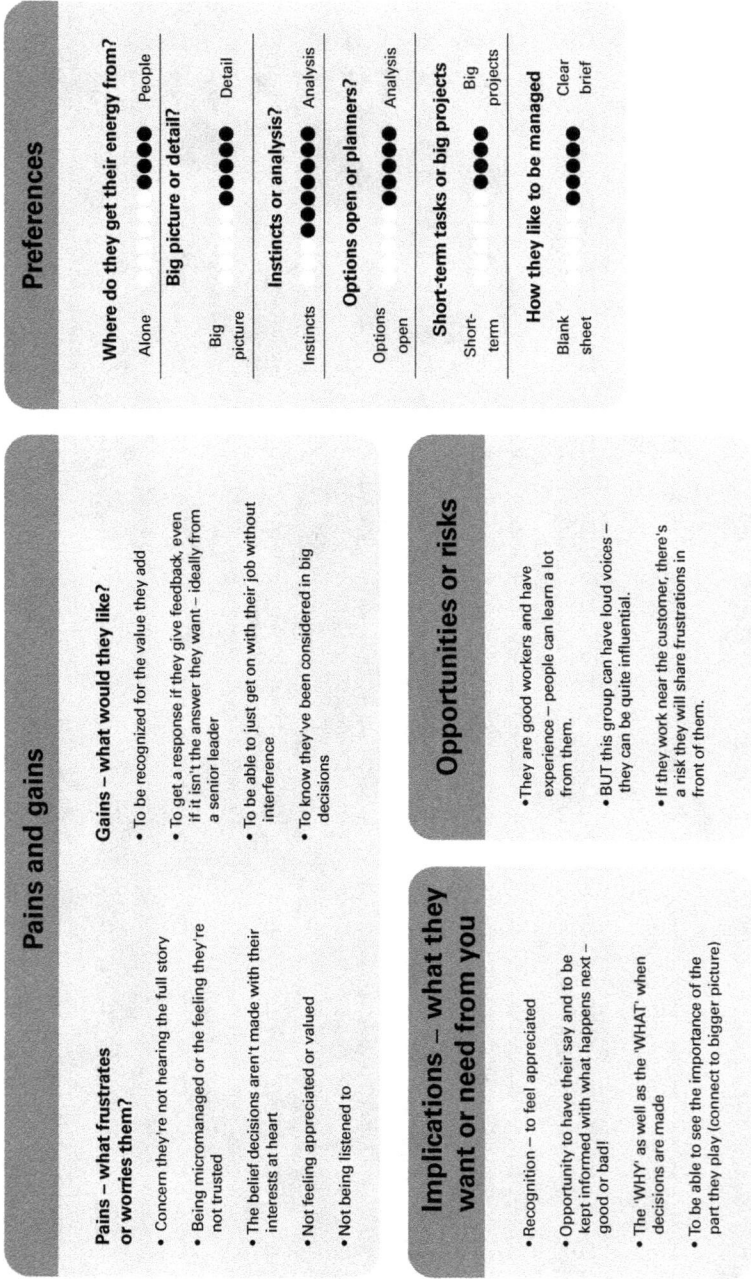

Preferences

Where do they get their energy from?

Alone ●●●● People

Big picture or detail?

Big ●●●●● Detail
picture

Instincts or analysis?

Instincts ●●●●●●● Analysis

Options open or planners?

Options ●●●●● Analysis
open

Short-term tasks or big projects

Short- ●●●● Big
term projects

How they like to be managed

Blank ●●●●● Clear
sheet brief

Pains and gains

**Pains – what frustrates
or worries them?**

- Concern they're not hearing the full story

- Being micromanaged or the feeling they're
not trusted

- The belief decisions aren't made with their
interests at heart

- Not feeling appreciated or valued

- Not being listened to

Gains – what would they like?

- To be recognized for the value they add

- To get a response if they give feedback, even
if it isn't the answer they want – ideally from
a senior leader

- To be able to just get on with their job without
interference

- To know they've been considered in big
decisions

Implications – what they
want or need from you

- Recognition – to feel appreciated

- Opportunity to have their say and to be
kept informed with what happens next –
good or bad!

- The 'WHY' as well as the 'WHAT' when
decisions are made

- To be able to see the importance of the
part they play (connect to bigger picture)

Opportunities or risks

- They are good workers and have
experience – people can learn a lot
from them.

- BUT this group can have loud voices –
they can be quite influential.

- If they work near the customer, there's
a risk they will share frustrations in
front of them.

Why bother with employee personas?

It's a fair question. Creating employee personas can take time and effort, so what makes them worth it? The answer is simple: personas make internal communication more human, more strategic and more effective. They bridge the gap between organizational intent and employee reality.

Here's what personas help us do:

- Identify with real people – personas humanize the data. They help us connect with real needs, frustrations and aspirations. This unlocks empathy and strengthens our motivation to make things better.
- Simplify complexity – personas distil complex insight into relatable stories. This makes it easier to make decisions, especially in cross-functional teams.
- Guide the ideation process – with personas in hand, it's easier to generate creative, relevant ideas. They help anchor brainstorming in lived employee experience.
- Surface the right questions – great personas help us to ask better questions. They reveal gaps, challenge assumptions and force us to think more deeply.
- Settle arguments – personas create a shared reference point across teams. When tensions arise about 'what people need', you can bring it back to the evidence.
- Drive behaviour change – personas help us design communication that feels personalized and emotionally resonant, which is essential.

In short, personas help us to stop designing IC 'for everyone' (which usually means no one) and start designing for someone real. And in doing so, they shift us away from generic, transactional communication and move towards meaningful, experience-led interaction.

Tips for creating great employee personas

You don't need a 12-month project to build brilliant personas, but you do need a thoughtful process. Here are some tips drawn from People Lab's 'Power of Personas' guide:

1. START WITH YOUR 'WHY'
- What problem are you trying to solve?
- How will these personas be used?

- Define your use cases up front, this keeps the personas practical and purposeful.

2. GO BEYOND DEMOGRAPHICS

- Ensure you gather data from a range of demographics, but don't include in the final version unless absolutely relevant.
- Focus on behaviours, attitudes, needs and motivations – this is what drives experience.
- Watch out for bias: remove unnecessary personal details (e.g. gender) that can feed stereotypes.

3. MIX YOUR DATA

- Use a blend of quantitative and qualitative insights.
- Surveys, interviews, focus groups, observation, internal comms metrics – they all play a role.

4. SPOT THE PATTERNS

- Look for themes across your data: shared frustrations, mindsets, goals or needs.
- Group similar types to form draft personas. This is more about common behaviours than common job titles.

5. KEEP THEM LEAN AND USABLE

- Aim for five to seven personas max. Any more becomes hard to manage.
- Make them visual, memorable and accessible – bring them to life with titles or icons but avoid clichés.
- Don't strive for perfection; aim for utility. Personas should be used, not just admired.

6. TEST AND ITERATE

- Use them in a real design workshop or planning session.
- Ask: Did this help us think differently? Did it shift our perspective? What needs refining?

7. PUT THEM TO WORK

- Use them in every project, planning session or leadership briefing.
- Share them widely – bring HR, L&D and leadership into the loop.
- Keep them visible, update them as context shifts and make them part of your everyday IC toolkit.

REAL-WORLD EXAMPLE
NATS – Embedding behaviour-based personas to power strategic IC

One organization that truly embraces the power of behavioural personas is NATS, the UK's leading provider of air traffic control services. Rather than using personas to fix a broken system, NATS worked with People Lab to proactively use them as part of a strategic reset, reimagining internal communication through the lens of employee behaviour, experience and motivation.

Their story illustrates what it looks like to apply people-first principles in practice: from deep discovery and journey mapping to live experimentation and capability building. This case study brings to life many of the tools and mindsets shared in this chapter and demonstrates how personas can move from static artefacts to living design tools that shift culture and unlock strategic impact.

The challenge

In early 2024, NATS' Internal Communications team found themselves at a pivotal moment. After a couple of years of navigating the after-effects of Covid-19 on the business and its employees, the team recognized the need for a strategic reset.

'We needed to reconnect our communications team with the organization's broader vision, reset our purpose and move from being reactive to truly strategic,' explains Lynsey Davidson, Head of Employee Communications at NATS.

As part of refreshing their five-year strategy, the team wanted to strengthen their foundations: reassessing channels, clarifying messaging and building closer links with HR and broader employee experience (EX) efforts.

Rather than fixing a problem, the team was proactively building towards a common objective: **To become a Top 25 employer in the UK by putting people at the heart of communication and experience design.**

To achieve this, they needed a deeper, evidence-based understanding of employees as individuals – not just broad functional or professional groups. In short, they wanted to move towards a people-first approach to IC.

That's where behaviour-based personas came in. 'We weren't fixing something broken – we were building on a strong foundation to stretch towards our objective of becoming a top 25 UK employer' (Helen Sierwald, Employee Communications Consultant at NATS).

What they did

1. *Discovery and planning*

They began with a discovery workshop to:

- understand NATS' operational, regulatory and cultural landscape
- review existing data
- design a phased approach sensitive to operational demands.

This early collaboration ensured the project aligned with the business context and strategic goals.

2. *Employee research*

They conducted:

- 16 employee workshops across different teams, locations and demographics
- 6 in-depth interviews to deepen understanding.

The focus wasn't just on feedback, it was on moments that mattered, best experiences, communication preferences and barriers to a great employee experience.

Far from a chore, employees found the sessions energizing: 'The process was genuinely positive. People appreciated the opportunity to reflect and share what really matters to them' (Helen Sierwald, NATS).

One team even requested to adapt the workshop format for their own internal use.

3. *Insights and opportunity mapping*

They consolidated insights into an **Employee Insight Pack** highlighting:

- cultural themes
- strengths and pain points
- employee preferences
- opportunities for better experiences across the life cycle.

This insight laid the foundation for persona development and for broader EX conversations across the organization.

4. Behaviour-based persona development

A set of behavioural personas was then created, grounded in real data, reflecting employees' motivations, needs and preferred ways of working.

Personas were designed to:

- challenge assumptions
- build empathy
- enable human-centred communication and design.

'Using personas challenged our assumptions. It forced us to move beyond instinct and really understand our colleagues as individuals' (Helen Sierwald, NATS).

5. Capability build and live application

They equipped the IC team with practical EX design tools, including empathy mapping, journey mapping, ideation and prototyping, using the personas as a foundation. The team then tackled a live challenge: reimagining IC channels through the eyes of the personas developed.

While stepping outside their comfort zones at times, the team found the experience energizing and transformational: 'It stretched us in a good way – it reminded us that to truly put colleagues at the centre, we have to use different perspectives, not just default to what's easy or familiar' (Lynsey Davidson, NATS).

The impact

Although it's early days, the impact is already clear:

- **Mindset shift:**
  New conversations about employees' real needs, moving beyond assumptions and instincts.
- **Strategic foundations:**
  Personas and EX design tools are now embedded into internal communications planning.
- **Stealth change:**
  Change is spreading organically through little victories and ambassador-style influence.
- **Cross-team interest:**
  Other departments, like HR, are already engaging with the approach.

The process was energizing, challenging in the best way and really rewarding. It's helping to future-proof our team – giving us skills that will keep us strategic, relevant and valuable in a world where the human touch matters more than ever (Lynsey Davidson and Helen Sierwald, NATS).

In a world of automation and AI, the ability to think empathetically and connect with people is how we'll continue to add value (Helen Sierwald, NATS).

What's next?

The persona work now sits at the foundation of NATS' refreshed five-year internal communications strategy. The focus for the year ahead is embedding this approach into major campaigns and communications, building EX maturity across the organization and continuing to strengthen the human touch that makes NATS a great place to work. 'This work feels like a reset – reconnecting us with why we work in communications: to make things better for people' (Helen Sierwald, NATS).

Putting personas to work

So you've spent time and effort developing a set of evidence-based employee personas. They detail employee needs and motivations; they're behavioural, not just focused on demographics. You're quite rightly proud of what you and your team have produced. You know they have the potential to help you design and deliver IC experiences which are going to make a real difference to your people. But what happens next?

It's often the case that personas are developed, but then forgotten, and left to gather dust. We hear this story time and again: 'We developed a set of employee personas, but they never really got used…' So how do you avoid the 'persona graveyard' and ensure you make use of all of this insight you've gathered? Let's for a minute remind ourselves of the purpose of employee personas. They are a 'thinking tool'. They are there to help to you, and anyone designing experiences (IC or otherwise) in your organization, understand things from different perspectives.

One of the best tools to help you put your personas to work is the 'empathy map'. Developed by Dave Gray and his team at XPLANE, this tool was designed to help develop a shared understanding of user experiences by mapping out what users say, think, feel and do. 'This particular tool helps teams develop deep, shared understanding and empathy for other people. People use it to help them improve customer experience, to

FIGURE 8.4 Empathy map

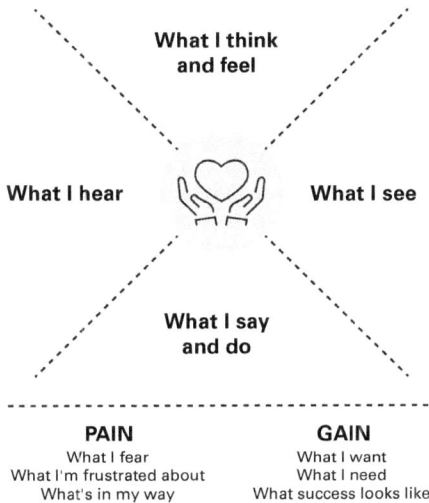

navigate organizational politics, to design better work environments and a host of other things' (Gray, 2017).

Empathy maps are a simple tool that can help you apply the insights from your employee personas to an IC experience, or an IC 'moment that matters'. Using an empathy map is quick and easy, and helps to overcome assumptions and biases you may have about what a good IC experience looks like. Creating empathy maps using your personas is a great way to interrogate and make sense of the data, as well as create and share insights. They help to externalize knowledge about employee needs and ensure a shared understanding. And they are a great tool to ensure you actually put your employee personas to work.

Let's look at an example

An IC team were redesigning their approach to 'employee voice'. Feedback from an IC audit had shown that employees didn't feel like they had a voice and that the current approach wasn't working. The audit itself didn't provide a great deal of insight as to why this might be the case; therefore, when looking to address this, they used their employee personas with an empathy map to understand the different perspectives of each persona in relation to employee voice. Let's look at some examples of what an empathy map might look like for two of their personas:

- 'I'll just keep my head down.'

- 'I'm new to management.'

On reviewing this employee persona, the team used an empathy map to fill in the gaps in relation to employee voice, here is what they came up with:

EMPATHY MAP EXAMPLE: I'LL JUST KEEP MY HEAD DOWN

THINK AND FEEL
- 'What's the point of speaking up?'

- 'If I say something, will it be used against me?'

- 'I care, but it's safer to stay quiet.'

- 'Nothing really changes anyway.'

HEAR
- 'Your feedback matters!'

- 'We're creating a listening culture.'

- 'Speak up – this is your chance.'

- 'Let's keep things constructive.'

SAY AND DO
- Says very little in meetings or forums.

- May contribute anonymously, if possible.

- Shares frustrations privately with trusted colleagues.

- Often avoids optional voice or survey activity.

SEE
- Confident employees dominate voice spaces.

- Feedback submitted but not acted on.

- Leadership rarely references past input or outcomes.

- No safe or informal spaces to raise concerns.

PAINS
- Fear of judgement or retaliation.

- Lack of psychological safety.

- Previous feedback ignored or dismissed.
- Feels invisible or undervalued.

GAINS
- A safe space to be heard without risk.
- Feeling valued and part of the bigger picture.
- Seeing real change from their input.
- Building trust in leadership and culture.

EMPATHY MAP EXAMPLE: I'M NEW TO MANAGEMENT

THINK AND FEEL
- 'I want to encourage input, but I'm not sure how.'
- 'What if I can't answer their questions?'
- 'I'm still trying to prove myself.'
- 'This is a big responsibility – I don't want to mess it up.'

HEAR
- 'You're the voice of leadership now.'
- 'Engage your team – be open to feedback.'
- 'Make sure you cascade the messages.'
- 'We expect managers to role model the values.'

SAY AND DO
- Shares updates but may not open space for discussion.
- Hesitates to invite tough conversations.
- Tries to protect team from overwhelm.
- Seeks help from peers or comms if unsure.

SEE
- Lack of clear guidance on employee voice.
- Senior leaders say 'we listen' but model top-down behaviour.
- Other managers disengaged or inconsistent.
- Generic tools that don't fit their team's needs.

FIGURE 8.5 Example behavioural persona B

'I'll just keep my head down'

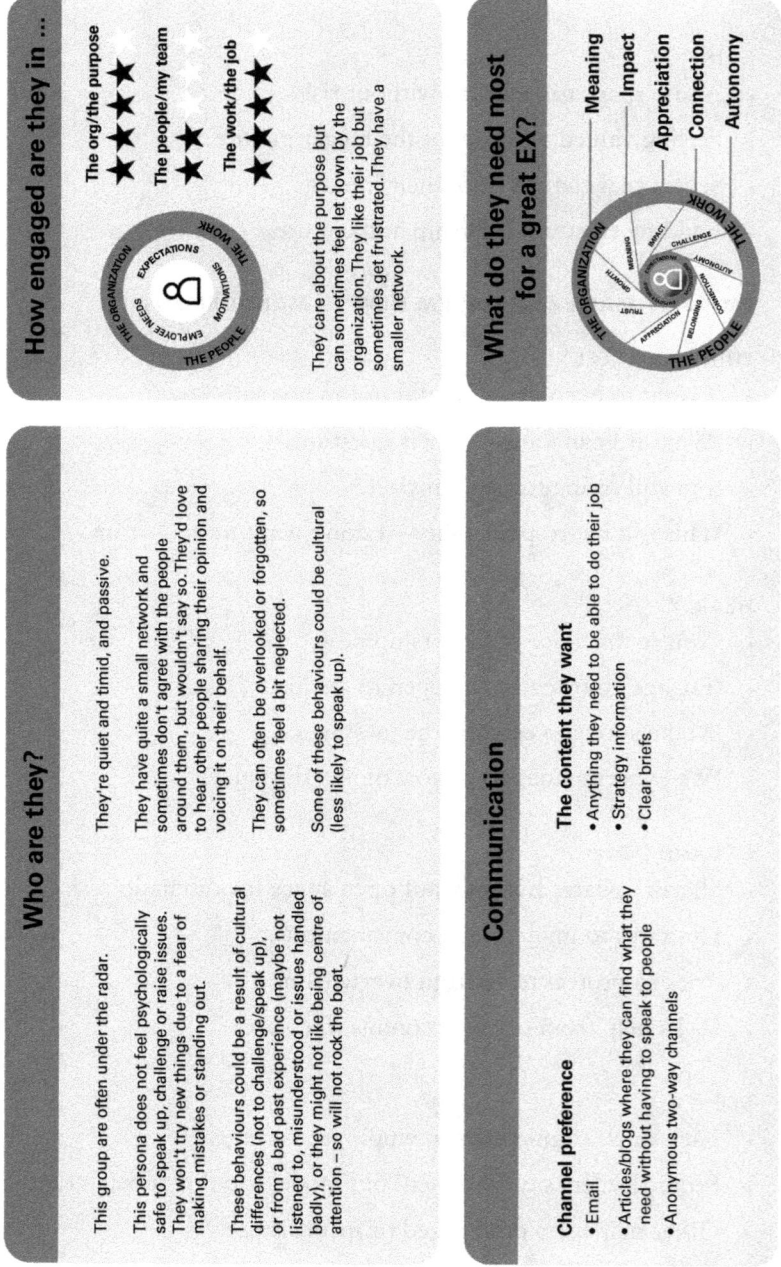

Who are they?

This group are often under the radar.

This persona does not feel psychologically safe to speak up, challenge or raise issues. They won't try new things due to a fear of making mistakes or standing out.

These behaviours could be a result of cultural differences (not to challenge/speak up), or from a bad past experience (maybe not listened to, misunderstood or issues handled badly, or they might not like being centre of attention – so will not rock the boat.

They're quiet and timid, and passive.

They have quite a small network and sometimes don't agree with the people around them, but wouldn't say so. They'd love to hear other people sharing their opinion and voicing it on their behalf.

They can often be overlooked or forgotten, so sometimes feel a bit neglected.

Some of these behaviours could be cultural (less likely to speak up).

How engaged are they in ...

The org/the purpose
★★★

The people/my team
★★★

★★

The work/the job
★★★

They care about the purpose but can sometimes feel let down by the organization. They like their job but sometimes get frustrated. They have a smaller network.

Communication

Channel preference
- Email
- Articles/blogs where they can find what they need without having to speak to people
- Anonymous two-way channels

The content they want
- Anything they need to be able to do their job
- Strategy information
- Clear briefs

What do they need most for a great EX?

- Meaning
- Impact
- Appreciation
- Connection
- Autonomy

FIGURE 8.6 Example behavioural persona B (continued)

'I'll just keep my head down' (continued)

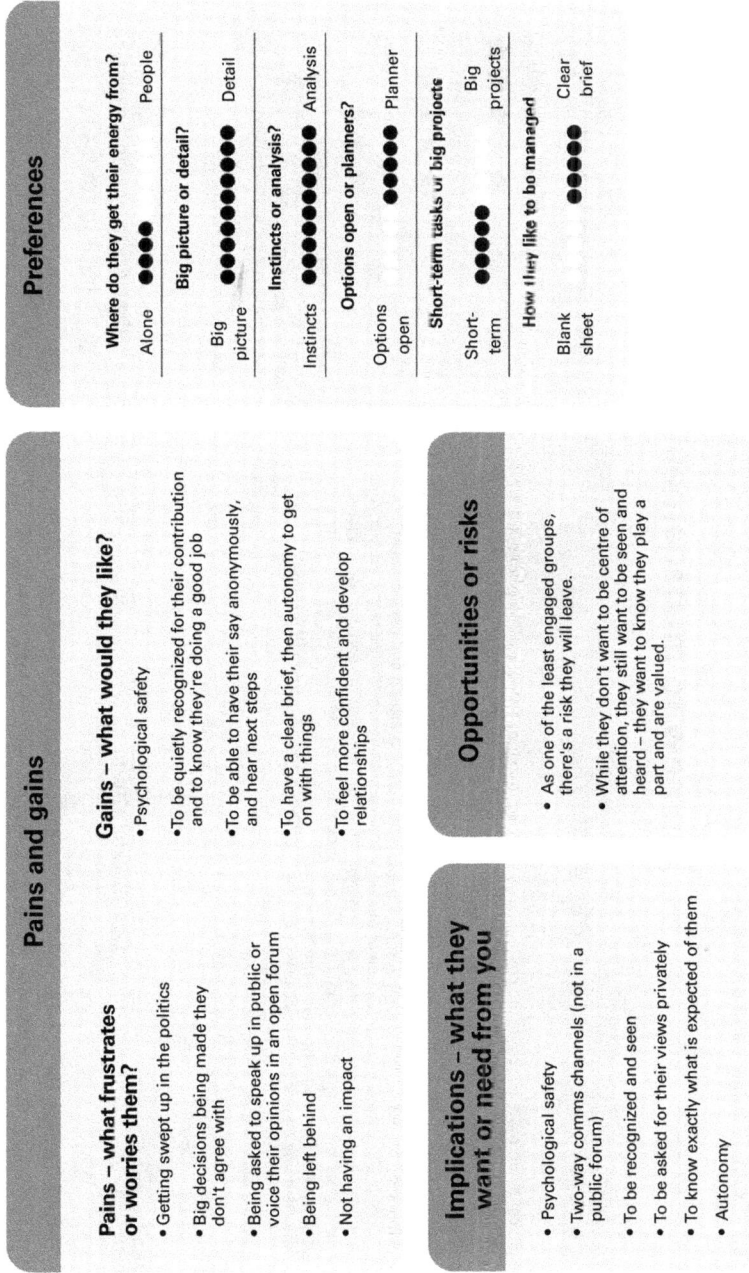

Preferences

Where do they get their energy from?

Alone ●●●● ○○○○○ People

Big picture or detail?

Big picture ●●●●●●●●● Detail

Instincts or analysis?

Instincts ●●●●●●●●●● Analysis

Options open or planners?

Options open ●●●●● Planner

Short-term tasks or big projects

Short-term ●●●●● Big projects

How they like to be managed

Blank sheet ●●●●● Clear brief

Pains and gains

Pains – what frustrates or worries them?

- Getting swept up in the politics
- Big decisions being made they don't agree with
- Being asked to speak up in public or voice their opinions in an open forum
- Being left behind
- Not having an impact

Gains – what would they like?

- Psychological safety
- To be quietly recognized for their contribution and to know they're doing a good job
- To be able to have their say anonymously, and hear next steps
- To have a clear brief, then autonomy to get on with things
- To feel more confident and develop relationships

Opportunities or risks

- As one of the least engaged groups, there's a risk they will leave.
- While they don't want to be centre of attention, they still want to be seen and heard – they want to know they play a part and are valued.

Implications – what they want or need from you

- Psychological safety
- Two-way comms channels (not in a public forum)
- To be recognized and seen
- To be asked for their views privately
- To know exactly what is expected of them
- Autonomy

FIGURE 8.7 Example behavioural persona C

'I'm new to management'

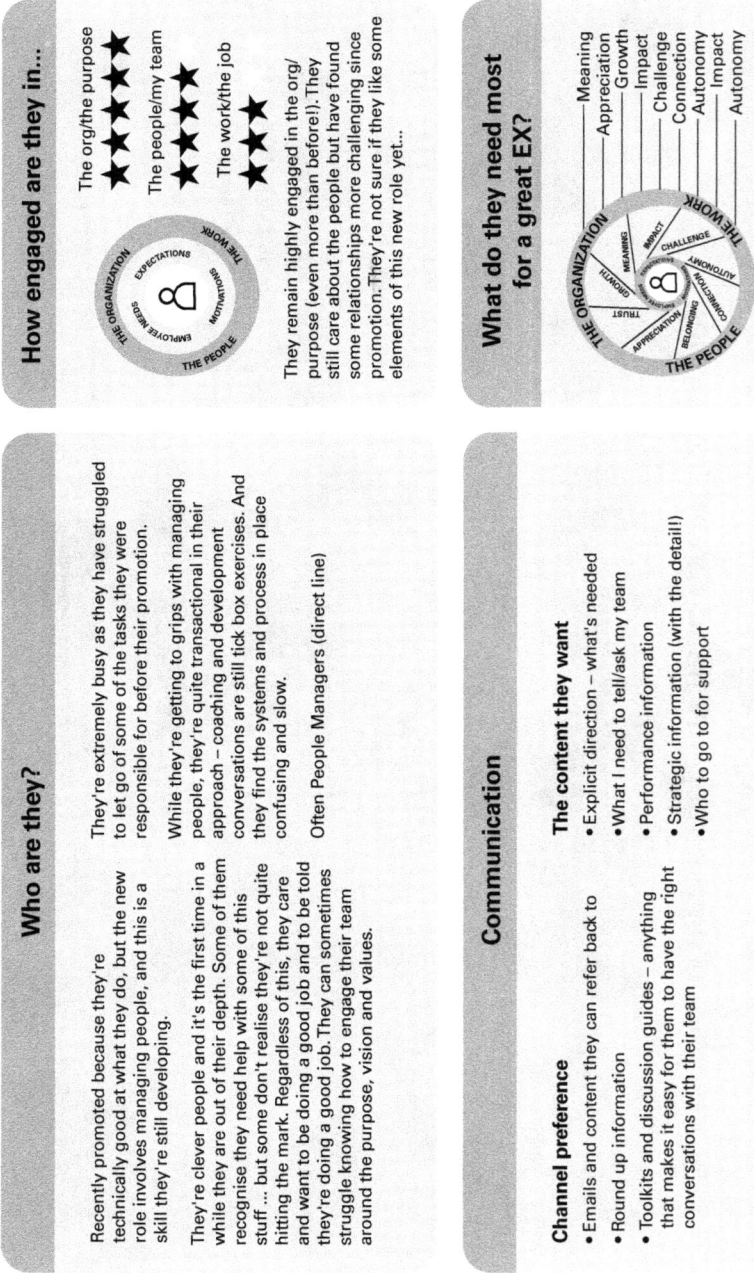

Who are they?

Recently promoted because they're technically good at what they do, but the new role involves managing people, and this is a skill they're still developing.

They're clever people and it's the first time in a while they are out of their depth. Some of them recognise they need help with some of this stuff ... but some don't realise they're not quite hitting the mark. Regardless of this, they care and want to be doing a good job and to be told they're doing a good job. They can sometimes struggle knowing how to engage their team around the purpose, vision and values.

They're extremely busy as they have struggled to let go of some of the tasks they were responsible for before their promotion.

While they're getting to grips with managing people, they're quite transactional in their approach – coaching and development conversations are still tick box exercises. And they find the systems and process in place confusing and slow.

Often People Managers (direct line)

How engaged are they in...

The org/the purpose
★★★★

The people/my team
★★★

The work/the job
★★★

They remain highly engaged in the org/purpose (even more than before!). They still care about the people but have found some relationships more challenging since promotion. They're not sure if they like some elements of this new role yet...

Communication

Channel preference
- Emails and content they can refer back to
- Round up information
- Toolkits and discussion guides – anything that makes it easy for them to have the right conversations with their team

The content they want
- Explicit direction – what's needed
- What I need to tell/ask my team
- Performance information
- Strategic information (with the detail!)
- Who to go to for support

What do they need most for a great EX?

THE ORGANIZATION
- Meaning
- Appreciation
- Growth

THE WORK
- Impact
- Challenge
- Connection

THE PEOPLE
- Autonomy
- Impact
- Autonomy

FIGURE 8.8 Example behavioural persona C (continued)

'I'm new to management' (continued)

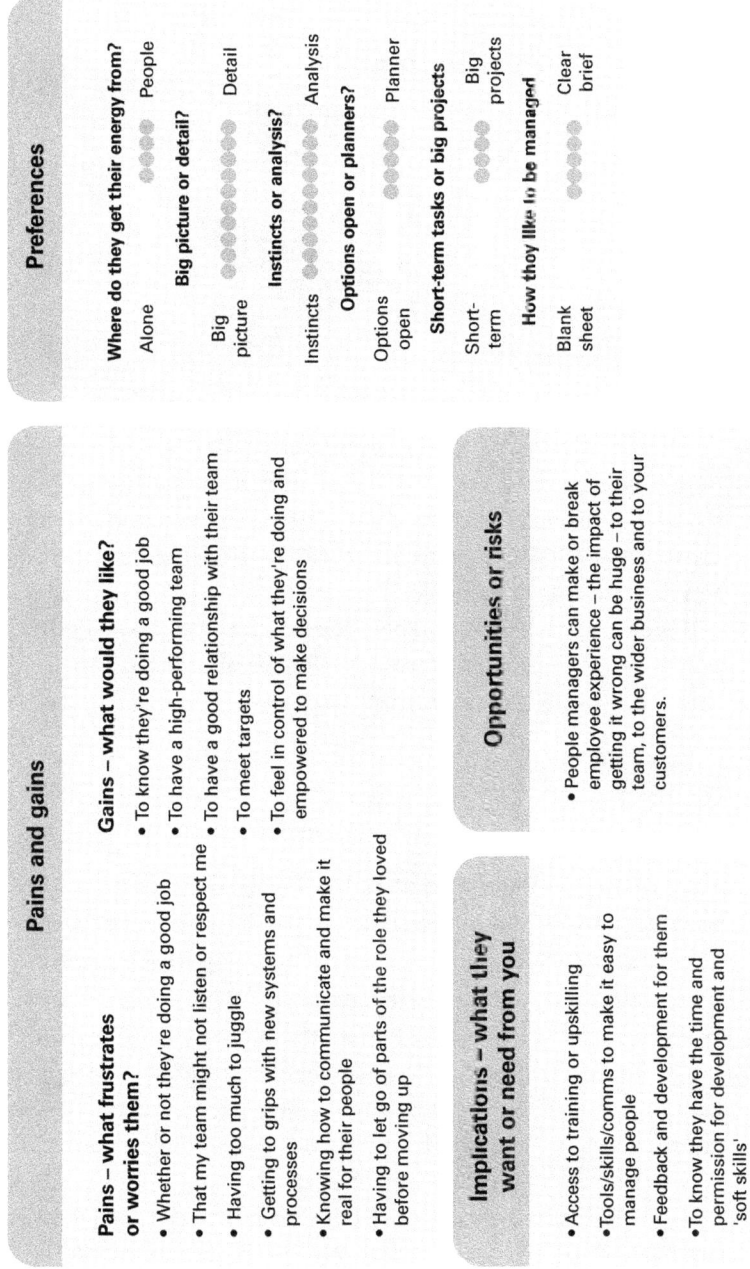

Pains and gains

Pains – what frustrates or worries them?

- Whether or not they're doing a good job
- That my team might not listen or respect me
- Having too much to juggle
- Getting to grips with new systems and processes
- Knowing how to communicate and make it real for their people
- Having to let go of parts of the role they loved before moving up

Gains – what would they like?

- To know they're doing a good job
- To have a high-performing team
- To have a good relationship with their team
- To meet targets
- To feel in control of what they're doing and empowered to make decisions

Opportunities or risks

- People managers can make or break employee experience – the impact of getting it wrong can be huge – to their team, to the wider business and to your customers.

Implications – what they want or need from you

- Access to training or upskilling
- Tools/skills/comms to make it easy to manage people
- Feedback and development for them
- To know they have the time and permission for development and 'soft skills'

Preferences

Where do they get their energy from?

Alone ●●●●○ People

Big picture or detail?

Big picture ●●●●●●●○ Detail

Instincts or analysis?

Instincts ●●●●●●○ Analysis

Options open or planners?

Options open ●●●●○ Planner

Short-term tasks or big projects

Short-term ●●●○ Big projects

How they like to be managed

Blank sheet ●●●●○ Clear brief

PAINS

- Uncertainty and lack of confidence.
- Fear of getting it wrong.
- Not enough time or support.
- Feeling stuck between leaders and team.

GAINS

- Simple tools that make it easier to listen well.
- Confidence from clear role expectations.
- Support from IC and HR.
- A more connected, engaged team.

The empathy map activity revealed a variety of different pains and gains for employee voice across the different personas; it was clear a 'one-size-fits-all' approach to employee voice was not working. Although psychological safety was needed for both, it was more of an issue for 'I'll just keep my head down'. And for 'I'm new to management', more support was needed to help to facilitate employee voice.

Using empathy maps enabled the team to design and deliver a much more personalized approach to employee voice and redesign their approach using detailed insights gained from this activity.

Deeper discovery tools

We've explored the power of employee personas and empathy maps to help us understand and design for the people at the centre of our communication efforts. Now, we're going deeper. We're going to share additional discovery tools that help you build richer, more empathic understanding of the people you're designing IC for. In traditional communication planning, discovery might involve scanning old engagement surveys, reviewing channel stats, or running one-off pulse polls. Useful, but often surface-level. People-first IC goes further. It borrows from human-centred design to deeply explore real IC experiences before we even start designing the solution.

Whatever the scope of project or size of team, your first step will be to discover more about the problem or opportunity. While a traditional approach may at best draw on survey data, in a people-first approach you'll explore the issue at a deeper level by combining discovery activities. This helps to overcome the say-do gap, expressed by famed US cultural anthropologist Margaret Mead (cited in Sunderland, P L and Denny, 2007) as: 'What people say, what people do, and what they say they do are entirely different things.'

We can use ethnographic research techniques to observe and deeply understand the human experience of different situations. Ethnographic research involves observing and/or interacting with people in their own environment to understand their experiences, perspectives and everyday practices, and involves different ways of achieving this:

- Hear it – interviewing, conversations, focus groups, workshops, stories etc.
- See it – observations.
- Live it – walk-a-mile immersion.

How you choose activities will depend on a number of factors:

- How much it will reveal about people's real needs, attitudes and beliefs.
- How many stakeholders you need to involve.
- How many end users, i.e. employees, you need to involve.
- How much time you have.
- Where your people are and how accessible they are.

Let's take a look at these discovery activities.

Interviews and conversations

Engaging directly with the people you are designing IC for is the most powerful way to reveal new insights and generate an emotional connection to the end user and their needs. If you need to take stakeholders on a journey, get them involved in interviewing. Tune in to the interviewee to know when to probe for more information, when to redirect the conversation and how to explore more deeply the meaning behind what they say. Workshops and focus groups work well too, the point is to hear about the IC experience direct from the people involved.

Observations

Observing is simply watching people and their behaviour in their own environment. For example, watch how someone uses your intranet, navigates your new office, uses collaboration tools or reacts to the latest company update at a town hall or team brief. Observation should, on the face of it, be straightforward. However, it's easy to fall into some traps if you're not careful. When practising observation, try the following:

- Be curious about what people are doing and why.

- Look at how they interact with each other, with objects and what they're frustrated by.

- Look for compensating behaviours or modifications they've made. This is where the person knows what job they want to get done, but there is no existing solution to help them do it – so they innovate or improvise (thought of as hacks). For example, a new starter creates a checklist on their phone to make sense of the overwhelming volume of information they receive on day one.

- Log exactly what you see, not what you expect to see (i.e. don't make assumptions).

- When making notes, make them specific and detailed and don't summarize.

- Take lots of photos, make sketches, create videos, etc. (without impacting what the people you are observing are doing), so you can replay with your team.

- Work in pairs (or more) and compare notes; seeing and hearing for yourself and agreeing on conclusions is a critical part of the process.

- Follow up with interviews to ask questions about what you've seen.

How to walk a mile in someone's shoes

'Walk-a-mile' takes you into another person's experience. You not only see it, or hear it, but you feel what it is like to live an experience as someone else. This could take a number of forms, for example using a blindfold to experience IC as someone with accessibility needs. Living an experience deepens your empathy for others and can provide first-hand knowledge of opportunities to improve it.

One word of caution – IC designers and end users should not be one and the same. Take the example of a parent returning from parental leave who needs to look into the IC support. If they are acting as IC designer and user, there's a real risk they will assume everyone's experience is the same as theirs.

Remember, discovery is iterative. One activity often sparks new questions or reveals new issues worth digging into. That's why rapid, layered research methods, especially those that bring users and stakeholders into the process, are so effective in IC design.

The tools we have shared here are just some that enable you to understand the behaviours, experiences and interactions of people in their natural settings. This is something that we have rarely seen IC teams make time for, but a practice that we highly recommend. By seeing things from the user's point of view, you can identify pain points and moments of delight that might not be obvious from the outside. This approach helps to create IC solutions that are not just practical but also emotionally engaging. These tools are useful because they bring real, first-hand insights into the design process, allowing IC to create more empathic and people-first experiences.

Sense-making in People-First IC

Now you're ready to revisit and review insights you've gathered so far and possibly redefine the IC experience you are working on through your people's eyes. Here is where you'll get really clear on the IC problem you are trying to solve or the opportunity you want to work on. This is where you'll review the insights gathered at every step of your journey; when you mapped journeys and identified moments that mattered in the scoping phase, when you completed your empathy maps from the perspective of different personas and more. But now is the time to pause, take stock, sense check your work to date and understand what the data and insights are telling you. Here is where you'll get really clear on the IC focus to generate ideas around and develop solutions to prototype and test in the final phase of the People-First IC journey. This critical step will give you the confidence that you are working on the right things and generating ideas and solutions that will make a positive difference to the IC experience.

The tools we'll share will help you to interpret and derive meaningful insights from the data gathered so far. They also provide a great opportunity to involve stakeholders at this critical point of the design journey:

- The employees who you are designing for can provide real-time feedback on the conclusions you are drawing.
- Key support teams can provide real-time input and hear first-hand where processes might be broken.
- Key stakeholders who sponsor the work hear first-hand about the work today and are involved in what comes next.

SENSE-MAKING IN ACTION: WHAT LEADERSHIP VISIBILITY REALLY MEANS

An internal communication team at a large financial services company was tasked with improving 'leadership visibility', a key driver of trust and engagement in the organization's engagement survey. The initial assumption was that visibility simply meant more content and channels: more videos, more blogs and more Q&A sessions. But the IC team decided to dig deeper before jumping to solutions.

They began their discovery by conducting informal interviews with employee resource groups (ERGs) and front-line teams. What they heard surprised them: people didn't want *more* content from leaders; they wanted more meaningful, human moments.

They followed this with a short diary study, asking employees to document moments they felt 'seen' or 'valued' by leadership during a typical week. The data revealed that visibility wasn't about volume, it was about relevance, authenticity and approachability.

To test their assumptions, the team then ran a series of virtual listening labs, inviting employees to co-create ideas for improving leader visibility. They also brought in behavioural science experts to help decode some of the more emotional responses.

The insight?

It's not about leaders being seen. It's about employees feeling seen.

That shift in perspective helped the team design a new approach: a leader-led 'spotlight' series focused on real employee stories, localized 'ask me anything' sessions co-hosted by employees and a toolkit that helped leaders communicate with emotional intelligence, not just broadcast updates.

This is People-First IC in action, layered, empathetic and insight-led.

Turning data into insight

Discovery activities produce data, but data alone isn't insight. Raw data tells you what's happening; insight tells you why it matters and what to do about it. In his book *How to Be Insightful*, Sam Knowles defines insight as: 'A profound and useful understanding – of a person, a thing, a situation, or an issue – that truly effects change' (Knowles, 2020).

Insight helps you move from 'What does this mean?' to 'What should we do as a result?' Let's consider the leadership visibility example we shared just now. Data tells us that:

- 'Only 38 per cent of employees feel they have enough access to senior leaders.'
- 'Employees say they want to 'see more of the leadership team.'
- 'Engagement survey comments mention lack of visibility from the top.'

These are useful findings; they describe what is happening. But on their own, they don't tell us why or how to act on it. Using discovery activities, we gain insights.

Employees don't just want to see leaders more often; they want to see them as real, relatable humans. Visibility isn't about volume. It's about authenticity, relevance and emotional connection. Or put even more succinctly, 'It's not about leaders being seen. It's about employees feeling seen.'

This insight reframes the problem and points to a new solution space. Instead of simply increasing leader comms output, IC can design for deeper connection, through story-led comms, shared platforms and co-created moments.

To get from data to insight, we need to make sense of what we've gathered. This process is known in design thinking as synthesis and involves:

- spotting patterns and connections
- prioritizing what matters most
- surfacing the unexpected
- creating a clear, evidence-based foundation for design.

Matt Cooper-Wright of IDEO puts it well:

'It may feel overwhelming at the beginning as you wonder if you'll ever be able to distil down the mass of evidence into something actionable and inspiring to design. The trick is to become comfortable with the ambiguity and take small steps. If your research was good, you'll find the answers you need.'

It's not always a comfortable process. Synthesis demands that we sit with ambiguity, lean into contradiction and look for meaning in the tension. But this discomfort is often where the richest insights live.

As AI becomes more integrated into our work, it can play a helpful, supporting role in this process, not to replace human judgement, but to enhance it.

Here's how AI can support IC teams in synthesis:

- Summarizing raw data from interviews, surveys or open-text responses quickly and efficiently.
- Highlighting recurring themes across large datasets that would take humans much longer to identify.
- Clustering responses visually or by emotional tone to spot patterns.
- Suggesting keywords or sentiment trends for further exploration.
- Spotting outliers or contradictions that might otherwise be missed.

This allows IC pros to spend less time wrangling data, and more time interpreting, empathizing and designing with intent. But, and this is important, AI can't feel. It doesn't know what makes a quote land in your gut. It can't tell when something rings true at a deeply human level. That's still your superpower.

To help you stay on track:

- Combine AI tools with human facilitation and emotional intelligence.
- Use AI to speed up the sorting, not to skip the sense-making.
- Prioritize insight that moves you emotionally, not just what appears statistically significant.

The tools we share here are designed to help you turn data into insight depending on the scale of the project, the volume of the data you've collected and when you want to involve stakeholders. You might want to use the tools in a single workshop or in a series of sessions. These activities can be run face-to-face or virtually using a collaborative whiteboard platform. You can cherry-pick or combine the activities to suit your needs – remember, make it work for you!

Gallery walk

This is a popular way to make sense of data. By bringing in stakeholders uninvolved in the discovery process, it removes the risk of the design team being unduly influenced by their own biases. This has the added benefit of bringing the opportunity to life for stakeholders and helping to ensure their commitment.

A gallery walk has two stages:

1 The first step is to select the most important data. Write it down on large posters, complete with pictures of employees you have interviewed and quotations. Hang the posters around a room.

2 Invite stakeholders to tour the gallery and write down on Post-It notes the data they see as essential for the solution. Then put stakeholders into small teams to share their observations, combine them and sort them by theme into clusters. The whole group then mines the clusters for insights. A healthy discussion should ensure that conclusions and assumptions can be challenged and insights emerge. Aim for a handful of insights only.

Sense-making workshop

A sense-making workshop is ideal for navigating large volumes of data in a short space of time. Rather than the team selecting data in advance, all the data is explored in the workshop. The aim is to reach a consensus around the most compelling insights and consistent problems and to create a story about why they are related. Because this is a collaborative process, it quickly aligns people around the key insights.

STEP 1 – GET IT OUT THERE AND BRING IT TO LIFE

Get the data into the open. Put it all in one place, ideally on a large whiteboard (or Miro board if online), where you can revisit and play with it to create a mental picture of everything that's been learnt. Never skip this step. If the content is hidden, you limit the team's ability to make sense of it. Moving pieces of the picture around – i.e. notes, photos, etc. is a powerful part of the sensemaking process.

STEP 2 – TALK ABOUT IT

Ask people involved in the discovery process to share their stories and talk about what they've learnt. Encourage everyone to explore and share what surprised them, what moved them and what they are curious about. This discussion will identify new connections between seemingly unrelated bits of data and help the team remember new things to share, things that previously might not have been obvious or seemed relevant.

STEP 3 – FIND PATTERNS

Now organize the data to find patterns and themes. At this stage, it is not the individual bits of data that are important but the relationship between them. Write data points on Post-It notes – observations, quotes and more and add to a new wall. It's not about recapturing everything but finding the standout points, surprises and revelations. Move the items into clusters of related themes. Don't worry about the exact nature of the groups; allow your collective instinct to lead.

Ask the group to look for themes and patterns. Rearrange the groups as you go along, removing some altogether as stronger patterns and connections emerge. If an idea doesn't fit, create a new group or simply park it and revisit it later. Continue until you have a manageable number of clusters you can agree on.

STEP 4 – FIND THE MEANING

Now you have clear groups of related themes, it's time to find the meaning. Take the groupings you identified and give them a name – don't overthink this. It's just about making themes easier to navigate. Then, for each theme, create an insight statement to transform a theme into a core insight of the research. The richest insights are supported by multiple research activities with data points, quotes, photos and observations all pointing to the same thing. Be wary of drawing insights from only one or two interviews as it may not be broadly applicable. Remember, a good insight statement should be simple and tell an emotional story to inform the design. Aim to identify between three and eight insights. Less might suggest you didn't speak with enough people. More suggests you've not been thorough in your sense-making and might be expressing the same insight multiple times.

'How might we' questions (HMW)

'How might we' (HMW) questions restate problems as invitations for exploration to drive the ideation process. Popularized by IDEO, the global design and innovation company, HMW questions are used within the design thinking framework, emphasizing their role in fostering collaborative and open-ended ideation.

Tim Brown, Chair of IDEO, explains in Warren Berger's book *A More Beautiful Question: The Power of Inquiry to Spark Breakthrough Ideas* (2014):

> 'The "how" part assumes there are solutions out there – it provides creative confidence. 'Might' says we can put ideas out there that might work or might

not – either way, it's OK. And the "we" part says we're going to do it together and build on each other's ideas.'

Framing the invitation in the form of 'how might we X in order to Y?' (or 'in what ways might we X in order to Y?') helps to create and sustain energy and optimism around the task. HMW questions are intentionally open-ended and generative, designed to spark ideas and unlock creativity without prescribing a single solution.

Here are some examples of IC HMW questions:

- How might we design comms that are heard and felt – not just read – in order to drive emotional connection and behavioural change?
- How might we make leadership updates more two-way in order to build trust and transparency across all levels of the organization?
- How might we reduce comms overload in order to ensure important comms actually land and stick?
- How might we empower line managers to communicate confidently in order to improve local engagement?
- How might we turn survey feedback into meaningful action in order to show employees they've truly been heard?
- How might we humanize digital communication in order to create more engaging, trust-building touchpoints?

Creating effective 'How might we' (HMW) questions is crucial for fostering a productive ideation session that can lead to innovative solutions.

They should feel:

- Optimistic: inviting exploration rather than focusing on what's broken.
- Actionable: not too abstract.
- Focused: specific enough to guide design, broad enough to allow multiple answers.

Let's revisit the empathy maps we completed for our two different personas when exploring how to improve employee voice. At the end of the empathy mapping activity, it is really useful to conclude with some HMW questions to guide the next step in our people-first journey, which is where we finally get to start developing possible solutions.

PERSONA: 'I'LL JUST KEEP MY HEAD DOWN'

Focus: Empower this persona to feel safe, seen and motivated to contribute their voice.

- How might we create safer spaces for quieter employees to share feedback in order to build trust and psychological safety across the organization?
- How might we invite contributions in more private, low-pressure formats in order to encourage honest input from those who rarely speak up in groups?
- How might we clearly show how employee voice leads to action in order to increase participation and close the trust gap?
- How might we design feedback experiences that remove fear of judgement in order to help more employees feel comfortable sharing openly?
- How might we use informal or anonymous channels to surface unheard perspectives in order to create a more inclusive communication culture?

PERSONA: 'I'M NEW TO MANAGEMENT'

Focus: Supporting new managers to facilitate and act on employee voice confidently.

- How might we provide simple tools in order to help new managers lead better team conversations?
- How might we normalize vulnerability and imperfection in leadership communication in order to reduce fear of 'getting it wrong' when giving employees a voice
- How might we equip managers to respond meaningfully to feedback even when they can't solve everything in order to build credibility and trust?
- How might we connect employee voice to leadership behaviours in order to reinforce its importance as part of the manager's role, not just a comms task?
- How might we spotlight great manager-led voice examples in order to inspire confidence and replicate success across other teams?

User stories

User stories can be used when working with insight to define the problem or opportunity statement, often as an alternative to using HMW questions.

First developed in the world of software engineering, they were popularized in Agile frameworks. Mike Cohn, an influential voice in Agile methodologies, further popularized the practice in his book *User Stories Applied: For Agile Software Development* (2004), establishing user stories as a cornerstone of Agile practices. User stories deliver the 'who', 'what' and 'why' of user requirements in a format that can be easily understood. They help chunk up a big opportunity into smaller, more manageable areas.

It works like this: As a [user description], I want [need/verb], so that [compelling insight].

Here are some examples below, again using the employee voice case study from the perspective of the two different personas we have been using:

PERSONA: 'I'LL JUST KEEP MY HEAD DOWN'
User story 1

- **As a** – less vocal employee
- **I want** – to share my feedback anonymously and safely
- **So that** – I can express how I really feel without fear of judgement or consequence

User story 2

- **As a** – front-line employee who doesn't usually speak up
- **I want** – to know that my input is valued and acted upon
- **So that** – I feel like my voice matters and contributes to real change

PERSONA: 'I'M NEW TO MANAGEMENT'
User story 1

- **As a** – newly promoted manager
- **I want** – practical tools and prompts to lead meaningful feedback conversations
- **So that** – I can build trust and encourage open dialogue with my team

User story 2

- **As a** – manager still building confidence
- **I want** – to know how to respond to tough feedback effectively
- **So that** – I don't feel stuck or exposed when I can't fix every issue raised

These stories can be a powerful bridge between insight and design, and used as a fuel for shaping comms strategies and solutions. User stories are a fantastic way to clearly articulate the needs and goals of different users in a structured format.

From insights to understanding

We began this chapter by asking internal communicators to rethink what it means to design truly meaningful communication experiences. What followed wasn't just a toolkit but an invitation to transform the way you work.

You've now seen that empathy isn't a fluffy 'nice-to-have' but a strategic advantage. From personas to empathy maps, from ethnographic research to user stories and 'How might we' questions, these tools help you shift from delivering messages to designing IC experiences. They help you move from assumption to understanding. From noise to nuance.

This is the real opportunity space: not just to tweak what's already there but to reimagine what IC can be – a discipline that's insight-led, human-centred and deeply embedded in the overall employee experience. A profession that doesn't just deliver messages but builds connection, earns trust and drives change.

Yes, this takes effort. It asks us to slow down, stay curious and make time for discovery. But the payoff is worth it. Because when we truly understand the people we're designing for, we create communication that doesn't just inform; it resonates. And in a world where AI is changing the game, the ability to create emotional, human connection is what will make internal communication not just relevant, but indispensable.

So as you move into the next phase of your People-First IC journey, ask yourself:

- What new opportunities have I uncovered?
- What assumptions have I challenged?
- And how will I now show up, not just as a communicator, but as an IC experience designer?

The tools are in your hands and the opportunity is in front of you. Now it's time to use both to design IC that connects, inspires and transforms.

CHAPTER IN SUMMARY

- People-First IC focuses on designing IC experiences rooted in empathy, shifting the mindset from broadcast to belonging.

- The opportunity space is where you deepen your understanding of the IC experience by seeing it through the eyes of employees, using insights to reframe problems and discover new possibilities.

- Employee personas are behavioural archetypes based on real data, not stereotypes, that help humanize insight, challenge assumptions and anchor IC experience design in real needs and motivations.

- Empathy maps translate persona insights into practical understanding, bringing nuance and emotion into IC planning.

- Deeper discovery tools, such as interviews, observations and 'walk-a-mile' immersions enable richer, ethnographic understanding of employee experience, revealing what people truly need, not just what they say.

- Sense-making activities help turn raw data into meaningful, emotional insight, clarifying where to focus IC design and involving key stakeholders in the process.

- 'How might we' questions and user stories bridge the gap between insight and action, helping to frame opportunity areas in open, optimistic ways that spark creative solutions.

- The opportunity space isn't about adding more to your IC workload; it's about transforming your approach to become intentional, insight-led and emotionally resonant.

- Done well, people-first discovery and sense-making shift IC from tactical content creation to strategic experience design, building relevance, trust and human connection in a way that AI alone cannot.

References

Berger, W (2014) *A More Beautiful Question: The power of inquiry to spark breakthrough Ideas*, Bloomsbury, New York

Cohn, M (2004) *User Stories Applied: For Agile software development*, Addison-Wesley, London

Cooper, A (1999) *The Inmates Are Running the Asylum: Why high-tech products drive us crazy and how to restore the sanity*, Sams Publishing, Indianapolis

Gray, D (2017) Updated empathy map canvas, Medium, medium.com/@davegray/updated-empathy-map-canvas-46df22df3c8a (archived at https://perma.cc/F5AL-HRZ7)

Knowles, S (2020) *How to Be Insightful: Unlocking the superpower that drives innovation*, Routledge, London

Sunderland, P L and Denny, R M (2007) *Doing Anthropology in Consumer Research*, Left Coast Press, Walnut Creek, CA

09

Designing IC solutions that work

We've made it to the solution space! This is the part of the People-First Internal Communication (IC) approach that will probably feel more comfortable and familiar. Here is where we get to use creativity and curiosity to come up with ideas and solutions, and use the expertise we've built as IC pros. This is our comfort zone, but while this space may feel familiar, it's not all business as usual.

The solution space is where we turn insight into impact. It's where we start to design real solutions based on what we've uncovered, not based on what we assume. And that's a crucial shift. Because while many IC pros excel at creativity, very few have the time, tools or confidence to truly test and prototype their solutions. We default to what we know. We go big, we go fast. But often, we scale without testing, launch without learning and deliver without truly designing with our people.

That's what this chapter is here to change. This is where curiosity and creativity come together, not just to produce something but to explore what might be. You'll learn how to generate ideas that respond to real needs, not just requests, and how to prototype and test quickly, cheaply and effectively, before you commit to full-scale delivery.

We'll explore simple but powerful ideation tools, share practical methods to bring your concepts to life and show you how to test early and often, so the solutions you scale are the ones that really work for your people. Yes, this is about getting creative. But more importantly, it's about being deliberately creative. The solution space is not the finish line; it's the space where evidence meets imagination, and IC begins to operate as a true experience design discipline.

Introducing ideation: from insight to imagination

Ideation is where we begin to unlock the creative power of the solution space in our people-first framework. This phase is all about generating, exploring and developing ideas that respond to the insights we've previously uncovered, not the assumptions we've long relied on. It's the beginning of a shift from 'what we know' to 'what could be'.

Ideation is more than just brainstorming. It's a structured, often collaborative process designed to challenge conventional thinking and uncover unexpected possibilities. As design thinking pioneer Tim Brown explains, 'Ideation is the mode of the design process in which you concentrate on idea generation... it's about pushing beyond the obvious to come up with fresh solutions' (2009).

For IC professionals, this means going beyond requests for 'more engaging comms' or 'better email subject lines'. It means asking, what are we really solving? Who are we solving it with? And how can we use our creativity not just to inform or align but to transform the IC experience?

This is a muscle IC pros already have but one we don't always flex. In fast-paced, delivery-focused environments, we often jump to solutions too soon. But great ideas rarely emerge fully formed. Ideation gives us permission to pause, play and explore the full range of possibilities before deciding what to build. As innovation expert Tom Kelley puts it: 'Fail often so you can succeed sooner' (Kelley and Littman, 2001).

It's a mindset of discovery, not perfection. Here, we'll explore how to use simple but powerful ideation techniques to generate ideas rooted in insight, not assumption. Because ultimately, ideation in internal communication isn't just about producing IC solutions, it's about shaping experiences. That's what makes this work not just creative, but meaningful.

REAL-WORLD EXAMPLE
People Activation in practice

So, what does it look like when insight meets imagination and results in real transformation? This example shows how one organization reimagined a tired, top-down activation by involving employees as co-creators. Their approach, rooted in emotional resonance, prototyping and human storytelling, unlocked not just better engagement but a whole new way of designing communication that reflects lived realities. This case is a vivid example of how ideation and iteration can be used to co-create IC experiences that really land.

Putting people first: how we co-create better employee experiences at
People Activation

People Activation is a live activations agency that moves people to action through
business and brand experiences. They help globally networked organizations bring
their strategies to life by transforming IC and employee experiences into moments
that drive real-world behaviour change. They are truly pioneers with n the world of IC,
using a people-first approach in the events and activations they design and deliver.
Here, they bring to life their human-centred approach and the difference it makes to
the people they work with. Over to Abi Humayun, one of the founders:

At People Activation, we believe the most impactful employee experiences are
not built *for* people; they are built *with* them.

Our human-centred approach ensures that every internal campaign and
activation we deliver is grounded in real insight, shaped through collaboration and
genuinely moves people to action. We do this not simply to be creative but because
research and experience consistently show that when people feel ownership and
agency in shaping an experience, its impact is exponentially greater.

Our ways of working reflect this philosophy at every level. Every member of the
People Activation team is trained in EITO – a human-centred innovation and
collaboration methodology that teaches us how to embed activation from the very
first steps of a project, not just in the final outcome. We use EITO tools and mindsets
to ensure that clients, leaders and employees are all actively involved in shaping the
experiences we create.

Additionally, our internal Human-Centred Design process provides a structured
approach to embedding co-creation into every stage of our work, from initial framing
to live delivery and legacy.

At the heart of this approach is a simple belief: employees are not passive
recipients of corporate communication – they are active shapers of organizational
culture. The more we involve them in the process, the more powerful and authentic
the outcomes become.

Human-Centred Design in action

Our Human-Centred Design process is deliberately iterative and collaborative, not
linear. We build in multiple points of interaction with clients and employees to
ensure the work remains grounded, inclusive and effective.

It begins with a Strategic Kick-Off, where we work with client stakeholders to
deeply understand both the brief and the needs and realities of the audience. Using
tools such as 'how might we?' (HMW) framing and empathy mapping, we

collaboratively define the opportunity and clarify the key behavioural and emotional shifts we want to achieve.

Next, in the Client Kick-Off Workshop, we engage a broader group of internal stakeholders and, wherever possible, employee representatives. Here, we facilitate structured conversations to gather insight and build alignment. We use EITO tools such as:

- Expert Interviews – capturing diverse internal and external perspectives that will inform the experience.

- Lightning Demos – surfacing relevant examples of great practice and inspiration, from both inside and outside the sector.

- Know-Feel-Do Mapping – clarifying what we want employees to know, feel and do as a result of the experience.

- The Boat – a visual metaphor exercise helping teams identify what is working well (the wind in their sails), what is slowing them down (anchors) and what opportunities and obstacles lie ahead. This helps surface both practical and emotional insights that shape the design.

Throughout the project, we view co-creation not as a phase but as a continuous process. We use:

- Brain Trust sessions (explained further on) to rigorously test creative thinking early and often.

- Content co-creation workshops with employee groups to ensure messaging and tone feel authentic and resonant.

- On-site Kanban boards during delivery phases to maintain visibility and invite client participation in the flow of work.

- Real-time feedback loops during and after activations to continuously improve and evolve.

The Brain Trust: building better ideas together

One of the most powerful tools we use to embed collaborative rigour in our creative process is the Brain Trust: a concept we've adapted from Pixar's renowned practice, as described in Ed Catmull's *Creativity, Inc* (2014).

At Pixar, the Brain Trust brings together a group of trusted peers to review films-in-progress with radical candour, not to impose solutions but to ask the right questions and help creators see their work more clearly.

At People Activation, we have embraced this model as a core part of our Human-Centred Design process. Our Brain Trust sessions are carefully structured checkpoints where cross-functional colleagues – from creative, strategy, production and client experience – come together to provide honest, constructive challenges to early creative thinking.

Importantly, these sessions are not formal approval meetings. They are designed to create a safe, open environment where feedback flows freely, without ego. The presenting team is encouraged to listen deeply rather than defend their ideas.

Typical questions explored include:

- Are we truly responding to what employees are telling us?
- Does the creative direction feel emotionally resonant, not just intellectually interesting?
- Is the experience inclusive and accessible to the full diversity of the audience?
- Are we making assumptions that need testing or challenging?
- Are there opportunities we are missing?

Psychologically, this practice aligns with what research tells us about innovation: teams that feel safe to share imperfect work and receive feedback without fear perform better and generate more creative outcomes (Edmondson, 1999). The Brain Trust helps us ensure that creative ideas are rigorously tested and iteratively improved – grounded in employee insight, not simply agency preference.

For clients, this results in stronger, more considered creative work that stands up to real-world employee expectations and a process that models the collaborative, inclusive values we want to reflect in the final experience.

Co-creation in action: a global pharmaceutical company

One of the most powerful examples of our co-creation approach in action was an anniversary activation for a global pharmaceutical company with 4,700 employees across 16 countries.

The goal was to celebrate 10 years of operation across EMEA (Europe, the Middle East and Africa), not through a corporate broadcast but through an authentic, employee-driven experience that would unite the region and energize people around the company's future vision.

Our design process was built around three simple, human questions, posed to all employees:

- What has surprised you?
- What has inspired you?
- What has made you feel proud?

The response was extraordinary: 535 stories submitted from every country and function. These became the raw material for the experience.

Rather than simply interpreting these stories ourselves, we worked in deep collaboration with employee representatives and client stakeholders through co-creation workshops. Together, we identified common themes and shaped how the stories would be brought to life through live performance, film, poetry and interactive broadcast.

Employees were not just consulted; they participated directly, performing live, contributing content and becoming the voices of the event. The result was a world-first interactive two-way broadcast, co-created by employees and celebrated by employees.

The impact was profound:

- 91 per cent of employees reported feeling motivated and positive about the company's future after the event.
- 89 per cent felt proud of their colleagues and organization.
- Engagement scores showed that employees who had participated directly in shaping the experience reported even higher levels of motivation and pride.

This was not a one-way communication – it was a two-way, co-created activation that reflected the authentic voice of the organization's people.

Why we work this way

The reason we take a people-first, human-centred approach is simple: it works.

Research consistently shows that when people feel ownership over an experience, they are more engaged and more likely to take action. The 'IKEA Effect' (Norton et al, 2012) shows that individuals place higher value on outcomes they have helped create. Self-determination theory (Deci and Ryan, 2000) confirms that autonomy and agency drive higher motivation and commitment.

In a world where employees are increasingly fatigued by passive communication and corporate spin, co-creation offers a more authentic, effective way to drive engagement, alignment and behaviour change.

Our Human-Centred Design process and EITO-inspired collaboration methods enable us to deliver experiences that employees see themselves in – experiences they feel connected to and proud of. And that is what moves people to action.

In summary

At People Activation, we exist to move people to action. Not through top-down messaging, but through experiences that employees help shape from the very beginning.

Through our Human-Centred Design process, our Brain Trust culture, our use of EITO tools and our deep commitment to genuine co-creation, we deliver campaigns and activations that drive not just understanding, but ownership, energy and action.

Because when employees see their voice reflected in an experience, it becomes their story too; and that is the key to forging better employee experiences and lasting organizational impact.

Who to involve in the ideation process

In the people-first approach, ideation is never a solo act. The best solutions emerge when we design with people, not just for them. That means deliberately involving a diverse range of collaborators, especially those closest to the problem. This isn't just about fairness or inclusion, it's about quality. Research shows that solutions co-created with employees are not only more innovative but more likely to succeed. As the authors of a 2019 report on employee-centred design in organizational change found, involving employees in co-creation enhances engagement, increases psychological ownership and improves the overall impact of change (Richards, 2019).

Let's explore who to involve and why.

EMPLOYEES: KEEP THE CHALLENGE REAL

Employees are your end users and your biggest asset in ideation. They bring lived experience and emotional truth to the table. Their perspective grounds the creative process, ensures relevance and unlocks insights others may miss. In design terms, they help us move from solving for people to solving with them, which is a fundamental shift at the heart of people-first IC. And by involving employees early, you build buy-in, boost momentum and create solutions more likely to land.

As IDEO puts it: 'The people who face a problem every day are the ones who hold the key to its answer' (IDEO.org, 2015).

DIVERSITY: MIX UP YOUR THINKERS

Ideation thrives on difference. Whether you're building on your initial discovery team or inviting new voices into the room, this is the time to stretch beyond the usual suspects. A diverse team brings a broader mix of perspectives, ways of thinking and creative inputs. And the data backs this up; studies have consistently shown that diverse teams outperform homogeneous ones in problem-solving and innovation (Page, 2007).

Think across:

- Functions: Comms, HR, IT, Ops, Finance.
- Levels: Front line to C-suite.
- Lived experiences: Demographics, roles, locations.

You don't need everyone all at once, but you do need to ask, 'whose perspective haven't we heard yet?'

CROSS-FUNCTIONAL ALLIES: FROM IDEAS TO IMPLEMENTATION

Ideation isn't just about generating great ideas; it's about finding feasible ones too. Involving people from other functions (such as Finance, IT, HR or Operations) opens the door to prototyping faster and scaling smarter. Bringing in functional partners early turns blockers into problem-solvers and future ambassadors for roll-out.

SENIOR STAKEHOLDERS: WHEN AND HOW TO INVOLVE THEM

Involving senior leaders can lend weight to the process, unlock resources and signal support. But tread carefully. Power dynamics matter in creative work. A senior voice can inadvertently shut down riskier ideas or rush the process toward a premature decision.

As innovation strategist Roger Martin argues, 'Innovation requires a space where new ideas can be explored without being immediately evaluated or judged' (2009).

Create that space and defend it fiercely.

Preparing to ideate

In the People-First IC approach, ideation isn't just a one-off brainstorm; it's a structured and intentional process that helps us move from insight to impact. Before jumping into generating ideas, there are two crucial steps: sharing the challenge and framing the ideation task. Together, these steps ensure that everyone involved understands the opportunity, connects with the people behind it and is clear on what success looks like.

1. Sharing the challenge

Great ideas are rooted in real human needs. That's why before any ideation activity, we need to reconnect with the insight that brought us here in the first place. Even if your team was part of the discovery process, it's helpful to revisit what you've learnt, especially from the perspective of those you're designing for.

This step isn't just about presenting data or research findings. It's about cultivating empathy. Use stories, photos, quotes or even short videos to make your insights tangible and personal. The purpose here is to help the team step into the shoes of the people experiencing the IC challenge. Doing this before the ideation session, through pre-reading, visual boards or briefing packs, gives participants time to reflect and ensures your ideation session starts with shared clarity and energy.

2. Framing the ideation task

Once the insight is clear, it's time to focus the group's creativity. This is where framing comes in: clearly defining what you want the ideation to achieve, without jumping to conclusions about the solution. This is where we bring out and use our 'how might we' questions (HMW), which we detailed in the previous chapter. These HMW questions turn challenges into open invitations for innovation. Here are two examples:

EXAMPLE 1: IMPROVING STRATEGIC NARRATIVE CUT-THROUGH
Insight: 'Employees told us they hear about the strategy, but they don't see their role in it. They feel overwhelmed by corporate messages and underwhelmed by relevance.'

HMW question: How might we bring the strategy to life in a way that feels personal, relevant and actionable for every team – especially those far from HQ?

EXAMPLE 2: REDESIGNING MANAGER COMMS
Insight: 'Managers feel stuck in the middle, expected to communicate information they don't always understand or agree with, without the tools or time to do it well.'

HMW question: How might we support managers to feel confident, credible and connected when communicating with their teams, especially during change?

Notice that neither question includes a 'pre-baked' solution, for example, a new toolkit, email series or training video, and that is deliberate. It keeps the solution space open, allowing unexpected and creative ideas to emerge. If your HMW question feels too vague or too prescriptive, pause and ask the team for feedback. Reframing is part of the creative process and the right question can unlock entirely new ways of thinking.

The six steps of people-first ideation

The People-First IC approach treats ideation not as a single brainstorming session but as a creative journey: one that is collaborative, iterative and grounded in human insight. Here we offer a structured six-step process adapted from experience design best practice and reframed for internal communication professionals. It draws heavily from the work of Emma and Belinda in *Employee Experience by Design* (2024), alongside design thinking principles from Stanford d.school and facilitation approaches like Liberating Structures.

FIGURE 9.1 The six steps of people-first ideation

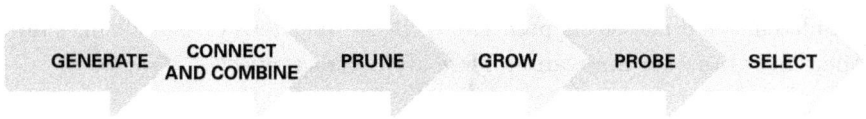

GENERATE   CONNECT AND COMBINE   PRUNE   GROW   PROBE   SELECT

These principles are helpful to guide your ideation work:

- **Defer judgement:** Don't critique ideas – yet.
- **Encourage wild ideas:** Bold ideas open new territory.
- **Build on the ideas of others:** Use 'yes, and...' to create momentum.
- **Go for volume:** Aim for quantity before quality.
- **One conversation at a time:** Maintain flow and clarity.
- **Make it visual:** Use sketches, symbols or maps to bring ideas to life.

Remember, this is a flexible framework, adapt it to suit your audience, format and timing. The magic lies in knowing where you are in the process: are you generating ideas, combining them or choosing what to test? This clarity helps maintain momentum and creativity.

Step 1: Generate ideas

This is where it all begins. In People-First IC, generating ideas is not just about being creative, it's about being inclusive. Ideation sessions that include employees, cross-functional partners and end users will draw out often unexpected insights and help to co-create solutions that reflect lived realities.

Goal: Go for volume. Aim for lots of ideas, not perfect ones. Use tools like brainstorming, role-play and sketching to open up thinking.

KEY TECHNIQUES FOR PEOPLE-FIRST IC IDEA GENERATION

When ideating in internal communication, your goal is to generate ideas that go beyond the obvious and reflect the lived experiences of your people. These creative prompts are designed to stretch your thinking, challenge assumptions and generate a diverse range of ideas because great communication design rarely comes from playing it safe.

Here are some techniques for you to try.

REVERSE THE QUESTION

Take your HMW question and flip it on its head. This technique disrupts conventional thinking and invites some dark humour, which can be a surprisingly effective way to surface the unspoken frustrations employees have about IC. Once you've got a list of terrible ideas, flip them again to discover more meaningful solutions.

EXAMPLE

HMW: How might we make our leadership communications more open and engaging to encourage employees to speak their truth?

Reversed: How might we make our leadership comms more closed-off, patronizing and tone-deaf to silence our people?

From there, your team might generate terrible ideas like 'only share toxically positive updates' or 'use buzzwords no one understands.' Then flip these ideas to find gold: 'be transparent about challenges,' 'use plain language' or 'tailor tone to audience feedback.'

PERSONALITY SWAP

A classic ideation exercise involves answering the HMW question from the point of view of a well-known brand or personality. This helps break the cycle of 'what we usually do' and opens up creative possibilities:

- Barbie: How would Barbie boost belonging in your internal campaigns?
- David Attenborough: What would he say about your tone of voice and storytelling?

- Monzo: How might a digital-first brand bring clarity and delight to dry policy comms?
- Spotify: How might a brand known for curation personalize the comms experience?
- Greta Thunberg: How might a climate activist inspire employee voice in purpose-led campaigns?

EXAMPLE

HMW: How might we use IC to help new hires feel part of the team from Day 1 to reduce turnover in the first six months?

Imagine you're Monzo: Maybe you'd send a custom onboarding playlist, create a Slack bot that introduces new starters through GIFs and fun facts, or build a simple welcome flow in your comms platform that mirrors a digital user journey.

BRAINSTORMING WITH AI

AI can be a powerful ideation partner, particularly when you're short on time or want to broaden your thinking beyond your own mental models.

Ways to brainstorm with AI in IC:

- Prompt it to generate ideas for your HMW question (e.g. 'Give me 20 creative ideas for making remote town halls more interactive').
- Ask it to play a personality (e.g. 'Answer this HMW as if you're Brené Brown or Patagonia').
- Use it to expand, remix or combine ideas generated by your team.

And remember, although AI can be a great sparring partner, the real power comes from combining its output with your contextual knowledge and your people's lived experiences.

1-2-4-ALL (TAKEN FROM LIBERATING STRUCTURES)

A people-first favourite, especially for inclusive teams. This approach lets everyone participate in idea generation by starting with 'solo and silent' thinking, then moving to pairs, then small groups, then the full group.

Example: you're reimagining your internal brand.

- Step 1: Everyone reflects on 'What one thing should our internal voice stand for?'
- Step 2: Pairs share and build on ideas.

- Step 3: Groups of four identify themes.
- Step 4: As a whole team, you prioritize and select the top three themes to take forward.

This technique helps prevent dominant voices from taking over and introverts get time to process. Everyone has a say and that's key in experience-led IC.

Step 2: Connect and combine

With hundreds of ideas flying around, the next step is to make sense of the chaos. Group similar ideas into themes. This isn't about picking winners yet but looking for patterns and connections. The goal here is to move from scattered Post-Its to organized possibilities. This starts with clustering ideas into similar themes, then discussing why these ideas connect. This stage also helps people feel heard and seen, a key tenet of experience design.

Step 3: Prune ideas

Now it's time to narrow the field. Pruning can be political, so keep things fair and transparent. The goal here is to reduce the volume to a set of promising concepts. You can use dot voting to prioritize themes and it helps to discuss trade-offs openly. Encourage the team to let go of ideas without defensiveness. Not every idea needs to survive to make the session a success.

Step 4: Grow ideas

Now is the time to expand the best concepts. The goal here is to develop rich, testable ideas. You can use storyboarding to bring the ideas to life or try role-playing or mapping an internal campaign. This is where IC professionals shine; you can bring a concept to life with compelling stories, touchpoints and empathy.

Step 5: Probe ideas

Good ideas are exciting. But great ideas are the ones that can actually work. This step uses critical thinking to surface assumptions. The goal here is to test feasibility without killing creativity. Ask questions here such as

- What needs to be true for this to succeed?
- Does it require executive sponsorship?

- Would it disrupt a cultural norm?
- Are key systems or budgets in place?

Just don't ask 'What won't work?' Ask what needs to be true for it to work.

Step 6: Select ideas

Finally, it's time to choose which ideas to prototype. The goal here is to prioritize high-impact, testable ideas. It can be helpful here to use a prioritization grid (high effort vs high impact), along with dot voting. Just ensure you have clear criteria, for example, people impact, speed to test, strategic relevance. Some teams pick quick wins; others go for bold experiments. The right idea to test is the one that will teach you the most, fastest.

By following these six steps, internal communicators can confidently move from insight to solution, grounded in empathy and fuelled by creativity. Remember, in a people-first IC approach, it's not just about coming up with ideas, it's about co-creating meaningful, sustainable experiences that work for your people.

INTRODUCING THE 4-STEP CONCEPT SKETCH

The 4-Step Concept Sketch is a structured ideation tool originating from the Google Ventures Design Sprint methodology, as detailed in Jake Knapp et al's book, *Sprint: How to Solve Big Problems and Test New Ideas in Just Five Days* (2016). This tool helps teams generate and refine ideas that are empathetic, inclusive and aligned with employee needs. It encourages individual reflection and creativity, ensuring that solutions are grounded in real insights rather than assumptions.

Step 1: Solo note-taking

Purpose: To reflect individually on insights gathered so far.
Instructions:

- Review key insights gathered so far, such as journey maps, empathy maps and 'how might we' (HMW) questions.
- Make notes on observations and reflections, focusing on employee experiences and needs.

Tip: Emphasize that this step is about understanding and reflecting, not about generating solutions yet.

Step 2: Idea generation

Purpose: To translate reflections into preliminary ideas.
Instructions:

- Choose one insight from your notes to explore further.
- Sketch out ideas related to this insight. These can be doodles, flowcharts or simple diagrams. Make it clear no one is going to see this; it's for their eyes only.
- Then look back at the notes and move on to something else and repeat.
- Repeat the process with other insights as time allows.

Tip: Reassure participants that artistic skill is not required; the focus is on conveying ideas. Explain that this might feel a bit tricky or messy and that's OK and normal at this stage.

Step 3: Crazy 8s

Purpose: To rapidly explore multiple variations of an idea.
Instructions:

- Take a sheet of paper and divide it into eight sections.
- Choose one idea to focus on.
- In each section, sketch a different variation of this idea, spending one minute per sketch.
- Stress it's normal to feel uncomfortable here!

Tip: Encourage participants to push beyond their first ideas as the most innovative solutions often emerge later in the process.

Step 4: Solution sketch

Purpose: To develop a detailed concept for presentation and feedback.
Instructions:

- Select your most promising idea from the Crazy 8s exercise.
- Create a detailed sketch of this idea, illustrating how it would work in practice.
- This should be self-explanatory and stress that ugly is okay.
- Ask them to give it a catchy title.

- Then ask each person to share their concept and explain it.
- Each member of the group is then able to ask questions about each other's concepts.

Tip: Focus on clarity and functionality rather than artistic quality.

Next steps: group review and selection

After all participants have presented their solution sketches, the group can discuss and vote on the ideas they'd like to develop further. Remember that unselected ideas are not discarded; they can be revisited and refined in future sessions.

Introducing prototyping

It's almost always the case that once we have landed on our solution in IC, we move straight into full-scale delivery mode. And with good reason; we are fixers and doers; we make things happen and at pace. But the problem is that sometimes this can lead to comms solutions that miss the mark, or IC experiences that fall flat, or fail to solve the real problem. This is something we have seen time and again in IC.

Prototyping is the pause that protects us. It's the moment where we get to test ideas and proposed solutions before they're polished. It's where we invite feedback before it's too late to change course, and where we get comfortable being curious instead of committed.

In a People-First IC approach, prototyping is critical, not just because it saves time and money (although it does) but because it respects your people. It gives you the chance to test whether your idea resonates, confuses, engages, alienates or inspires before you scale it across a global workforce or invest weeks (or months) of resource. We previously shared the real-life example of the IC team that invested in a shiny recognition app to improve employee recognition and gather stories to showcase values in action. This proved to be an expensive mistake; the app didn't solve the problem and definitely wasn't the right solution. If the team had only taken the time to prototype their proposed ideas and solutions, they would have avoided this situation.

The guidance we share here will help you embrace prototyping as a mindset as well as a method. You'll learn that prototyping is not about perfection; it's about learning fast, failing small and evolving ideas into solutions that actually work.

Why prototyping matters in IC

In IC, we're often under pressure to act quickly. But great communication is rarely about speed; prototyping helps you to deliver comms solutions with real insight that actually work.

Some of the benefits of prototyping are:

- It deepens understanding of the IC ideas you are proposing.
- It invites feedback from end users, which results in better solutions.
- It reduces risk by identifying what doesn't work before it's too late.
- It boosts creativity by inviting experimentation without pressure.
- It builds buy-in from stakeholders who want evidence, not just ideas.

What is prototyping?

The aim of prototyping is to communicate an idea and get feedback; it's that simple. A prototype should be just enough to bring an idea to life and get feedback. 'Prototypes are not meant to be perfect. They are designed to ask questions and get some reactions' (Tim Brown, CEO of IDEO).

A prototype might involve:

- a rough sketch of a campaign on A3 card
- a sample intranet post written in three styles
- a quick video recorded on a phone to test tone and clarity
- a role-played team briefing delivered to a test group.

The point isn't polish, it's learning. A prototype helps you explore a hypothesis: If we communicate X in Y way, people will feel or do Z. You're testing ideas, not launching them. That applies just as much to IC as to any other employee experience challenge. Complex problems rarely have a single, perfect solution. Prototyping helps you explore a range of responses, quickly, cheaply and collaboratively.

A first prototype, perhaps the first few iterations, is often a very rough execution of an idea. For example, it's more likely to be a sketch of an idea or a storyboard of an online experience rather than a website or functional process. Rough and ready is the key. As you move through the process, your prototypes might move from low-fidelity to high-fidelity, but the purpose is always the same: to communicate your ideas and proposed solutions to get feedback before you scale up.

To be really clear, prototyping is not the same as a minimum viable product (MVP). An MVP is something you give to a test group to use. A prototype is something you give to others to react to. In IC terms, your MVP might be a pilot version of a new communication tool. Your prototype might be a sketch of how it would work, a sample content calendar or a rough demo of a new team newsletter. We've worked with teams who have created prototypes in LEGO, through role play, as well as with a bunch of craft materials. There's nothing like building something together to drive team bonding, boost energy and create a shared sense of where you're heading.

Prototyping works best when we're not too attached to our ideas. That's not always easy, especially in creative roles. But the goal here is not to be right, it's to be better. The earlier you invite feedback, the easier it is to let go of weak ideas and grow stronger ones. When we prototype, we have to learn to be open to feedback, which can include criticism; we have to be open to going back to the drawing board, and we have to listen to understand. This can sometimes feel uncomfortable, not least when we have put in time and effort to get us to this stage of the process. The IC superpowers we detailed in Chapter 4 can help develop the right mindset to embrace prototyping, and even enjoy it! Let's take a closer look:

- **Empathy**: Prototyping only works when it starts with people. Your ability to deeply understand your employees, to walk in their shoes, listen without judgement and tune into what they really need, helps ensure you're designing with, not just for, your people. Empathy keeps your prototypes grounded in real insight, not assumptions.

- **Curiosity**: A curious communicator doesn't just accept the first answer; they explore, question and stay open. Prototyping is powered by curiosity. It's about asking 'What if...?', 'Why not?' and 'How might we make this even better?' Curiosity helps you see possibilities others might miss and stay in learning mode.

- **Resilience**: Not every idea will work and that's the point. Prototyping is designed to reveal flaws early, before they become expensive mistakes. That means you'll encounter feedback, failure and dead ends. Your resilience helps you bounce back, adapt and keep going, knowing each 'not quite' gets you closer to a 'just right'.

- **Creativity**: Prototyping is a creative act. It invites you to imagine, make, test and remake. It doesn't demand polished final products, just tangible expressions of an idea. Your creativity helps you visualize new approaches, sketch bold alternatives and reframe problems in ways that spark innovation.

- **Influence**: You'll need others to come on the journey and you may need to sell the value of prototyping to stakeholders who are used to seeing only finished work. Your influencing skills help you build buy-in, frame prototypes as low-risk experiments, and shape the environment where testing and learning are embraced.

- **Courage**: Prototyping is brave work. It means putting rough ideas out into the world, knowing they may be challenged. It also means pushing back on the instinct to over-polish or over-control. Your courage helps you take creative risks, speak truth to power and champion people-first design even when it goes against the grain.

When you lean into your IC superpowers, you stop seeing prototyping as a threat to your ideas and start seeing it as a path to better outcomes. You shift from a mindset of perfection and protection to one of possibility and progress. Instead of fearing criticism, you welcome feedback. Instead of aiming to get it right first time, you get excited about iterating your way to something better. Prototyping becomes less about defending your work and more about designing what truly works. And that's where the magic happens, not just in the solutions you create but in how much more energizing, inclusive and effective the process becomes.

How to run a prototyping session

Prototyping in internal communication isn't about perfect deliverables, it's about learning fast, failing safely and putting people at the centre of the solution. Yet, in many IC teams, this way of working still feels unfamiliar. We're used to creating polished campaigns, beautifully crafted copy and fully formed strategies before anything sees the light of day. But prototyping asks us to flip that, to get rough and ready early.

Design thinker Tim Brown describes prototypes as 'conversations made tangible' (Brown, 2009). And that's exactly what we're doing here, creating quick, imperfect artefacts to prompt dialogue, gather feedback and learn what works before we scale.

LOW-FIDELITY, HIGH LEARNING
In early-stage IC design, we're not building finished intranet pages, newsletters or video scripts. We're sketching storyboards, mocking up a comms

moment, role-playing a conversation or creating a paper-based version of an experience. These are what we call low-fidelity prototypes and they're rough (in a good way), inexpensive and fast to build.

They might look like:

- a set of sample headlines and email subject lines
- a hand-drawn journey map for an IC experience
- a short, narrated video mock-up
- a role-played leadership Q&A, using real employee questions.

Low-fi prototyping isn't just more accessible, it's more inclusive. Tom Wujec has spoken extensively on design thinking and visual collaboration. In his TED Talk 'Build a Tower, Build a Team,' Wujec discusses how rough, incomplete sketches encourage more honest and constructive feedback during the design process. 'The less complete something looks, the more people feel empowered to give honest feedback' (Wujec 2010).

And in IC, that's exactly what we want.

SET EXPECTATIONS

Internal communicators often pride themselves on clarity, polish and professionalism, which is exactly why prototyping can feel uncomfortable at first. To help teams shift gears, start by setting expectations:

- Show examples of low-fi prototypes (your own or sourced online).
- Share the purpose: we're not creating the answer, we're exploring possibilities.
- Normalize messiness: great insights often come from awkward beginnings.

If you're in a room together, a physical box of craft supplies (paper, markers, sticky notes, LEGO) can quickly signal this is a creative space. If you're virtual, prompt people to grab simple materials from their home or use digital tools like Miro.

KEEP IT SIMPLE

Remind the group that a prototype is not the solution but a way to test parts of the solution. Encourage questions such as:

- What's the smallest piece of this idea we can test right now?
- What's the fastest way we can make this tangible?

For example, instead of building a whole campaign, prototype just the first message. Instead of scripting a full video, storyboard the key scenes. Instead of designing a full feedback tool, mock up one screen or question set. The aim is to spark feedback, not applause.

STOKE THE ENERGY
Prototyping should feel energetic, creative and collaborative, but that doesn't mean it will always stay that way. If momentum dips:

- Play upbeat music to lighten the mood.
- Use time-boxing and countdowns to prompt faster decisions.
- Switch team members between groups to inject fresh thinking.

Bringing in people with different perspectives, especially end users, also boosts energy and relevance.

FOCUS ON THE TEST
Throughout the session, anchor the team in what they're trying to learn:

- What assumption are we testing?
- What feedback do we need?
- Who do we need to hear from?

Keep reminding them: The goal of the prototype is learning, not launch.

You might even use an AI co-pilot like ChatGPT or Claude to help prep your testing questions, simulate audience feedback or turn insights into quick refinements. Used well, AI can be a creative sparring partner in rapid prototyping, especially when time or resources are limited.

Introducing the prototype pro forma

We have reinforced the idea that prototyping isn't about testing polished outputs, it's about learning. This tool helps your team clarify the why behind the prototype:

- What are we trying to understand?
- What feedback do we need?
- And how will we use it to shape better IC experiences?

You can use the prototype pro forma to capture your thinking, stay focused on your learning goals and prepare for meaningful feedback. It's a simple yet powerful way to shift from launching assumptions to learning through evidence.

Worked example: testing a new leadership Q&A format

Imagine you're redesigning a quarterly leadership Q&A session based on feedback that employees feel it's too formal, too scripted and too disconnected from their concerns. You've ideated a new format that's more conversational, includes upvoted employee questions and uses a live moderator. Before rolling it out company-wide, you decide to prototype it with a small group.

PROTOTYPE PRO FORMA (WORKED EXAMPLE)

What are you trying to achieve with your prototype?   To test whether a more conversational and interactive format for leadership Q&A increases perceived authenticity and relevance for employees.

Brief description   A 30-minute pilot version of the Q&A hosted in a regional office. It will feature a moderator from the comms team, three real questions submitted by employees in advance and a 'quick-fire round' where leaders answer unscripted questions.

What are you seeking to learn from your prototype and how will you generate that learning?

- Do employees feel the session is more authentic and engaging?
- Does the format encourage leaders to show more personality and empathy?
- What tone, structure and pacing feel right?

We'll gather feedback through:

- a five-question pulse survey sent immediately after the session
- informal follow-ups with attendees
- observation notes from the comms team and facilitator.

Who are you going to test your prototype with?

- 12 employees from the regional office (mixed levels and roles)
- 2 senior leaders
- 1 member of the comms team acting as moderator
- feedback reviewers from HR and employee networks.

This tool not only helps guide better prototyping, it also builds buy-in by clearly showing the logic behind what you're doing and why. When used well, it keeps the process focused, human and evidence-based, helping to bring people-first IC to life.

Early-stage prototypes

What low-fidelity prototypes lose in resolution, they make up for in flexibility. Here are some examples, most of which can be created in as little as an hour:

- Sketches are a visual way to make an idea more tangible. You don't need any artistic skills to create shapes, stick people and speech bubbles.

- Storyboards are a series of sketches or pictures that demonstrate an end-to-end solution. We use cartoon strip boxes to help people think through a scenario. Storyboarding is a great way to ensure the IC experience is at the heart of the solution.

- Paper interfaces are a way of creating a real interface where people can pretend to tap and click as if they are on a screen. They are useful for prototyping digital products. You can create paper interfaces by sketching or by drawing and cutting out usable parts of a user interface (e.g. text field or navigation such as dropdown menu). They can equally be used to bring a physical object to life, such as a book.

- Modelling is a fun, playful experience that people love. LEGO and Play-Doh are popular ways to create early prototypes, which can be shared and are versatile, as the models can easily be tweaked or changed completely.

- Role-play, or experiential prototypes, are where you re-enact scenes and situations you are trying to improve. While the thought of role play might fill you with dread, we are always surprised by groups' willingness to embrace this as a way to communicate their idea. Not only is it a way of getting feedback from end users, but the experience of being in the moment can also create new energy and often provides insight around the problem for the design team. You can add levels of detail to the role-play, including simulating a physical environment with props.

- Wizard of Oz prototypes sit halfway between a low and high-fidelity prototype and create an illusion of the functionality you want to test, without actually providing it. It's about smoke and mirrors. A team we worked with came up with an idea for an AI-powered 'ask comms' assistant. The internal comms team has identified a recurring issue: employees didn't know where to go to get quick answers about internal updates, events or policy changes. As part of an ideation sprint, the team developed a concept for a chatbot-style 'Ask Comms' assistant embedded in the intranet. It would use natural language processing to answer questions like 'When's the next town hall?' or 'Where can I find the brand guidelines?'

Eventually, the team wanted this assistant to integrate with the intranet's search function, pull in real-time updates from the comms calendar and use AI to suggest the most relevant answers.

Instead of building the bot right away (which would take significant IT and AI support), the comms team created a mock-up chat interface using Typeform that looked and felt like a chatbot. When an employee submitted a question, a member of the comms team manually read it and responded behind the scenes in near real time, creating the illusion of an intelligent assistant. They also set up a Slack integration where responses appeared within minutes and A/B tested two different tones of voice (formal vs conversational) to see what employees engaged with most.

THE TEAM WANTED TO FIND OUT

- Were employees likely to use a tool like this?
- What types of questions are most common or most useful?
- What tone and interface feel right for internal comms?
- How quickly do employees expect a response?

This approach allowed the team to test the core assumptions and user experience of the 'Ask Comms' assistant but without having to build the tech first. This Wizard of Oz method kept things fast, flexible and focused on real feedback. And by the time they were ready to scale, they had more evidence to inform each design choice.

Higher-fidelity prototypes

Low-fidelity prototypes are brilliant for fast learning and early testing. But as your ideas evolve through feedback, iteration and increasing clarity, you may need to build something more robust. That's where higher-fidelity prototypes come in.

In internal communication, this might mean moving from a rough storyboard of the comms experience for a new manager onboarding experience to running a live pilot, or shifting from mocked-up comms journeys to clickable digital mock-ups. These higher-fidelity prototypes are still for learning, not perfection, but they test your ideas in more realistic contexts. At this stage, you're no longer asking, 'Does this idea have potential?' You're asking, 'How well does it work in the real world?'

To make higher-fidelity prototyping effective, purpose is everything. If you build something polished but haven't defined what insight you need, or how you'll test it, you risk ending up with a shiny artefact but no actionable learning.

Ask these questions before you build:

1 The build
   What's the simplest way to test the key behaviour, experience or assumption? Do you really need a microsite or could a mocked-up email journey work just as well?

2 Resources
   What tools, platforms, budget and time do we realistically have access to? Who can help us create a real-world version of this idea?

3 Testing plan
   How will we test the experience? Where, when and with whom? What are we observing or asking to evaluate it?

4 Stakeholders
   Which leaders, team or influencers do we need to involve to ensure buy-in and scalability? How can we keep them in the loop and aligned?

5 Insight capture
   How will we collect, reflect on and act on the insight we gather from testing? What feedback methods (interviews, surveys, analytics) will we use?

Worked example: higher-fidelity prototype – 'Real Talk' for new managers

CONCEPT
After testing a rough storyboard of a 'Real Talk' conversation kit for new managers to guide open team discussions about culture and communication, feedback was positive. People liked the idea, but wanted to try it in action.

OBJECTIVE
Test the effectiveness and usability of the 'Real Talk' kit in live sessions with real teams.

PROTOTYPE PLAN

- Pilot the kit with five newly appointed managers across different departments.
- Equip them with facilitator guidance, printed kit materials and a cheat sheet on managing discussion dynamics.

- Observe sessions and record reflections afterwards, capturing what worked, where people got stuck and how the kit was used in practice.

- Follow up with a short feedback survey and optional interviews with both managers and team members.

KEY INSIGHTS TO CAPTURE

- Did the kit build confidence in new managers?
- Were teams more engaged or open in conversation?
- Did it surface useful data for the comms or culture teams?

This prototype may not be a final product, but it's enough to validate (or challenge) core assumptions, before investing in full-scale design, roll-out or digital tooling.

You've got a prototype – what's next?

The real value of a prototype isn't in what it looks like, it's in what it teaches you. Higher-fidelity prototypes give you a window into how your solution performs in the wild. Now we'll focus on testing and iterating, so you scale the solutions that actually work, not the ones that just sound good in theory.

Testing your prototype: learning before launch

In many internal communication teams, the default mindset is to launch and then (maybe) learn. But people-first IC flips that script. Instead of assuming we've nailed it, we test before we scale, because real insight comes from real experiences, not just good intentions.

Testing your prototypes is about getting rough ideas in front of the right people, learning from their feedback, and evolving your approach based on what actually works. This stage is critical but so often overlooked in traditional IC, where timelines and expectations push teams to jump straight to delivery. As with all people-first design, testing means involving your people, and this might include:

- end users, e.g. employees, managers, team leads
- business partners, e.g. HR, IT, legal, project teams
- sponsors and stakeholders, e.g. senior leaders or influencers
- neutral observers who can give objective feedback.

By bringing a diverse group into your testing loop, you'll see your prototype from different perspectives, helping you strengthen your solution and uncover hidden gaps.

Testing low-fidelity prototypes

Low-fidelity prototypes are simple, fast and imperfect. They're sketches, scripts, mock-ups, or even walkthroughs of a potential experience. To get meaningful feedback, follow these four golden rules:

1 Make people feel safe: Emphasize that honesty is welcome. You're not testing them – you're learning from them.

2 Introduce, don't sell: Share your prototype as a work-in-progress. Position it as something you're co-creating.

3 Say less: Let the prototype speak for itself. Resist the urge to explain every decision.

4 Detach emotionally: Don't defend the idea. Listen. Learn. Be grateful.

You can use a simple feedback grid to structure what you hear using these prompts:

- I like…
- I wish…
- I wonder…
- I've got an idea…

This makes the insight easier to reflect on and share with your wider team. It also keeps the feedback focused on experience, not just opinion.

After the session, reflect with your team:

- What surprised you?
- What assumptions were challenged?
- What needs iteration or deeper testing?

Testing higher-fidelity prototypes

As you iterate and refine your idea, your prototype may get more detailed. That could mean:

- a live trial of a new manager toolkit
- a fully designed intranet mock-up
- a click-through prototype of a new content hub.

At this stage, your questions become sharper. Remember, at this stage, you're no longer asking, 'does this idea make sense?' but rather 'how does it work in practice?'

Before you test, get clear on:

- What are we testing? What's the hypothesis or behaviour we want to validate?

- What's the build plan? What's the simplest way to bring the idea to life?

- Who's involved? Which functions (e.g. HR, Tech, Change) need to help us test this?

- What's our feedback method? Surveys, interviews, observation, data capture – pick what's right for your test.

- What will success look like? Define clear criteria to evaluate whether to scale or pivot.

Worked example: testing a higher-fidelity prototype

PROTOTYPE: 'REAL TALK' CONVERSATION KIT FOR NEW MANAGERS

Following positive feedback from a low-fidelity storyboard and rough kit outline, the team builds a working prototype of 'Real Talk,' a set of facilitated conversations to help new managers build communication confidence.

OBJECTIVE

Test the kit in live sessions with new and experienced managers.

TESTING PLAN

- Pilot with five newly appointed managers over a six-week period.
- Weekly sessions focus on key themes:
  - Building trust.
  - Managing performance.
  - Navigating conflict.
  - Leading change.
- Each session includes:
  - a short scenario-based role-play
  - peer discussion
  - structured feedback forms.

FEEDBACK SAMPLE
New managers said:

- 'I like the realness of the scenarios; this is the stuff I face every day.'
- 'I wish we had time to explore how other managers handle things.'
- 'I've got an idea – could we get access to a library of role-play examples?'

Experienced managers said:

- 'I like how engaged the group is, this builds a community.'
- 'I wish we could do follow-up check-ins.'
- 'I've got an idea to pair new managers with a 'practice buddy' between sessions.'

RESULT
The team decided to roll out a three-month pilot with:

- facilitator training for experienced managers
- a buddy system for new managers
- digital library of scenarios
- agreed success criteria comparing engagement and performance with a control group.

REAL-WORLD EXAMPLE
Prototyping for front-line impact

Background and challenge

An internal communications (IC) team at a large utilities company had received troubling insights from their annual survey. While engagement was relatively strong in office-based teams, front-line employees, including engineers, field technicians and depot teams, reported feeling disconnected, unheard and often forgotten by internal communication efforts.

Comments included:

- 'We never hear anything until it's already happened.'
- 'It's like we don't exist unless something goes wrong.'
- 'Comms feel like they're for office people, not us.'

The IC team knew they needed to act, but they also knew traditional top-down campaigns wouldn't cut it. So, they turned to People-First IC design principles, embedding experience design and prototyping into their solution.

Insight and ideation

Following discovery interviews, observation and journey mapping across various front-line roles, the team developed three potential concepts:

1 'Shift start snapshots' – a mobile-first daily update for team leaders to share with crews during morning briefings.
2 'Ask me anything (offline)' – a physical poster campaign with QR codes and hotline numbers to submit questions to leadership.
3 'Voices from the front line' – a rotating slot in leadership town halls featuring short video stories from field staff.

Rather than jumping straight to delivery, the IC team used rapid prototyping and testing to explore what would work and why.

Testing approach

To learn fast and fail smart, the team sought to validate which solutions improved perceived visibility, connection and trust among offline employees, and identify barriers to scale.

They involved:

- depot team members (across four regions)
- IC business partners
- line managers
- field supervisors.

What they did:

- low-fidelity prototypes (mocked-up posters, printed 'snapshot' sheets, simple video clips)
- show-and-tell interviews
- Wizard of Oz testing for digital functionality
- feedback captured using the 'I Like / I Wish / I Wonder / I Have an Idea' grid.

Wizard of Oz testing

To simulate the 'Shift Start Snapshot', the team created mocked-up versions of the daily update and distributed them manually to team leaders for three weeks. Each update included:

- key operational messages
- a message from leadership (video transcript or quote)
- a 'Quick Voice' question of the day (with space for handwritten responses).

Rather than building a full digital system, the IC team manually collected responses and feedback. Behind the scenes, a comms partner acted as the 'wizard,' customizing and delivering each update while gauging engagement.

WHY IT WORKED

The experience felt real to the front-line teams. By simulating the end product without the technical investment, the IC team was able to test what mattered: usability, tone and emotional resonance.

Feedback from testing

Depot team members said:

- 'I like that this came from the people upstairs – it felt more personal.'
- 'I wish we could hear more from different teams, not just head office.'
- 'I wonder if we could add birthdays or team shoutouts.'
- 'I have an idea to use this for safety reminders too.'

Line managers said:

- 'It helps me start the shift in a more positive way.'
- 'I wish I didn't have to print it myself – maybe it could come as a WhatsApp PDF?'

What they learnt

After three weeks of testing, the team held an insight workshop to synthesize findings. They mapped feedback to the adoption curve: from awareness to buy-in to behaviour change.

KEY INSIGHTS

- Simplicity and tone matter more than format.
- Local managers are critical conduits of trust.
- Personalization boosts relevance.
- Visibility without feedback loops reduces impact.

Outcome and next steps

Based on this feedback, the IC team committed to a three-month pilot of the 'Shift Start Snapshot,' delivered weekly via depot printers and WhatsApp groups. They also:

- built a mini training guide for managers
- created a submission box for shoutouts
- assigned IC business partners to support local implementation.

Key learnings

- Prototyping builds trust: it shows you're willing to test *with* people, not just launch *at* them.
- Wizard of Oz techniques can simulate tech-based solutions without the resource investment.
- Feedback loops must be baked in: 'saying thanks' and 'acting on input' increases credibility.
- IC superpowers make a difference: empathy, curiosity and influence helped the team listen, explore and co-create with confidence.

This case study highlights how People-First IC reframes the role of internal communication moving to experience design. By prototyping with intent, the team built solutions that front-line teams saw, felt and valued and laid the groundwork for meaningful, measurable change.

Testing is where feedback becomes fuel. In People-First IC, we don't chase perfection, we test, learn and adapt. When you build the muscle of prototyping and testing, you build trust. You design with, not for your people. And you scale what works, not just what sounds good. 'If a picture is worth a thousand words, a prototype is worth a thousand meetings' (IDEO.org, 2015).

From IC pro to IC experience designer

Prototyping is much more than a set of practical steps in the design process. It embodies a mindset that will transform the way in which IC pros design and deliver solutions. In a profession where we are often under pressure to deliver fast, go big and move on, prototyping invites us to pause, test and learn. And when we make the time to do this we shift our focus from launching polished IC campaigns and solutions to delivering meaningful IC experiences that are grounded in insights.

When we embrace prototyping, we move away from fear of failure or judgement and towards curiosity, creativity and experimentation. We test ideas not to defend them but to evolve them. We listen more closely and this means that we can learn more rapidly. And ultimately, we build solutions that actually work because they are shaped with the people they are meant for.

And it's here that the IC superpowers come into their own. Empathy allows us to design with people in mind. Curiosity fuels better questions and bolder thinking. Resilience helps us navigate uncertainty and let go of attachment to the 'perfect' plan. Creativity gives form to new possibilities. Influence helps us bring others on the journey. And courage gives us the confidence to test what we don't yet know.

So as you move forward from this chapter, remember: prototyping isn't a luxury, it's an essential. It's the difference between comms that land and comms that resonate. Between campaigns that are seen and experiences that are felt. And between being a communicator of information and a designer of change.

CHAPTER IN SUMMARY

- The solution space is where insight meets creativity. It's here we really make the shift from assumption to action, by designing communication experiences rooted in real employee needs.

- Ideation is a structured, collaborative process that moves beyond brainstorming, which focuses on possible solutions and what might work.

- Involving a range of people in ideation helps to not only come up with better solutions but also secures early buy-in to what comes next.

- Prototyping is a great way to bring possible solutions to life quickly and simply before investing in full delivery.

- Feedback loops are critical, prototyping encourages a test–learn–iterate mindset, where feedback strengthens solutions rather than threatens them.

- Here is where the IC superpowers come into their own, enabling IC to design experiences that resonate and drive change.

References

Bridger, E and Gannaway, B (2024) *Employee Experience by Design: How to create an effective EX for competitive advantage*, 2nd ed, Kogan Page, London

Brown, T (2009) *Change by Design: How design thinking creates new alternatives for business and society*, Harvard Business Press, Boston

Catmull, E and Wallace, A (2014) *Creativity, Inc.: Overcoming the unseen forces that stand in the way of true inspiration*, Bantam Press, London

Deci, E L and Ryan, R M (2000) The 'what' and 'why' of goal pursuits: Human needs and the self-determination of behavior, *Psychological Inquiry*, 11 (4), 227–68

Edmondson, A (1999) Psychological safety and learning behavior in work teams, *Administrative Science Quarterly*, 44 (2), 350–83

IDEO.org (2015) The field guide to human-centered design, IDEO.org (archived at https://perma.cc/T6EQ-YUUS)

Kelley, T and Littman, J (2001) *The Art of Innovation: Lessons in creativity from IDEO, America's leading design firm*, Currency/Doubleday, New York

Knapp, J, Zeratsky, J and Kowitz, B (2016) *Sprint: How to solve big problems and test new ideas in just five days*, Simon & Schuster, New York

Martin, R (2009) *The Design of Business: Why design thinking is the next competitive advantage*, Harvard Business Press, Boston

Norton, M I, Mochon, D and Ariely, D (2012) The IKEA effect: When labor leads to love, *Journal of Consumer Psychology*, 22 (3), 453–60

Page, S E (2007) *The Difference: How the power of diversity creates better groups, firms, schools, and societies*, Princeton University Press, Princeton

Richards, H (2019) *Design Thinking in Change Management: Engaging employees through co-creation* [Internal research paper]

Wujec, T (2010) Build a Tower, Build a Team (online video), TED Conferences, www.ted.com/talks/tom_wujec_build_a_tower_build_a_team (archived at https://perma.cc/Y2E4-2U3U)

10

Empathy in action: planning and delivering People-First Internal Communication

Making it happen

Over the last four chapters, we've deep dived into the world of experience design and design thinking. We've shared many of the practical tools and techniques you'll need to adopt a genuinely people-first approach to internal communication. Whether the tools and methods we've described here are completely new to you or build on ways you're already working, you're now set up for success! You've scoped, empathized, ideated, prototyped and tested. You've engaged your people and applied design thinking, mapped the moments that matter, built your activity around human experience, tested, tweaked and refined.

Now comes the part that should feel very familiar: delivery. This is where we're at our most comfortable. It's our craft. We know how to roll-out messages, build campaigns and launch initiatives. We're experts at making things happen. But here's the challenge: the old ways of delivering IC – big campaigns and initiatives, email alerts, cascade toolkits and fixed channel plans – just won't cut it anymore. Not if we're serious about People-First Internal Communication.

Delivery in a people-first world is not the final step in a linear process; it's the start of the lived employee experience. This chapter is all about helping you deliver solutions in a way that honours all the work that's come before – the insights, the testing, the human connection – and keeps people at the centre, not just in theory but in practice.

In this chapter we'll explore how to:

- Build delivery plans that reflect employee needs, not just campaign milestones.

- Make choices about channels and tactics through a people-first lens.
- Equip managers, leaders and champions to communicate with empathy and confidence.
- Stay open to iteration and feedback, even post-launch.
- Embed change by creating experiences – not just messages.

What you've designed *with* people must now be delivered *for* and *through* them. And that means rethinking not just what we deliver but how, with whom and why. Or at least recalibrating how we do what we do.

For many of us, becoming a people-first internal communicator will be less about taking a giant leap and more about dialling up some of the great things we're already doing. There are growing numbers of IC professionals who are already working in a more human-centric way. But there are many who have not yet discovered tools and techniques such as journey maps or personas, and have yet to use them to transform their work.

Now is the time to double down on our people-first principles. That means creating delivery journeys – not just deployment plans. Empowering others – not just informing them. Iterating in real time – not ticking boxes and moving on. Because when we deliver with people first, we embed behaviour, build culture and create meaningful, lasting change.

Championing an experience mindset

As we move into the implementation phase, it's vital that we keep that word, *experiences*, front and centre. This is the point at which the pressure to fall back into 'push comms' mode is at its most extreme – and at times, it'll be hard to resist.

All too often, delivery is seen as the final stage of the journey – the tactical execution of a strategic plan. But in People-First IC, delivery *is* the experience. This is where the magic happens, the moment where intentions become reality, messages and plans become experience, and where your credibility as a people-focused communicator is ultimately tested. This is where People-First IC lives or dies.

This is where many well-intentioned and perfectly planned People-First IC programmes could come unstuck. Internal communicators are world-class fixers; we excel at execution and delight in delivering solutions. However, in the context of People-First IC, this deep-seated strength can be a weakness. Because we are so solution-orientated, the temptation to shift into tick-box implementation can be hard to resist, but resist we must!

People-First IC isn't about set-piece solutions or off-the-shelf campaigns. It's not about doing what your expert learning and past experience tell you to do. It's about listening, learning and co-creating, iterating and experimenting. Our mission right now is to ensure we remain rooted in empathy, relevance and impact, even in the hustle of execution.

Superpowered delivery

It's here that you will need your IC superpoweres more than ever. The delivery phase isn't just operational, it's profoundly human. It demands much more than robust air traffic control or expert channel execution. At its best, it builds on the communicator's core human strengths:

- Empathy helps us understand what people are going through, in real time, enabling us to adjust and fine-tune our delivery. Listening isn't a once-and-done exercise; it's a constant. You'll need to stay in tune with your people as you progress and stay alert to shifts in individual circumstances and/or the 'mood' of the organization.

- Curiosity drives us to keep listening, learning and asking: 'What's really going on here?' You need to keep digging below the surface and asking insightful questions throughout the delivery phase. In the words of Stephen Covey: 'seek first to understand, then to be understood' (Covey, 1989, p. 239).

- Resilience enables us to keep on when the going gets tough or when feedback is difficult to hear. You'll need to maintain a flexible, optimistic approach as you push forward. Delivery rarely goes to plan – it's an endurance sport!

- Creativity enables us to craft and adapt comms in ways that surprise, connect and inspire – especially in low-trust or change-weary environments. You'll need to work hard to keep things fresh over time, regularly revisiting and reframing problems and recalibrating your activity to take account of changing circumstances.

- Influence helps us keep leaders, managers and advocates engaged so we can co-deliver communication in credible, compelling ways. To succeed, it's vital you keep on walking the talk during the delivery phase, demonstrating the right behaviours and showing the sceptics there's a better way.

- Courage empowers us to speak truth to power, challenge ineffective delivery tactics and push for communication that truly serves employees. You'll need to keep challenging the prevailing wisdom, push back on stakeholder demands and stay true to the principles of People-First IC.

These aren't soft skills, they're razor-sharp delivery capabilities. They underpin every decision about how, when and through whom, comms are delivered and what happens as a result. And they help IC professionals stay people-first, even under pressure. Practising these deeply human strengths makes the difference between a message that is simply transmitted and one that genuinely lands and inspires real change.

What can customer experience (CX) teach us about delivery?

When it comes to communication delivery, there are lots of moving parts. Every project is different. It could be the introduction of a new enterprise social network, the roll-out of a new strategy, bringing organizational values to life or delivering the communication workstream for a large-scale transformation programme. It's impossible for us to provide a playbook for each and every scenario, but we can provide you with a set of guiding principles. And thankfully, we have somewhere to look for inspiration.

Customer experience professionals have long understood that delivery defines perception. No matter how polished a brand's values, how well packaged the product or how creative its advertising, ultimately, customers judge a business by how it behaves in the moments that really matter: the store visit, the help desk call, the online checkout, the return or exchange when things don't go to plan.

Internal communication can take a leaf from the CX playbook. Employees, like customers, are increasingly experience-savvy – they expect a similar level of clarity, responsiveness and relevance in their workplace communication experience. They don't distinguish between internal and external experiences in the way we do; they now expect a consumer-grade experience at work.

New-Zealand's Haka House Hostels provides a powerful real-world example of these principles in action. We caught up with Haka's Kirsty Lloyd to discuss how she used an experience design approach to reimagine internal communications at the business, working hand-in-hand with employees.

REAL-WORLD EXAMPLE
Reimagining internal communication at HAKA Hostels

When Haka House Hostels underwent rapid growth – from 18 to 170 employees across 15 properties in just six months – it became clear that its small company approach to internal communication had to evolve. And fast. Against a backdrop of change, Kirsty Lloyd, Head of People and Capability, recognized the need to rethink how people across the business connected, communicated and celebrated.

With support from the Excellent's EX Design School and sister company Humankind, and a strong grounding in design thinking, Kirsty led a transformational journey to co-create a simple, human-centric communication approach that worked for everyone – from housekeepers without email to senior leaders – and could be scaled as the company grew.

Making IC fit for purpose

Prior to the redesign, internal communication at HAKA was informal and inconsistent – suitable for a small startup but not fit for a rapidly scaling, multi-site organization. As Kirsty explained: 'There were definitely areas of the business where people felt communicated with – and others where they had no clue what was going on until it was happening.'

Without a consistent system or shared expectations, critical updates were missed, achievements went uncelebrated and employee voices were often unheard. Senior leaders assumed the biggest issue was pay. But Kirsty knew assumptions weren't enough.

Uncovering the real problem

Kirsty began by applying design thinking principles – starting with deep listening and empathy. She started the project with a series of 'Know, Think, Suspect' workshops with both the leadership team and hostel managers, inviting them to reflect on what they believed employees might say about their experience.

Kirsty said: 'Most leaders assumed the team would say they wanted more money. But when I did open discovery interviews with staff, the average employee experience score was 8 out of 10. What they actually wanted was better communication and more celebration.'

This insight reframed the problem – from dissatisfaction with pay to a genuine need for inclusion, visibility and human connection.

From discovery to design: co-creating the solution

Next, Kirsty formed a cross-functional working group, including front-line staff such as IT team members and housekeepers, many of whom didn't even have email accounts. The group worked through a classic design thinking process: Define, Design, Deliver.

Kirsty utilized a variety of people-centred techniques as she worked through the process:

- Open discovery interviews involved dozens of staff members across locations and levels.
- 'How might we' questions were used to define the design challenge. For example, 'How might we create a communication framework so that we ensure consistent communication that includes all employees?'
- Paper prototyping was used to test different formats.
- Feedback loops captured input at each stage, including from those in hard-to-reach roles.
- Low-fidelity Mural boards were used for collaboration.

Despite the diversity of roles and preferences, a surprising consensus emerged: 'I thought we'd need to spend thousands on a fancy comms tool. But what they wanted was a simple newsletter emailed to their payroll address – and for some, printed and pinned up in hostels.'

The outcome: the Haka communications playbook

The final output wasn't a tool or platform – it was a mindset shift, operationalized through a communication playbook. This document:

- Set clear expectations for the frequency, tone and delivery of internal messages.
- Defined who was responsible for communicating what.
- Included multichannel delivery (email, printed newsletters, digital noticeboards, team meetings).
- Provided an ongoing feedback mechanism to improve communication iteratively.

Crucially, the playbook was embedded into onboarding and performance KPIs. Leaders were now accountable for ensuring communication reached their people – not just relying on HR to do it for them.

Kirsty said, 'There's now a shared responsibility. If people aren't hearing things, we ask: has their manager shared it with them in the way we agreed?'

Making a difference

These changes sparked a shift in culture – not just in communication.

Psychological safety has increased significantly. Staff now knew how to raise concerns, give feedback and get updates.

Employees have started contributing communication content. Newsletter submissions started pouring in from front-line staff, well-being ambassadors and leaders.

Awareness of valuable employee benefits has improved. Staff began accessing previously unknown benefits – like learning funds and policy information – simply because they were better communicated.

Leadership development was catalysed. Many participants in the co-design group showed measurable growth in their confidence, influence and understanding of the wider business – and they have started using these tools and approaches with their own teams.

Kirsty said, 'If you take those people and compare their performance to others, they're far exceeding. Because they now feel part of it.'

Reflections and advice

Kirsty's background in animation and design gave her an instinctive feel for prototyping and iteration and a natural leaning towards design thinking – but her greatest learning was around humility and trust.

She said, 'Don't make assumptions. The solution you're seeking lies with the people you serve.'

Her top tips are to:

- Get senior sponsorship early: 'You don't need every stakeholder on board, but you need at least one influential ally.'
- Be ready to get messy: 'Perfect today might not be perfect tomorrow. Just start.'
- Close the loop: 'If you ask for feedback, act on it. Don't leave people hanging.'
- Shift ownership: 'Comms isn't just HR's job – it's every leader's job.'

What's next for Haka?

The success of this project has had ripple effects across Haka. Leaders are now applying design thinking to challenges like onboarding and housekeeping standards. The annual *hui* (Māori for gathering) will shift from presentations to employee-led design workshops.

Kirsty said, 'They've seen the power of co-creating solutions. Now they want to use it in every part of the business.'

Three guiding principles for people-first delivery

The many lessons we have learnt from the world of CX have helped us develop three powerful guiding principles for delivering People-First IC that go beyond good intentions to drive meaningful action. Use these overarching principles to guide your delivery approach:

- Think journeys, not campaigns.
- Create moments that matter.
- Orchestration, not execution.

Let's explore each of these in turn.

1. Think journeys, not campaigns

Campaigns comprise a series of coordinated messages and activities, delivered over time and designed to achieve a specific goal, such as raising awareness, changing attitudes or influencing behaviours. Campaigns make use of multiple channels and are aimed at a target audience. Campaigns are built around timetables and schedules, are heavily planned and structured and usually run for a fixed period.

Today, campaign-thinking permeates nearly every aspect of internal communication practice and influences so much of what we do as IC professionals – from goal setting, planning and audience segmentation to creative work, planning and air traffic control. It is a concept that has served us well and helped us make the transition from scattergun messaging to more targeted delivery, from relaying information to driving real behaviour change, from craft to profession. But, while most of us continue to plan and deliver in this way, we believe the concept of the campaign is past its sell-by date.

The truth? Campaigns were built for another era.

In the age of People-First IC, we need to shift from campaigns to journeys, from pushing messages to shaping experiences.

The difference between these two approaches is quite profound. Campaigns are short-term, message-driven and typically designed by experts for employees. They aim to grab attention and persuade but risk being performative, disconnected from daily experience and easily forgotten. Journeys, by contrast, are people-centred, experience-driven and aligned to real moments that matter. They're co-designed with employees, integrated into day-to-day work and more likely to create lasting impact because they meet people where they are.

Delivering people-first communication means obsessing not about what we send out, but about what people experience. It means stepping into the shoes of the employee, anticipating their questions, distractions, emotional state and conflicting priorities. It means choosing the channels and timing that work for them, not for us. Whereas campaigns are designed around the message, journeys are designed around the employee.

Table 10.1 summarizes the key differences between campaigns and journeys.

TABLE 10.1 Campaigns versus journeys

Aspect	Campaign	Journey
Mindset	Message delivery	Experience design
Focus	Short-term event or intervention	Ongoing lived experience across key moments
Timing	Fixed duration (start and end dates)	Continuous or aligned to life cycle and need
Audience role	Passive recipients	Active participants and co-creators
Design process	Planned centrally by comms team	Co-designed with employees, based on real needs
Tone	Persuasive, polished	Empathetic, conversational, authentic
Measurement	Reach, awareness, clicks	Understanding, usefulness, behaviour over time
Delivery channels	Formal comms (email, intranet, posters)	Formal + informal (manager comms, peer-to-peer, EX touchpoints)
Influence strategy	Push messaging to change beliefs	Shape experience to influence feelings and behaviours
Change sustainability	Risk of one-off impact	Designed to embed change and sustain over time
Risks	Performance theatre, disconnection from reality	Requires systems alignment and more investment upfront

Why are journeys so transformational?

Shifting from campaign-thinking to journey-thinking completely changes how you deliver your internal communication programmes:

- Journeys shift the focus from outputs to outcomes, enabling IC professionals to deliver experiences that support employee success over time. They align internal communication with real-life employee moments, connecting comms to the actual challenges, questions and emotions employees face.

- Journeys recognize communication as an experience, not an event, making IC a vital part of how people feel, learn and act. They also drive consistency and coherence across touchpoints, helping deliver a joined-up rather than fragmented experience.

- Journeys encourage co-creation and empathy, helping the IC team see the organization through employees' eyes – leading to more relevant, human and inclusive communication.

2. Create moments that matter

People-First IC is about designing experiences and experiences are wrapped up in moments. By switching the focus of our delivery from messages to moments, we can create more meaningful, human and lasting connections between people and the organization.

People remember moments, not messages. Research shows that people don't remember every detail, but they do remember how they felt during key moments. The Peak-End Rule, proposed by psychologist Daniel Kahneman, suggests that people judge experiences based largely on how they felt at the most intense moment (positive or negative) and at the end of the moment (Kahneman, 2011). In other words, we don't form our overall impression of an experience by averaging every moment but by recalling its emotional highs and the way it concluded.

This explains why certain moments, such as your first day at work, how you are given negative feedback, how success is celebrated or even how you exit a company, can have disproportional influence on how you perceive your relationship with the organization. Recognizing that not all touchpoints are equal, communication at these points of emotional intensity should be more human, more thoughtful and more empathetic.

Shaping moments helps shape culture. If handled well, key moments become signals of what the organization values, reinforcing desired behaviours and mindsets more effectively than any values campaign ever could. The truth is, how organizations show up in moments that matter says more than any corporate value statement. A people-first approach ensures communication is aligned with experience, not just intent, helping close the 'say–do' gap.

3. Orchestration, not execution

In IC, execution (another widely used term we cannot abide) is about delivering content: writing messages, publishing updates and running campaigns. It's task-focused, often reactive and usually centred on getting information out to employees via established/formal channels. While execution in this sense is essential, it's only part of the picture. It tends to reinforce a view of communication as a set of isolated outputs, rather than as part of a broader experience or system.

Our alternative is orchestration, a far more strategic and human-centred approach. It means coordinating messages, channels and moments so they work together in harmony. It's inherently about people, too. Just like a conductor doesn't play every instrument but ensures the whole orchestra is in sync, the internal communicator enables others – leaders, managers, teams – to play their part. Orchestration recognizes that communication doesn't just happen through formal channels but through relationships, behaviours and informal conversations.

Making the shift from execution to orchestration elevates the role of internal communication, moving the function from being a service provider to a strategic enabler. Instead of just writing and distributing content, internal communicators become conductors of the whole communication 'system', creating coherence, enabling others, building dialogue and designing communication as a core part of the employee experience. Whereas execution is about delivery, orchestration is about creating the right conditions for communication to land, stick and inspire action.

Orchestration acknowledges that communication happens beyond the comms team, and it ensures the voices of leaders, line managers, champions, peers and others are enabled, equipped and harmonized. In a world where people trust people more than channels, orchestration means enabling trusted messengers, not just broadcasting through formal tools.

Orchestration also recognizes that organizational change is complex and adaptive. Instead of a fixed plan and outputs, it emphasizes ongoing tuning, feedback and responsiveness.

These three guiding principles capture the essence of People-First IC delivery and, between them, signal a step change in how we implement on a day-to-day basis. Seeing yourself as someone who orchestrates journeys and creates experiences and moments is truly transformational. As conductor, you realize you're never alone but surrounded by people who can help you make the music of communication. Thinking journeys shifts you from one-off delivery of stuff to shaping seamless experiences across multiple touchpoints. Where campaigns end, journeys evolve. And a focus on meaningful moments enables us to impact not just what people see and hear but how they feel, creating connection, not just comprehension.

Embedding the principles in practice

These guiding principles aren't intended as a tick-box checklist. They represent a mindset shift. Delivering People-First IC means treating employees not as an audience to be managed but as real people to be supported and enabled.

That doesn't mean abandoning rigour or strategy though. It means applying those things in the service of experience. It means testing and learning. Above all, it means caring deeply about how communication feels, not just how it looks.

Evaluation, which we'll discuss further in the next chapter, plays a crucial role in people-first delivery. When we measure what matters, not just outputs like clicks but outcomes like understanding and trust, we gain the insight needed to refine both content and delivery. This transforms communication from a broadcast function into a continuous learning loop.

In fast-paced organizations, it's easy to compromise on delivery. We meet the deadline, hit 'send', move on. But people-first practitioners ask different questions: Did this land in the way we hoped? Did it help? Did it honour the human on the other side? When the answer is yes, that's when internal communication makes a real difference.

Iteration: feature not flaw

Perhaps one of the most uncomfortable aspects of shifting from expert-led IC to People-First IC is the concept of iteration. This is the idea that we don't just deploy 'once and done', but instead constantly listen, learn and adapt as we deliver.

In CX, feedback is continuous. Products and services are constantly improved based on customer input. Similarly, in People-First IC, feedback is built into the very fabric of delivery. People-First IC delivery means evaluating impact continuously, listening before, during and after implementation, and using that data to adapt and fine-tune your activity. It means treating delivery as a learning loop. Are people engaging? Do they understand? Are we achieving the intended emotional response? If not, adapt.

To achieve this, it helps to learn to think like an anthropologist. That means approaching the organization as a complex human system, one shaped by beliefs, rituals, behaviours, power dynamics and shared (or contested) meanings. Once again, it relies on those deep human strengths such as curiosity, observation, empathy and cultural awareness to help communicators truly understand how things work beneath the surface.

WHAT IT MEANS TO THINK LIKE AN ANTHROPOLOGIST

Anthropologists are social scientists who study human beings, cultures and societies, both past and present. Their mission is to understand how people live, think, interact and make meaning of the world around them, what it means to be human and how different environments, cultures and systems shape our ways of thinking, feeling and acting.

Anthropologists are especially interested in:

- cultural practices (e.g. rituals, language, traditions, values)
- social structures (e.g. family, hierarchy, roles)
- beliefs and behaviours (e.g. what people consider normal, taboo, sacred or just)
- everyday life (e.g. how people work, relate, celebrate or grieve).

In the workplace, anthropological thinking can help internal communicators uncover the unwritten rules, hidden dynamics and lived experiences that shape how people really engage with their organization.

One particularly powerful practice is their use of ethnographic research methods – like observation, interviews and immersion – to learn from the inside, not just the outside. We discussed this in more depth in Chapter 8. Anthropologists don't just look at what people say but how they live – what they do, how they behave and what those behaviours mean.

So how can we start to operate more like an anthropologist?

Observe before advising

Instead of jumping in with a comms plan, take time to watch, listen and learn. Notice how people really communicate and interact with each other: What do they say in meetings and how does that differ to what they say in the canteen? Who gets heard? Who has influence? Who doesn't?

Understand the hidden dimension

Anthropologists look beyond what is visible in society – the formal policies and structures – to the unwritten rules and social dynamics that actually guide behaviour. In IC, this means understanding power dynamics, subcultures, influencer networks and how trust (or fear) is distributed.

Ask deeper questions

Anthropologists don't just ask what people think; they explore why. Asking great questions is a core skill for many internal communicators – use them to dig into stories, language, symbols and behaviours to reveal what really matters to people and how they make sense of their environment.

Embrace diverse perspectives

Organizations are a web of overlapping cultures and identities. Thinking like an anthropologist means accepting that there are many different realities at play – not assuming there's one unified experience or voice.

Make the familiar strange

Anthropologists often study their own culture by stepping back and treating it as unfamiliar. This lens helps internal communicators challenge assumptions, notice what's being taken for granted and design more inclusive and effective strategies.

Value lived experience over corporate narrative

Anthropological thinking prioritizes how people actually experience the organization, rather than how leaders say it works. This can expose disconnects between stated values and day-to-day reality – the so-called say-do gap – and help bridge it.

Design with empathy and insight

By uncovering what people really need, communicators can move beyond blanket messaging to culturally relevant, human-centred communication that resonates and respects.

Make it easy!

When it comes to internal communication, less is often more. Deborah Hulme highlighted the growing body of research on our limited cognitive capacity in Chapter 3 – human-centred delivery means reducing the cognitive load for employees by focusing on clarity and simplicity. When employees are overwhelmed with competing priorities, tired, unsure or confused, offering clarity in messaging is not only helpful, it's kind.

To achieve this, communication must be direct, accessible and easy to act on. Avoid vague calls to action, overly creative treatments and long-winded, dense language that only serve to distance people from the message. Instead, focus on making every interaction as smooth and seamless as it can be, from the first touchpoint to the last.

Use simple, everyday language – no jargon. Structure your information in discrete, digestible chunks and use visual elements and signposting to clarify important points. Communications should prioritize clarity over cleverness.

This relates to channel choice too. In digital delivery, ensure that all messages are mobile-friendly and accessible across devices so employees can access them whenever and wherever is most convenient for them. Provide clear, actionable next steps, and make it easy to follow through – whether it's filling out a form, attending a meeting or reading a document.

Think of your job as being to reduce the friction that often prevents employees from engaging with the content. When information is easy to consume, simple and intuitive, employees are more likely to engage and act, ensuring the message is not only heard but also understood and acted upon.

A PRACTICAL EXAMPLE: THE SYSTEM ROLL-OUT

To bring all this to life, let's consider a challenge many internal communicators are tasked with – the roll-out of a new organization-wide IT platform. This is a great example because it's part communication (there is practical information to share, messages to land) and part behaviour change (as a core work tool, it will require new ways of working). It's also strategically important for the organization.

For simplicity, we'll use two extremes here – contrasting traditional internal communication *at its worst*, and people-first communication *at its best*. In reality, most internal communicators will be operating somewhere between these two ends of the spectrum – doing some elements in a human-centred way and others in a more traditional organization-centric way. We hope, however, that this crude example demonstrates how a people-first approach leads to a very different *experience* for employees.

The first difference is when the project starts. In the past, internal communicators were invited to the table at the eleventh hour – at best, a few weeks before go-live. The message? 'Can you create some comms to announce the change?' The launch date is fixed, there's a locked-down and largely impenetrable PowerPoint deck built by the IT team and a list of 'key messages' written by the project committee.

In People-First IC, the communication professional is involved from day one – as a strategic partner, not a delivery channel. Using design thinking, the team starts with empathy – understanding pain points with the current platform via interviews, work shadowing and employee journey mapping. The communication strategy is co-developed with these insights in mind, building human needs into every step of the change.

When it comes to understanding the problem itself, the two approaches are worlds apart. In old-school internal comms, we assume the problem is already solved: 'We're implementing this because it's what the business has chosen.' There's no pushback or challenge, no exploration of whether this meets actual employee needs; we take our instructions from leaders and go deliver.

The people-first approach, meanwhile, begins with curiosity and empathy – interviews, surveys and observation are used to uncover what's frustrating or slowing people down in their current experience. The problem is reframed from 'we need to announce the new system' to 'how might we support people in doing their best work with these new tools?'

The differences continue. Armed with their brief, the traditionalists disappear into a quiet meeting room to develop their plans and materials, which are then signed off by a senior project leader without any employee input.

Meanwhile, with an experience mindset, the people-first communicators host a series of co-creation workshops where employees help generate ideas for communication formats, training approaches and messaging styles. Ideas are prioritized in these sessions using criteria like usefulness, empathy and inclusivity. It doesn't stop there. Now the draft messages, comms assets and training materials that emerged from the workshops are then prototyped with real users. What's unclear? What's missing? What works? Feedback is gathered and changes are made before wider roll-out. Here iteration is a feature, not a flaw.

By this stage, the old-school communicators are nearing completion of their journey! Following a few rounds of amendments, the timings are locked down and the 'final versions' of the comms issued via the intranet and email, with no testing or adaptation. There are a few posters placed around the building too, to maximize awareness.

In contrast, the people-first team adopts an agile, iterative approach, using feedback loops (e.g. pulse surveys, digital analytics, team check-ins) to continuously improve the experience as it rolls out, phased over time.

In one scenario, communication is delivered as a journey, in the other as a campaign. In People-First Internal Communication, the communication is human, story-driven, and supported and amplified by managers. The launch of the new system is just one milestone in a longer 'experience arc' designed around what people need, when they need it. Messaging adapts as people progress from awareness to advocacy.

For the people-first communicators, it doesn't stop there. Guided by behavioural science and human-centred learning principles, and working collaboratively with the L&D team, the people-first communicators ensure employees receive just-in-time learning, are offered a choice to reflect their different learning preferences and hands-on support is embedded into workflows. Change champions, power users and communities of practice are cultivated too, to sustain peer-to-peer learning and promote best practice over time.

When it comes to evaluation and measurement, the traditional communicators are armed with a wealth of output data (email open rates, training completions, etc.) while the people-first communicators highlight the difference all this is making to employee confidence, workflow and customer experience. Feedback is collected continuously, and insights feed back into further improvement as the journey continues.

The people-first communicators don't need to justify their existence though – their value has been evident throughout. However, measurement is baked into their approach, and they focus on assessing employee experience and impact. Are people more confident? Is their workflow easier?

The differences between the two approaches are stark – one is a journey, an experience that builds trust, improves outcomes and makes people feel valued. The other is a transactional campaign with a focus on delivering what the project team dictates is needed. At its worst, traditional internal communication is reactive, transactional and employee-blind, whereas People-First Internal Communication is proactive, participatory and human.

The blurring of boundaries between communication and change is very evident in this example. Approaching this challenge from a deeply human perspective leads us to focus on human behaviours – equipping employees to be able to use the new system, change their ways of working and improve their workflow over the long term. The journey doesn't finish when the system is switched on. In a world where change is constant, the way we communicate change is just as important as the change itself.

By contrasting the traditional approach with the people-first approach, we see that design thinking and people-first communication principles can significantly improve employee engagement, reduce resistance to change and ensure a smoother roll-out of a new system. The people-first approach creates emotional resonance with employees and ensures that communication is human-centred, making it more effective in driving successful organizational change.

Planning through a people-first lens

You could be forgiven for thinking that in the iterative, experimental, agile world of People-First IC, planning takes the back seat. But the reality is that human-centred internal comms needs to be planned and executed just as robustly as traditional internal comms.

Notice here that we're emphasizing planning over plan. This is not about the fancy document or punchy PowerPoint deck; it's about strategic thinking in action. Planning is the dynamic process of thinking, co-creating, aligning and adapting, whereas the plan is the static output. Planning is collaborative, iterative and insight-led – it's where you engage your stakeholders, clarify outcomes and think about how you'll measure success. A plan is only ever a snapshot in time. A good plan should emerge from good planning, but if it becomes too rigid, it quickly loses its value.

In People-First IC, the process of planning is slightly different to traditional IC planning. Rather than focusing primarily on the mechanics of communication – the channels, tactics, messages and timing – we focus instead on experiences. It's a subtle but transformational shift of emphasis. Think back to those three guiding principles – this is about intentionally planning those journeys and moments. For us, planning is an active, iterative process that starts at the very beginning of the design process, with deep listening and insight gathering. In People-First IC, planning is a collaborative undertaking – co-designed and co-delivered with employees and with stakeholders who don't just sign off your plan, but shape it with you.

Ultimately, it's about mapping the overall experience – including key moments and emotional touchpoints – not just sending stuff out. It's about prioritizing personas, not segmenting audiences. It's about choosing channels based on audience need and viewing people as a primary channel. It's about using constant dialogue and feedback to adjust your activity in real time. It's about embedding flexibility, not being driven by a schedule.

It won't come as a surprise that this echoes the experience design process we've shared in previous chapters – planning isn't a prelude to the real work; it is the real work. If you've worked through the previous chapters, you'll have already completed much of the traditional work of planning as part of the overall people-first journey. That spirit of co-creation, so central to the design process, should extend into the delivery phase as well, by involving employees in both the planning and delivery of your programme.

Pulling it all together: recalibrating the traditional IC plan

Our stakeholders still expect to see a plan and they want something concrete to review – we totally get that! So how do we capture all this in a document we can share? The good news is it's not an enormous leap to reshape your traditional IC plan into something that's fit for purpose. It's just a question of emphasis.

TABLE 10.2 Recalibrating the IC plan: what's in and what's out

What's in	What's out
Moments that matter	Rigid calendar plans
People journeys and needs	Channel-led thinking
Delivery through people	One-size-fits-all messaging
Co-owned delivery (not just IC doing all the doing)	Communicator as gatekeeper
Flexibility and iteration	Cascade-only thinking

We need to recalibrate our plans to make them people-first. For us, planning and delivery are two sides of the same coin. Good planning sets up human-centred delivery. So let's walk through each section of the People-First IC Plan.

1. PURPOSE STATEMENT
We start with a crisp, clear articulation of why the communication is happening, from the angle of both the business and the employee. This dual

perspective is vital as it anchors the plan in shared value, setting the tone and direction for everything that follows.

2. INSIGHT SUMMARY

Next comes a synthesis of employee input from your listening activities (surveys, interviews, feedback) and a summary of the insights you've gleaned from elsewhere. Its role is to ensure the plan is grounded in evidence-based reality, not our assumptions.

3. PEOPLE EXPERIENCE

Here we capture the intended mindset, emotional response and behavioural outcomes for employees. Put simply, this is where we shift the focus from what we want to say to the experience we're aiming for.

4. EMPLOYEE JOURNEY AND MOMENTS

Hardwiring your plan to the employee journey is a key point of difference with traditional communication planning. Mapping the key points in the employee experience where communication adds value, drives an experiential approach and helps connect comms to lived experience. It ensures timely, meaningful interventions that support key transitions or pain points.

5. EMPLOYEE PERSONAS

We discussed the power of behavioural personas in Chapter 8. These are empathetic profiles representing employee needs, context and preferences. Including personas shifts us away from surface-level audience segments based on role, grade or location, towards something much more real and human. They encourage a more inclusive approach and support personalization and tailoring.

6. STRATEGIC OBJECTIVES

Here we define the 'why' behind communication efforts. It outlines the specific outcomes the plan aims to achieve, both for the organization and crucially, for employees. These objectives are not about messages or channels (outputs), they're about change: in awareness, understanding, behaviour, culture or trust (outcomes).

7. KEY NARRATIVE THEMES

The difference between key narrative themes and the more traditional 'key messages' is subtle but significant. While key messages focus on what we say, narrative themes focus on why it matters. They provide the emotional and strategic backbone of people-first communication – helping employees connect the dots, see meaning and feel part of something bigger. These aren't discrete facts or points to convey but rather bigger ideas and storylines that help shape understanding. Rather than focusing on what needs to be said, they focus on what needs to be felt, believed and acted upon.

8. CHANNEL STRATEGY

Here we're in familiar territory! But, in a People-First IC Plan, the channel strategy section is fundamentally different – focused on access, relevance, trust and experience, rather than logistics, reach, or convenience. This isn't about what we can control as gatekeepers, but about delivering in a way that reflects the reality of employees. It's about prioritizing people-based channels (line managers, champions, team discussions) and ensuring delivery happens where employees are most likely to engage with them. It's not about what's available, it's about what's accessible, trusted and human.

9. DIALOGUE AND FEEDBACK LOOPS

Feedback isn't an afterthought; it's part of the conversation. Here we capture the vital mechanisms for listening during delivery – the key to making communication a shared, two-way experience rather than a one-way broadcast. This isn't about an optional post-implementation survey, but rather how we bake listening into the everyday. It takes place before, during and after the communication and makes use of both formal and information listening channels. It treats employees not as an audience but as co-creators of meaning.

10. ROLES AND RESPONSIBILITIES

This section defines who is responsible for creating, delivering, supporting and reviewing communications. It recognizes that People-First IC doesn't belong to and can't be controlled by one team but is co-delivered by the organization – through line managers, peer networks and leaders. The section makes shared ownership explicit, ensuring that everyone involved knows what they need to do to create a trusted, human-centred communication experience – and that they have the support they need to do it well.

11. EVALUATION APPROACH

This is where we focus on demonstrating our value. It blends data with dialogue and helps IC earn its place as a strategic, empathetic contributor to employee experience. We'll discuss measurement and evaluation more in the next chapter.

Each of these sections plays a distinct but interconnected role in building your People-First IC Plan. Together, they ensure that communication is not only aligned with business needs but truly designed for and with the people it aims to serve.

You can use the following People-First IC Plan template as a basis for your own plan, but don't be afraid to adapt it for your specific circumstances. There's no single best way to do this – it's about finding what works for you and your organization.

PEOPLE-FIRST INTERNAL COMMUNICATION PLAN TEMPLATE

Use this template to build a communication plan that puts people – not just processes – at the centre. It's designed to be flexible, co-created and grounded in real employee insight.

1. Purpose statement

Why are we communicating? What's the shared business and employee value? For example, 'To support our organizational change by helping employees feel informed, involved and confident about what's coming next.'

2. Insight summary

What have we learnt from employees so far? What do they need, feel, or find challenging?

- [Key themes from listening sessions or surveys]
- [Direct quotes that capture sentiment]
- [Known barriers to understanding, trust or engagement]

3. People priorities

What do we want people to *think*, *feel* and *do* as a result of this communication?

4. Employee journey moments

What are the key points in the employee experience that we need to support?

5. Audience personas

Who are we communicating with, and what do they need?

6. Strategic objectives

What outcomes are we trying to achieve – for the organization and for employees?

- [Organizational goal #1]
- [Employee experience goal #1]
- [Behavioural or cultural shift goal #1]

7. Key narrative themes

What are the consistent messages or ideas we want to reinforce across all communication?

- [Theme 1 – e.g. Transparency / Purpose / Togetherness]
- [Theme 2 – e.g. Empowerment / Support / Shared success]

8. Channel strategy

Which channels will we use – and why?

9. Dialogue and feedback loops

How will we listen and respond during delivery?

- [Pulse survey questions]
- [Check-ins or listening sessions planned]
- ['You said, we did' moments]
- [Space for open dialogue or reactions]

10. Roles and responsibilities

Who is involved in delivering this plan?

11. Evaluation approach

How will we know it's working? What does success look like?

From planning to delivery – communicating through people

DELIVERING THROUGH PEOPLE

When it comes to putting all this into practice, a key step is to make a conscious choice to deliver through people wherever possible. People-First IC plans are co-created with employees. But if delivery is then controlled rigidly from the centre, the sense of ownership quickly evaporates. Delivery must mirror the inclusivity of planning.

Research highlights that most of what employees believe comes from what they see and hear around them – from managers, peers and informal, impromptu conversations. The Edelman Trust Barometer (Edelman, 2023) reports that employees are four times more likely to trust information from their immediate manager than from a senior executive – a clear signal that human delivery matters more than polished messaging.

People-first delivery shifts the role of internal comms from 'gatekeeper' to 'enabler'. This requires an increased focus on equipping others to bring the comms to life. That might be line managers holding meaningful conversations with their team members, team champions facilitating Q&As or peer advocates sharing their lived experiences.

This means giving teams autonomy to adapt messages for local relevance. It means trusting leaders and champions to deliver in their own words. It means allowing for dialogue, not just dissemination. We need to see every communication as an opportunity to build trust, empathy or belonging – or to damage it.

Tone matters. So does humility. So does genuine human presence. And it can be much more impactful when messages are delivered through people, rather than by email, text message or newsletter.

Framing a message with empathy and humility ensures that employees feel respected and heard. When communicating difficult news, honesty and transparency build trust, while celebrations of success should feel genuinely personal, rather than automated, acknowledging the collective effort and pride that goes into a shared achievement.

It may seem obvious, but People-First Internal Communication is about human connections – tapping into the powerful informal social networks, peer-to-peer influence and trusted relationships that naturally exist within teams and across the organization. At its core, every piece of communication is about being human, showing up authentically, acknowledging emotions and responding with respect.

People-First IC means prioritizing people, not just as contributors, but as collaborators. This isn't about IC doing everything. It's about empowering others to communicate well. Of all the decisions we make as we move forward with delivery, this one is arguably the most critical – clarifying the role that people need to play. And there's a lot to think about.

The magic in the middle

Line managers play a pivotal role as communicators. When they deliver messages locally with credibility, empathy and authenticity, it will often be far more effective than top-down, one-size-fits-all business-wide messages.

As the interface between senior leadership and front-line employees, managers often have the most direct access to teams and the greatest influence over 'everyday experience'. They are largely responsible for translating strategy into action by making the big picture meaningful for teams and individuals, and also provide an 'emotional filter' by sheltering their teams from unwelcome noise or distractions.

Research by Gallup (2020) has consistently found that managers account for around 70 per cent of the variance in employee engagement. And Edelman's Trust Barometer (Edelman, 2021), found nearly 60 per cent of employees trust their immediate supervisor over other channels of communication.

Of course, none of this is new. We have known about the importance of line manager communication for decades and yet, in Gallagher's 2024 State of the Sector (2024) report, 60 per cent of respondents reported that people managers' communication skills were below expectations. If ever there was a time to focus on line manager communication, this is it.

INFORMAL NETWORKS AND PEER-TO-PEER INFLUENCE

Informal social networks, the very real but often invisible web of human connections in the workplace, often carry more weight than formal communication channels because they are based on trust. Echoing the same dynamic we see outside work – what we call the 'Trip Advisor Effect' – employees are increasingly likely to listen to and trust 'someone like me' than to an official communication coming from the corporate communications team or C-suite executive they have never seen in person.

According to a study by McKinsey & Company (McKinsey, 2012), informal networks are two to five times more effective than formal communication channels at transferring knowledge and aligning employees with the company's goal. Peer-to-peer influence is one of the most powerful drivers of behavioural change inside organizations.

This idea aligns with Dr Leandro Herrero's concept of Viral Change, which emphasizes that change within an organization is most effective when it spreads organically through social networks, rather than mechanistically through the hierarchy (Herrero, 2008). Herrero argues that rather than relying solely on formal, top-down communication, change initiatives should harness the power of informal networks and influential individuals to accelerate adoption. According to Herrero, 'change is not something you manage; it's something that is created by the interactions and behaviours of individuals' (Herrero, 2015, p 19). When peers lead by example and share their experiences, they become change agents who foster engagement and inspire others to adopt new behaviours, thus creating a more sustainable and widespread transformation across the organization.

A study published in the *Harvard Business Review* (Knight, 2018) supports this, highlighting that peer-led initiatives often lead to higher engagement levels because they feel more personal and less hierarchical. These individuals are seen as less 'corporate' and more in tune with the concerns and preferences of their colleagues, making them trusted sources of information.

Creating a conversation culture

In People-First IC, we shift the emphasis from messaging to conversation and recognize that, even in the age of AI, talking is the lifeblood of the organization.

Research by Gallup (2016) shows that organizations that engage employees through regular conversation are more productive and innovative. Regular dialogue also helps employees feel heard and valued, which enhances their commitment and motivation. Encouraging managers and peers to regularly check in with employees – whether through one-on-ones, team meetings or informal catch-ups – creates an ongoing feedback loop that strengthens relationships and improves the quality of communication.

Equipping leaders and managers to be able to lead conversations that focus on active listening, empathy and respect, and that foster a culture of psychological safety, is a vital part of our future roles. Creating a workplace climate where people feel safe to communicate openly, share their thoughts and be vulnerable in front of each other is key to ensuring successful communication through people.

KEY TAKEAWAYS

- Trust: Employees trust their colleagues and managers more than formal, top-down messages, making peer-to-peer communication a uniquely powerful tool.
- Engagement: Two-way communication fosters engagement, innovation and commitment by making employees feel needed, valued and heard.
- Empowerment: Providing employees with the tools and knowledge to communicate effectively – whether through managers, peers or communities – ensures messages resonate and builds lasting change.
- Authenticity: Messages from credible, authentic voices are more likely to land and inspire action than impersonal or overly corporate messaging.

Shifting the emphasis

By communicating through people, IC professionals can create a more connected, engaged and trust-based culture, where messages don't just flow top-down, but are embedded in the relationships and networks that already exist within the workplace. And when you switch the focus from formal channels to human connections, you start to see just how many opportunities we have to make a difference to the lived experience.

This approach can make your job easier and more fulfilling, too. Rather than being a lonely, under-resourced, overworked IC expert, the people-first internal communicator is actually blessed with a rich and diverse support network that is just waiting there for you to activate it. Leaders, managers, champions and communities – all of these are available right now to tap into as part of your people-first approach!

In the age of AI, this is where we should be spending the bulk of our time – not on managing formal channels or crafting campaigns, but on the deep human work of delivering through people.

So where do formal channels fit?

We are not saying that the formal channels of communication have no place in People-First IC – far from it! As we stated at the start of this book, the process factors remain vitally important – we just need to be more intentional in our use of them. Rather than defaulting to what is easiest and most controllable from the centre, think instead about the nature of the communication and the needs of employees.

If you need to communicate something simple and urgent, like the fact that the lift at head office isn't working, then a well-placed poster is a fantastic option! Targeted at those who are impacted, it points the way to the staircase or alternative lift. Job done. But if you're trying to introduce a new way of working and need to change behaviours, a poster will never be enough.

Intentionality extends to the style and content of communications too – and there are numerous opportunities to inject more humanity into our channels and content. We asked Nick Andrews, business development director at Sequel Group and a former chairman of Communicators In Business (now the IOIC), to share his thoughts around making content more human.

REAL-WORLD EXAMPLE
Making it happen: design to delivery

BY NICK ANDREWS

Great internal communication should create meaningful and creative experiences for employees, so why do so many internal comms plans fail to recognize the need for human-focused channels and campaigns?

Some might say it's because hard-pressed IC managers don't have the time or budget to create moments that matter, but that is an easy cop-out; a best-in-class plan carves out time and resource to ensure communication appeals to the hearts and minds of a diverse employee base.

For me, that means any meaningful IC plan is based on a matrix of job roles, channels and – crucially – the elements that will truly engage colleagues from the shopfloor to the C-suite.

So, yes, the plan needs a structure and a framework for reference. Your C-suite will want to see evidence that you have something robust in place. And members of any IC team need a set of KPIs against which their success will be measured. Without that measurement and a clear demonstration of value add, it's unlikely that future budget and resource will 'set you free' to do what you want to do.

But within that structure, there needs to be freedom. Freedom to be creative, to have fun and to communicate in a way which recognizes and taps into the way people across an organization behave.

Too many companies still persist in producing the status quo of 'tick box' comms with a lack of heart and wonder why their employees don't feel excited about their role.

Central to this is a reluctance or inability to reflect the needs of the audience. After more than 40 years in this industry, I remain part amazed and part depressed by the lack of interest or understanding in and of the people we are here to serve.

In my early days editing a magazine for factory workers making teabags for a household manufacturer (clue – chimps were involved in their advertising), I was informed by the PR team managing the magazine that they had never visited a factory. It was almost a badge of honour.

And even to this day, a sizeable number of communicators do not take the time to 'walk in the shoes' of the people they are trying to engage with. How are we going to build a culture of people-first, human-centred communication if we don't build relationships across the business?

Get out there. Talk to Dave who makes widgets every day. Take a ride with Sharon who delivers goods to customers. Spend some time with Martin managing a team of sales reps. Ask to shadow an exec for a day. Try to understand what the IT team really think! You get the picture – by being part of these different worlds, you'll build your own picture of how your organization operates and how you can truly make a difference. Without actually talking to the people you're communicating to, your IC plan is based on hunch, supposition and a repeat of what's gone before.

Consider, therefore, the disparate audiences who need to feel that your communications plan has been created with them in mind.

Do your leaders believe that you understand their vision and can present it in a way which means they come across as authentic? Do your line managers have the tools they need to explain the corporate objectives in a way which resonates with their teams.

Is the shopfloor community able to easily understand why this 'head office noise' not only applies to them but can help them to get more job satisfaction and feel they are part of something with purpose? Are your customer-facing employees able to use the information you share with them to act as ambassadors for the business, able to articulate what makes the organization better than your competitors?

And does your network of comms champions – you need one, by the way – feel empowered and excited enough to be the bridge between you and the rest of the business?

If you're able to answer yes to these questions, it means you'll have taken considerable time out to truly understand the way they work, the obstacles they face and the comms they need to do their job to the best of their ability.

It also means you can tailor your comms tactics to engage hearts and minds in a way which makes the corporate messages interesting.

And that means using the wide range of tools and channels available to appeal to those different audiences with content that grabs attention and makes the process more personal (and even fun!).

Any of the following might work for you, depending on your organization. Consider:

- People-first email newsletters, magazines and films telling stories with humans at their heart.
- Using employees to create user-generated content at all levels, e.g. the diary of a senior exec, a guided tour of a factory.
- Making use of the interactive elements of your intranet, e.g. community and special interest groups.
- Using new technology to bring the best elements of consumer communication to the internal environment, e.g. apps, digital walls, instant feedback/polling.
- Running events with a difference, e.g. hackathons, touring expos, themed-based weeks.
- Beefing up your recognition schemes and celebrating those people making a difference.
- Involving the family and friends of your people, e.g. through open days, bringing a relative to work.
- Making more use of internal and external social media, showcasing those employees who are the characters that truly represent the organization.
- Enlisting representatives from across the business to help shape your comms.

And as part of your IC plan, don't be afraid to try new things. And occasionally fail. At a time when internal communicators are (again) under pressure to prove their value, and against a backdrop of AI and the rise of the robots, there's a compelling need to demonstrate empathy, intelligence (in every sense of the word) and agility.

Above all, be human...

But I'm the expert! Changing how we show up

Finally, one of the most challenging aspects of People-First IC delivery is that it requires us to let go and open ourselves up to co-creation and iteration. The age of expert-led IC is over, as AI ushers in 'accessible expertise', our deep subject matter knowledge is devaluing rapidly.

The commoditization of expertise fundamentally changes what makes an internal communicator valuable. Many of us, the authors included, have built our entire professional reputations and careers around knowledge. We have spent years (many decades in our case!) reading, learning, studying, conducting research, sharpening our specialist knowledge and training others. We've contributed to industry think tanks, served time on committees, written books, articles, blogs and more – we have become bona fide experts in our field. But now, anyone armed with a mobile phone and an ability to ask good questions, can tap into our entire collective wisdom in seconds! This is a deeply uncomfortable truth, but denial is not the answer. The answer is to find a new source of value.

In the early 2000s, we came across the work of David Maister and specifically the book *The Trusted Advisor*. At the heart of the book is the notion that being a deep subject matter expert and being a trusted advisor are two very different modes of operation. Two decades on, it's more relevant than ever.

In simple terms, an expert offers solutions based on specialist knowledge and skill – they are the go-to person on a particular topic. Sound familiar? A trusted advisor, on the other hand, spends their time building strong relationships, earning trust, asking questions, listening deeply and tailoring advice to context.

According to Maister, 'the advisor's job is to be helpful, providing guidance, input and counselling to the client's own thought and decision-making processes' (Maister, 2005).

When you think about what's required to be a great advisor – as opposed to an expert – you quickly realize that it's not about knowledge at all, but rather about deeply human strengths like emotional intelligence, contextual understanding and mutual respect. It's about co-creation, shared ownership and long-term capability-building.

Trusted advisors strike a balance between advocating for their clients' best interests and providing objective advice. They offer independent perspectives, challenge assumptions and present alternative solutions when necessary. As Maister says: 'People rarely trust you because you're smart. They trust you because you're emotionally intelligent and consistently show you're on their side' (2000).

In practice, this underlines the need to strengthen those six IC superpowers and, in particular, hone our coaching and facilitation skills. Areas to focus on are your ability to ask better questions, to enable reflection, to support the growth of others, to create safe spaces for dialogue and to help groups think and act together – the very capabilities that underpin People-First IC.

Over the last decade or so, we've started to see the term 'trusted advisor' appear in an increasing number of ads for senior HR, internal comms and engagement roles. It's already a highly valued way of operating for anyone whose role it is to advise senior leaders – but now it becomes core to our future-proof professional skill set.

Letting go of your expert status isn't about diminishing your professional experience – it's about redeploying it in more human, more powerful ways. Once again, it is human strengths that distinguish future-ready practitioners. In the age of AI, value lies not in knowing, but in enabling. Be the guide, not the hero.

Delivery at scale: using AI to power People-First IC

Building trusted advisor relationships takes time and in the past, that is something internal communications have lacked. But, in the age of AI, we have a gifted and always-alert companion who can free us up to focus on people and supercharge our delivery.

AI enables us to scale communication and deliver the right message, to the right person, at the right time. But People-First IC ensures that message is worth receiving. When we combine these forces thoughtfully, we move from communication delivery to creating communication *experiences* – and that's where the real impact lies.

There are so many ways AI can support People-First IC delivery and the use cases are expanding every day. Here are just a few of the ways you can utilize AI right now:

1. Personalization at scale

- AI can tailor comms based on role, location, behaviour or preferences.
- Example: An AI agent sends a summary video to a front-line worker, while a manager receives a leader briefing with talking points tailored to their team's feedback trends.

People-First IC means **meeting people where they are.** AI helps us do that – without burning out the comms team.

2. Real-time adaptation

- AI can track how messages are landing in real time (open rates, sentiment, engagement) and recommend and implement changes in real time.

- Example: If data suggests uptake is low in one region, AI prompts a local leader nudge or content tweak.

This allows delivery to become a **live experience,** not a static campaign.

3. Supporting managers and leaders

- AI can coach managers and leaders with just-in-time nudges, draft templates or feedback.
- Example: 'Your team hasn't heard from you in eight days. Here's a quick message draft you could personalize.'

This helps scale *human delivery* by giving your front-line communicators the tools, confidence and support they need to succeed.

4. Automated experience orchestration

- AI can help coordinate message sequencing, timing and format across complex delivery journeys.
- Think of AI as your **orchestration engine** – ensuring harmony between comms, not noise.

But remember that while AI can optimize delivery, only you can design an experience that feels *real, relevant and human.*

Your role as an IC professional is to guide the **tone, timing and truth** of the message – ensuring every touchpoint builds trust and connection, not just efficiency.

AI AS CO-PILOT IN PEOPLE-FIRST DELIVERY

Designing and delivering a truly People-First Internal Communication experience requires a blend of human empathy, creativity and judgement – augmented by AI-enabled scale, personalization and responsiveness.

In Table 10.3, we've captured some of the many tasks that are required to plan and deliver People-First Internal Communication – then we've split out the activity to show how AI can be utilized as a delivery partner.

TABLE 10.3 Partnering with AI on planning and delivery

Task	Human	AI
1. Strategic direction	Define the communication purpose, experience vision and desired behaviours.	Provide trend analysis and identify communication gaps from past data.
2. Audience insight	Use personas, empathy maps and journey mapping to define needs and context.	Analyse audience behaviour and sentiment data to refine segmentation.
3. Messaging	Set tone, emotional nuance and storytelling structure.	Draft first-pass messages and adapt content to tone and audience preferences.
4. Channel planning and orchestration	Determine ideal moments and messenger roles (e.g. peer vs leader).	Optimize delivery timing, suggest best-performing channels and sequences.
5. Empowering communicators	Coach leaders and managers, role-model communication behaviours.	Provide AI-generated talking points, nudges and suggested responses.
6. Personalization	Ensure relevance and inclusivity based on audience insights.	Tailor messages based on role, geography or communication style.
7. Listening	Facilitate qualitative feedback loops and surface emotional responses.	Track sentiment and engagement in real time, flag drop-off points.

This stack outlines how both human and AI can work side-by-side to create delivery that is not only efficient but emotionally intelligent and experience-driven.

AI enables us to scale communication and deliver the right message, to the right person, at the right time. But People-First IC ensures that message is worth receiving. When we combine these forces thoughtfully, we move from communication delivery to creating communication *experiences* - and that's where the real impact lies. Adopting a human-centred approach gives us direction. AI gives us pace, empathy and efficiency. Together, they help us deliver internal communication that makes a difference.

AI doesn't replace the human side of IC, but it does free us up to double down on it. While AI handles some of the mechanics of delivery, we can focus on designing moments that matter.

Delivery as experience

Ultimately, People-First IC isn't about pushing messages – it's about shaping experiences. It means letting go of the control-at-all-costs campaign mindset we've been trained in and instead thinking in journeys. It means stepping back from execution and stepping up to orchestration. It means moving from content creation to experience design, from knowing to feeling, from telling to enabling others.

When we focus on the moments that really matter, we stop chasing attention and start building something deeper – trust, commitment, engagement. When we think like anthropologists, we see the organization through the eyes of our people – not just the lens of leadership. And when we design with empathy, relevance and intention, communication becomes more than noise – it becomes a force for good.

CHAPTER IN SUMMARY

- **This is the experience**: In People-First IC, delivery isn't the ending, it's the experience. It's where empathy, intention and planning become real for employees.

- **From campaigns to journeys**: Campaign thinking is outdated. People-first delivery is built around *journeys* that meet people where they are, designed with their needs in mind.

- **Design moments that matter**: Focus on emotive moments – like onboarding, feedback or exits – and the everyday experience – to influence how people feel, remember and act.

- **Orchestrate, don't execute**: IC's role isn't to push content, it's to *orchestrate* a system of communication, empowering others to deliver with empathy and impact across formal and informal channels.

- **Deliver through people**: Employees trust people more than corporate channels. Equip, empower and support them to bring messages to life with authenticity.

- **Plan the experience, not the output**: People-first planning is iterative, collaborative and based on deep insight. It's about shaping *experiences* – not just messaging schedules.

- **Iterate relentlessly**: People-first delivery is not one-and-done. Treat it as a live process – listen, adapt, improve. Think like an anthropologist to uncover hidden needs, norms and signals.

- **AI as co-pilot**: AI can help personalize, sequence and optimize communication – but it's human strengths that ensure communication is meaningful, trusted and emotionally resonant.

- **Shift from expert to enabler**: People-First IC dismantles the expert model. The future-ready communicator is a facilitator, coach and trusted advisor – co-creating and enabling others, not controlling every message.

People-first delivery isn't a tactic. It's a shift in mindset – a commitment to meet people where they are, with what they need, in a way that respects their time, intelligence and fundamental humanity. And that's what makes internal communication not just effective – but deeply meaningful.

References

Covey, S R (1989) *The 7 Habits of Highly Effective People*, Free Press, New York

Edelman (2021) 2021 Edelman Trust Barometer, www.edelman.com/trust/2021-trust-barometer (archived at https://perma.cc/2J66-EAKW)

Edelman (2023) Edelman Trust Barometer 2023: Special report – trust in the workplace, https://www.edelman.com/sites/g/files/aatuss191/files/2023-08/2023-Edelman-Trust-Barometer-Special-Report-Trust-Work.pdf (archived at https://perma.cc/7ULQ-WLAS)

Gallagher (2024) State of the sector 2023/24: Internal communications and employee engagement, www.ajg.com/-/media/files/gallaghercomms/gcommssite/state-of-the-sector-2024.pdf (archived at https://perma.cc/U6LP-W73E)

Gallup (2016) State of the global workplace, www.gallup.com/workplace/238079/state-global-workplace-2017.aspx (archived at https://perma.cc/5JJ9-8LGN)

Gallup (2020) State of the American manager: Analytics and advice for leaders, www.gallup.com/services/182138/state-american-manager.aspx (archived at https://perma.cc/UJN6-VFM5)

Herrero, L (2008) *Viral Change: The alternative to slow, painful and unsuccessful management of change in organisations*, 2nd revised ed, Meetingminds Publishing, Buckingham

Herrero, L (2015) *Homo Imitans: The art of social infection: Viral Change™ in action.* 2nd ed, Meetingminds, UK

Kahneman, D (2011) *Thinking, Fast and Slow*, Penguin Books, London

Knight, R (2018) How to increase your influence at work, *Harvard Business Review*, 16 February, hbr.org/2018/02/how-to-increase-your-influence-at-work (archived at https://perma.cc/A8F6-446T)

Maister, D H (2005) Do you really want relationships? davidmaster.com/articles/
do-you-really-want-relationships (archived at https://perma.cc/XX8P-73SH)

Maister, D H, Green, C H and Galford, R M (2000) *The Trusted Advisor*, Free
Press, New York

McKinsey Global Institute (2012) The social economy: Unlocking value and
productivity through social technologies, www.mckinsey.com/industries/
technology-media-and-telecommunications/our-insights/the-social-economy
(archived at https://perma.cc/U49H-PBSK)

11

Measuring what matters

Let's be honest: measurement is something internal communication (IC) pros are often challenged by. In their *State of the Sector 2024* report, Gallagher highlight the ongoing struggle with measurement and data literacy, with their research finding a lack of analytics and measurement to be one of the top five barriers to IC success. This is nothing new; demonstrating impact and value has often eluded the IC profession. Back in 2019, CIPR Inside, in partnership with the Institute of Internal Communication (IoIC), published their *Measurement and ROI for Internal Communication* report. In it, they explored the ongoing challenges IC pros face when measuring their work and demonstrating return on investment (ROI). Their findings included:

- A strong perception that effective internal communication positively impacts organizational performance and productivity.
- A lack of consistent frameworks and standardized metrics across the IC profession.
- Practitioners often struggle with measurement due to time, budget constraints and the qualitative nature of communication outcomes.
- The absence of clear ROI evidence undermines IC's credibility and influence at the senior leadership level.

The report proposed a framework for measurement, with the authors calling for a cultural shift in the profession towards strategic measurement. And yet here we are many years later and little has changed.

But here's the truth: if we want to demonstrate the real value of internal communication, we need to measure what really matters. And we believe that the People-First IC approach can help us to do this. The problem is that measurement in IC often ends up as an afterthought, something we scramble to justify after the work is done, usually by counting the easy stuff like clicks and likes. But these surface-level metrics don't tell us whether we've actually made a difference, and they don't earn us credibility with our stakeholders.

When it comes to measuring deeper, more meaningful outcomes, many IC pros struggle. Why? Because in the traditional IC approach, we often move straight to solutions, without getting clear on the problem we're trying to solve or what success looks like. And this can help explain why meaningful measurement is a challenge – because we've skipped the vital first steps. We've jumped straight into solution mode – launching a new intranet, planning a town hall, running a campaign to 'embed the values' – without stopping to ask why. What's the problem we're trying to solve? What change are we trying to create? Without clarity at the start, meaningful measurement at the end is almost impossible.

The people-first approach flips this. It bakes measurement into the process right from the start. That's where the people-first approach makes the difference. It holds your hand through the process, starting with the scoping phase and opportunity framing. Instead of rushing to solutions, we slow down and get intentional. We ask better questions and in doing so, we get crystal clear on the outcomes we're after. Once you know the specific shift you're trying to create, whether that's improving trust, increasing confidence or changing behaviour, it becomes far easier to measure it. By focusing first on people, their real experiences, needs and barriers, we can get super clear on our objectives. And when we know exactly what we're trying to shift, we're in a far better position to track whether we've actually achieved it. Rather than relying on metrics, such as clicks and open rates, we can start to track what really matters. In People-First IC, measurement isn't an afterthought, it's part of the design from day one.

Let's reframe what measurement means and make it meaningful.

Why measure

We all know that communication matters. But for years, internal communication professionals have struggled to prove just how much, especially when it comes to anything beyond the basics. While clicks, views and email open rates are easy to count, they rarely tell us whether we're making a meaningful difference. Measuring deeper outcomes like trust, clarity, behaviour change, connection or belonging has often felt more difficult. But what if the real challenge isn't measurement itself but how we're working in the first place?

When IC is treated as a delivery function, brought in late to push out comms or run campaigns, there's rarely the clarity or context needed to measure impact or outcomes. We're often unclear on exactly what the problem is we're solving, what change we're trying to create, or even who it's really for. So we default to what's easy to measure, rather than what matters most.

The People-First IC approach changes this. It bakes measurement into every stage of the process. From the start, we ask better questions, like 'How might we improve trust in leadership in order to increase confidence during change?' and therefore we get clearer on our objectives. We focus on outcomes, not just outputs. And that makes it much easier to track whether we're actually making a difference.

We can begin to explore what ROI in internal communication might look like. That might mean linking strategic communication activity to business outcomes like employee retention, engagement, well-being, customer satisfaction or even productivity. For example:

- Poor communication is a key reason people leave their jobs. If IC plays a role in reducing voluntary turnover by improving onboarding or manager communication, that's a measurable cost saving.

- A clear, consistent narrative during change can reduce resistance, improve understanding and increase speed of adoption, all of which impact productivity.

- Equipping line managers with better communication tools can improve team connection and trust, leading to higher engagement and performance.

Here are some examples of the types of useful data points that support this kind of thinking:

- 82 per cent of employees stay longer at companies with strong onboarding and 70 per cent are more productive (Glassdoor, 2015).

- 50 per cent of employees have left a job because of poor management communication (Gallup, 2015).

- 61 per cent of employees have considered leaving their job due to poor internal communications, with 26 per cent identifying it as a major factor in their decision-making process (Staffbase and USC Annenberg School for Communication and Journalism, 2024).

This isn't just theory. John Kotter and James Heskett's (1992) longstanding research into culture found that companies with strong, aligned cultures, supported by effective internal communication, outperformed their peers dramatically:

- Revenue grew 4× faster.
- Stock prices increased 12× faster.
- Profits climbed by 750 per cent.

In a people-first approach, internal communication isn't just a way to share news; it's a strategic lever that shapes culture, connection and performance. And when we take the time to scope properly, define clear outcomes and measure meaningfully, we can show the real return of effective internal communication.

REAL-WORLD EXAMPLE
A worked example: reducing early attrition through People-First IC

Imagine your organization is facing high turnover among new employees; many are leaving within the first six months. It's expensive, disruptive and a clear sign that something isn't working. The average cost to replace an employee is estimated at over £12,000 once you factor in recruitment, onboarding, training and lost productivity. Multiply that by dozens or even hundreds of new starters each year, and the financial impact is significant.

A scoping activity, using the People-First IC approach, digs beneath the surface. Through interviews, empathy maps and journey mapping, the team uncovers a common theme: new hires feel disconnected. They don't understand how things work, where to go for information or how their role fits into the bigger picture. Line manager communication is inconsistent, and there's no clear narrative helping them feel part of the culture. What they were promised during the interview process doesn't match their reality. They feel like outsiders and so they leave.

Instead of defaulting straight to solutions like an 'onboarding comms pack', the People-First IC team reframes the problem:

'How might we help new employees feel connected, informed and part of the organization in order to improve retention in the first six months?'

With this focus, the team co-designs a new communication experience for onboarding. It includes:

- a structured 90-day communication journey that supports each stage of the new hire experience

- a digital onboarding hub with clear pathways for getting started
- personalized messages from leaders and peers at key moments in the first six months
- tools and scripts for line managers to help them welcome and integrate new team members
- regular check-ins and feedback loops to continuously improve the experience.

Because the problem was scoped clearly, measurement becomes straightforward. The IC team partners with HR to track:

- voluntary turnover in the first six months
- time to productivity
- new hire engagement scores
- qualitative feedback from new hires on their early experience with the company
- manager feedback on onboarding communication quality.

After six months, early attrition has reduced by 25 per cent. Based on the average cost per leaver, this translates into an estimated cost saving of £250,000 for that period alone. And that's before factoring in the improved engagement and reduced pressure on hiring teams.

This is what return on internal communication looks like. When we are clear on the problem we're solving and design intentional communication experiences, we can have a real and measurable impact, not just on people but on the business.

What are we measuring?

When we're clear on the problem we're trying to solve, understanding how to measure success becomes easier. At some point during the design process, you'll want to define clear objectives, to give your work direction and to ensure it aligns with wider business priorities.

Defining decent objectives can take time. A simple and effective framework for setting measurable objectives is the OKRs model, which stands for objectives and key results. Originally developed at Intel by Andy Grove and later popularized by John Doerr (2018) through his work with companies like Google, it's used by organizations around the world to clarify direction and measure impact. Setting OKRs helps to ensure we're really clear about what we are doing and how we'll know when, and if, we're successful. The beauty of this approach is in considering how you'll measure your objectives it ensures that the objectives you set are more likely to be meaningful. If you're struggling to understand how you'll actually measure the objective, described in the key results, then the objective probably isn't right in the first place. The people-first process helps with this too, because the clearer you are on your why, the easier it is to define the what.

While the OKRs approach is simple and powerful, to put it into practice often requires some serious thinking and discussion time, but it is a really critical process to go through. Once you have your OKRs in place, the direction is clear and the plan comes together – everyone understands what they need to do and how they'll know when they get there. In summary:

- Your objective is what you want to achieve – the people-first goal.
- Your key results are how you'll measure whether you've achieved it, the tangible, trackable indicators of success.

Let's take a few examples of what this might look like in internal communication:

Objective: Improve the onboarding communication experience to reduce early attrition.

KEY RESULTS

- 30 per cent reduction in turnover within the first six months
- 85 per cent+ positive feedback on onboarding experience survey
- 90 per cent of new hires say they understand how their role contributes to the company strategy
- Employee Net Promoter Score (eNPS) of 75+ among new joiners

Objective: Equip people managers to communicate more confidently and consistently during change.

KEY RESULTS

- 70 per cent increase in manager confidence scores (pre/post survey)
- 60 per cent decrease in 'lack of communication' comments in employee feedback on the change
- 20 per cent improvement in change adoption speed

These objectives and key results are more than a list of metrics; they're a reflection of meaningful, people-led goals. Where possible, they link internal communication directly to business outcomes like retention, engagement and performance. And they give communicators a much stronger voice at the table.

Using the OKRs approach as part of the people-first framework is also a great way to unpack big, conceptual objectives and make them more tangible. Rather than trying to reverse-engineer a strategy from a vague IC vision, we start by understanding people's experiences, scoping the real opportunity, and setting clear objectives that reflect both organizational intent and what matters to employees.

One of the reasons internal communication has struggled with meaningful measurement is that we often start with statements that sound inspiring but are hard to pin down. Goals like 'engage our people in bringing our values to life and help create the culture to make it happen' might sound impressive but what does this actually mean? What would success look like? And how on earth would we measure it?

This is exactly the kind of challenge the People-First IC approach is built for. Rather than jumping to campaigns or cascading messages, we go deeper. We explore what the real problem is, and what experience people are actually having, not just what we hope they're having. Let's work through this step by step.

We start with scoping

We begin by gathering insights. In this example, let's say a recent employee survey revealed that while people can name the values, they don't *see* them lived and breathed in the organization. There's a disconnect between what's said and what's done, and people have noticed. So we start by mapping the current experience. We explore where employees should be encountering the values: during onboarding, in team meetings, through recognition, in decision-making, etc. We look at what the current experience actually feels like in each of those moments.

Then we co-create a future-state vision: What would it look like if our values were truly part of the culture? What would people be seeing, hearing and feeling? What would leaders and peers be doing differently?

This becomes our north star – a grounded, people-shaped picture of success.

Then we explore the opportunity and reframe

Next, we use empathy mapping to dig deeper. What are different people thinking, feeling, saying and doing when it comes to values and culture? For example, new hires, front-line managers, longer-tenured employees and leaders?

From there, we develop a set of 'how might we' questions to guide ideation. Here are some examples:

- How might we help people recognize and celebrate our values in action, every day, so that we build pride and reinforce a consistent culture?
- How might we make it easier for managers to role-model the values in a way that feels real, so that their teams feel inspired and supported to do the same?
- How might we bring our values into moments that matter – like onboarding, 1:1s and performance reviews – so that they shape meaningful experiences and decisions?
- How might we turn our values into behaviours that are visible and meaningful to everyone, so that they guide daily actions and strengthen trust across the organization?

Next we ideate and prototype

From these questions, we generate ideas, collaboratively, creatively and with the end-user in mind. Maybe we land on:

- a values storytelling programme, with employees sharing real examples in their own words
- a recognition platform that links shout-outs to specific values
- a toolkit for line managers to bring values into team conversations and decisions
- a reworked onboarding journey that introduces values not as words on a wall, but as real behaviours people can expect.

We test and prototype these ideas, quickly and lightly, with the people they're designed for.

Then we define objectives and key results

Through this process, we naturally arrive at much clearer objectives and measurable outcomes. That big, conceptual goal becomes something we can actually work with. For example:

ORIGINAL STRATEGIC GOAL

Engage our people in bringing our values life – and help create the culture to make it happen.

PEOPLE-FIRST IC OBJECTIVE

Embed our values more meaningfully into everyday employee experiences, so people see and feel them as part of our culture.

KEY RESULTS

- 30 per cent increase in employees who say they see the values in action day-to-day (pulse survey).
- 70 per cent of managers use the new values conversation toolkit within the first three months.
- 20 per cent increase in values-related stories submitted to internal channels.
- 85 per cent of new hires report understanding how the values show up in team behaviours (onboarding feedback).
- 15 per cent decrease in comments about 'values not being lived' in employee feedback.
- 90 per cent of performance reviews include documented examples of how employees demonstrated company values in their work (reported through HR systems or manager audits).

Now, we've gone from a lofty aspiration to a clear, people-led strategy. We know what success looks like. We know how to track it. And we've built it on real insight and collaboration, not assumptions. By moving through this process, we start to see the real shape of our work and understand how we'll know if it's working. We're not just aiming to 'create culture' in the abstract. We're tracking real signals that show whether it's happening.

This is the power of the People-First IC approach. It takes the conceptual and makes it concrete, not by reducing the ambition but by designing it with people in mind, from the start. This approach doesn't just make communication better; it makes it measurable. And when we can measure what matters, we can demonstrate value, secure buy-in and have far more impact.

The beauty of this approach is that it builds measurement into the work from the start. Rather than trying to prove impact after the fact, we define success early, and we design our work with the end in mind. In People-First IC, setting objectives isn't a bureaucratic step, it's a powerful part of the process that helps us deliver real, measurable value.

How to measure the impact of People-First IC

Your OKRs are the best place to start when it comes to measuring the impact of the work you do. In the People-First IC approach, these outcomes are defined early in the process, so by the time you get to evaluation, you already have a clear focus on what matters.

Measurement isn't just about proving value after the fact. It's about learning, adapting and continuously improving. And when IC is treated as a lived experience, something people are part of, not just recipients of, the way we measure also becomes more human, more meaningful and more aligned with real outcomes.

We use a simple framework to evaluate the impact of internal communication, aligned to three levels:

FIGURE 11.1 Process/impact/outcome measurement framework

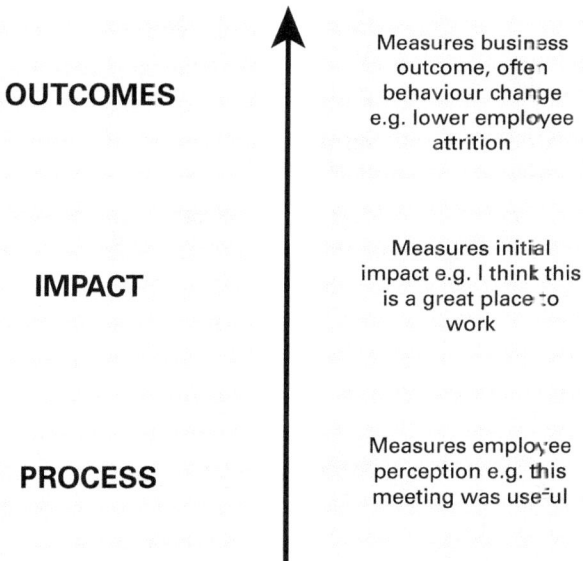

OUTCOMES

Measures business outcome, often behaviour change e.g. lower employee attrition

IMPACT

Measures initial impact e.g. I think this is a great place to work

PROCESS

Measures employee perception e.g. this meeting was useful

1. Process evaluation

This looks at how people experience the communication itself; for example, was it clear, useful, respectful of their time and context? This is an assessment of employee perceptions. It focuses on the perception of their IC experience, whether or not it was positive. Examples of process questions could include:

- The information shared in the session was clear and relevant.
- I had opportunities to ask questions or give feedback.
- The briefing session was a good use of my time.

2. Impact evaluation

This assesses the immediate effects of the communication, such as changes in understanding, clarity, confidence or alignment. Example questions could include:

- I understand the purpose behind this change.
- I feel confident explaining our strategy to others.
- I believe the decisions being communicated are in line with our values.

3. Outcome evaluation

This measures longer-term shifts in behaviour, sentiment or business outcomes that internal communication aims to influence. These are the indicators that often matter most to leadership, and they show how communication connects to organizational performance. Example measures might include:

- Increase in engagement scores across teams.
- Higher uptake of new processes or behaviours.
- Decline in 'poor communication' as a reason for attrition in exit data.

Choosing the right methods

Once you're clear on what you're measuring, the next step is to decide how to measure. You don't always need a large-scale survey; sometimes the richest insight comes from a small group discussion or an informal feedback loop. The method you choose should reflect the question you're trying to answer.

Table 11.1 provides a quick comparison of quantitative and qualitative methods.

TABLE 11.1 Quantitative and qualitative methods

Approach	Quantitative	Qualitative
Objective	To track measurable changes and trends across a large group (e.g. improved understanding, reduced confusion).	To explore how people feel, what's working or not, and why communication is (or isn't) landing.
Methods	Surveys, polls, pulse checks, usage stats, analytics.	Interviews, listening groups, empathy mapping, observation, open feedback.
Sample	Larger, often representative.	Smaller, targeted and purposeful.
Data	Numbers, trends, tracking change over time.	Stories, insights, context, nuance.

Methods you might use

Depending on your objectives, you might consider:

- online pulse surveys
- face-to-face or virtual listening groups
- one-to-one interviews or manager feedback sessions
- in-the-moment feedback tools (e.g. during events or campaigns)
- observation (e.g. how meetings are run, how leaders communicate)
- existing data from HR, engagement platforms or even comms channels
- comments from exit interviews or onboarding surveys.

Increasingly, tech tools can support this work, from real-time feedback apps to AI-powered sentiment analysis. But no matter how advanced the tool, your best guide is always your purpose. Don't be dazzled by dashboards if they aren't giving you insight into what really matters.

MEASURING YOUR IMPACT: TURNING COMMUNICATION INTO BUSINESS VALUE

In People-First IC, we don't just measure what was sent or seen, we measure whether it made a difference. Did it create clarity, confidence or connection? Did it lead to people doing something differently?

Measurement starts by going back to your objectives. These should have been shaped early in the process, through scoping and stakeholder conversations. Now you ask: How will we know if we've achieved what we set out to do? And remember, if it's difficult to answer, your objectives might not be tangible enough. Strong objectives naturally point to measurable results.

Example measurement plan

Communication challenge

You've been asked to support a major transformation programme – the organization is shifting to a new operating model. Previous change efforts have faltered due to confusion, inconsistent messaging from leaders and a lack of employee trust in the process.

People-First IC objective

To create a clear, confident and consistent communication experience that enables people to understand, engage with and adopt the new operating model.

PROCESS MEASURES (PERCEPTION OF COMMUNICATION)

- The comms I received about the transformation were clear and consistent.
- My concerns and feedback were acknowledged during the change process.
- I knew where to find reliable information and updates about the transformation.

IMPACT MEASURES (IMMEDIATE EFFECTS)

- I understand why the transformation is happening and what it means for me.
- I believe these changes are right for the organization.
- I trust that leaders are making thoughtful, transparent decisions.

Outcome measures (longer-term impact):

- 30 per cent increase in change understanding and confidence scores in quarterly pulse surveys.
- 40 per cent decrease in 'mixed messages' or 'unclear direction' comments in employee feedback.

- 20 per cent faster adoption of new processes or tools (measured via ops/HR systems).

- 15 per cent improvement in team-level performance KPIs in impacted areas within six months.

Taking this approach can help you to embed measurement into your communication planning, not as a tick-box exercise but as a meaningful reflection of the change you're working to create.

Rethinking the IC audit: from one-off check-in to ongoing curiosity

In traditional internal communication, the IC audit is often seen as the moment we learn how we're doing. An audit is a temperature check that's meant to guide decisions for your IC strategy, but they only tend to be run every few years, if that, given the time and expense involved in conducting them. But in a People-First IC world, that's not how we operate.

We don't wait for an occasional IC audit or even the results from IC-related questions in the annual engagement survey, to tell us what's working. We're constantly listening, and we're intentionally curious by design. Every part of the process, from scoping to prototyping and iteration, is built around gathering insight, seeking feedback, involving people and staying close to the real experiences of our people.

That said, a structured IC audit can still play a valuable role, so long as we are clear that the insights provided are only one piece of the puzzle. We have had considerable experience of running IC audits for large organizations all around the world. So we know that when used well, an audit can offer a helpful, independent view of your current communication landscape and highlight patterns or blind spots you might otherwise miss. It can be particularly useful:

- When you're new in role and need a baseline view.

- When you're refreshing your IC strategy and want evidence to inform your direction.

- After major change or disruption, as a 'reset' moment like the appointment of a new CEO.
- When leadership is asking for 'proof' or a more formal review of the comms function (though by this stage it may be too late to be useful!).

A well-designed IC audit can:

- Identify which elements of the IC approach support, or get in the way of, a good IC experience.
- Help you understand what's really happening 'on the ground'.
- Explore how people really feel about communication – not just what they receive.
- Assess the maturity of your IC approach and establish how near or far you are from being people-first.
- Identify IC moments that matter that for your people.
- Reveal mismatches between what leaders think is happening and what people experience.
- Uncover whether line manager communication is working or not.
- Help you prioritize quick wins and longer-term shifts.
- Capture both the current state and the culture around communication.

Auditing with a people-first lens

Traditional IC audits have typically focused on the 'nuts and bolts', looking at how and what we communicate. They evaluate channel use and effectiveness, test message delivery and if we're lucky, explore line manager communication and employee voice. While these areas are still important, the People-First IC approach calls for a broader, more human-centred way to understand how communication is actually experienced. We recommend using your audit not just to check what's being said or sent but to assess how it's landing, how it's shaping culture and what it feels like to be on the receiving end of internal communication.

Before you start your audit, it's essential to get really clear on the purpose. Are you aiming to inform a new strategy? Evaluate the impact of a campaign? Or understand cultural gaps? Audits come in many shapes and sizes, but whatever the scope, we strongly recommend broadening your lens to explore the experience of internal communication, not just the mechanisms.

When approached through the People-First IC lens, the audit becomes less about the standard channel review and more about understanding the

IC experience. This is where real insight lives. It's a snapshot in time, but it's also a chance to pause, reflect and re-centre around your people. The **People-First IC audit** reimagines the process, shifting the focus from *what's being sent*, to *how communication is felt, used and acted on*. It's less about coverage and consistency, and more about clarity, connection and impact. Table 11.2 summarizes the key differences between the traditional IC audit and a People-First IC audit.

TABLE 11.2 Traditional IC audit versus People-First IC audit

Aspect	Traditional IC audit	People-First IC audit
Primary focus	Channels, volume, frequency, accessibility	Experience, outcomes and alignment with people's real needs
Questions asked	'Did employees receive the newsletter?' 'Are messages consistent?'	'Did this communication help you feel more confident/informed?' 'What does a brilliant IC experience look and feel like for you?'
Methods used	Surveys, analytics, channel reviews	Mixed methods: empathy mapping, interviews, pulse checks, observation
View of success	Efficiency of delivery, aligned messaging	Clear outcomes, changed behaviour, improved employee experience
Use of data	Metrics-focused: clicks, opens, readership	Insight-focused: perceptions, feedback, emotional and cognitive response
Tone	Diagnostic, compliance-driven	Exploratory, human-centred, iterative
Strategic use	Often used to defend budget or validate current strategy	Used to inform, evolve and co-create future strategy

Some principles to keep in mind:

- Make it part of a wider listening strategy. The audit isn't your only insight source – it complements your ongoing curiosity.
- Use mixed methods. Combine surveys, interviews, listening groups and existing data (like channel metrics or engagement results).
- Frame the questions around people's experiences. Move beyond 'did you receive it' to 'did it help you feel more confident, informed or included?'
- Share back the findings transparently. People are more likely to participate in audits if they see their input leads to action.

A one-off audit won't fix poor communication, but it can spark reflection, reveal surprising patterns and inform change. When used as part of a People-First IC approach, it's a helpful way to deepen understanding, generate strategic insight and build a richer picture of how communication is really experienced in your organization. And you can take elements of the audit that uncovered rich insights and start using them much more regularly.

Your guide to designing a People-First IC audit

This guide provides a structured, people-first approach to running an IC audit. It combines best practice audit areas along with a framework to evaluate intent, implementation, perception and outcomes. It also addresses key experience layers and contextual relevance to your organization.

1. MAPPING INTENT TO OUTCOME

Corine Boon (2019), Associate Professor at the University of Amsterdam and Director at the Amsterdam People Analytics Centre, recommends making the distinction between intentions, what is actually implemented, employee perceptions and outcomes. Inspired by her framework, this section will help you to identify gaps between what you *intend* to communicate and how it is *actually* experienced by employees. Put simply:

- Intended: What are we trying to do, e.g. provide a consumer-grade IC experience for induction or make it easy for people to find the information they need quickly and easily.
- What is actually implemented: An induction programme.
- Perceived: This is essentially the experience, and how your people experience what you offer, e.g. that was a fantastic induction experience. You can evaluate how near or far the reality of the IC experience is from the intended IC experience.
- Outcomes: What happened and what was the result, e.g. employees are more likely to stay now we have this new induction and their engagement is higher.

Mapping intent to outcome is a powerful tool because it shifts your IC audit from being a checklist of activities to a strategic exploration of impact. It helps you design a smarter, more people-first audit by getting really clear on what you're auditing. For example, rather than just checking if employees read the weekly newsletter, you might ask questions to evaluate the IC experience and assess the outcome. Using this lens helps us to move from activity-based questions to experience and impact-based ones.

Mapping outcome to intent also reveals any gaps between what's intended and what's perceived. Questions here will look at how near or far the IC experience is from what was intended. Mapping intent to outcome helps you uncover:

- where things are being lost in translation
- what parts of the comms ecosystem aren't landing or resonating
- where perception and outcomes don't align.

Your audit can then probe those specific areas, e.g. '*What messages from leaders feel most (or least) authentic?*'

This framework also enables you to move beyond counting beans. Switching from 'how much' to 'how well' involves developing questions that seek to understand shifts in motivation and behaviour. This mindset elevates your audit from a usage report to an impact evaluation.

Taking this approach also supports a focus on experience-based design. When looking at intent to outcome, we might develop empathy-based questions to understand what this is really like for people and flag any missed opportunities to improve the experience.

And finally, when we use this framework, it naturally guides us to select the right methods to gather insights, for example, a survey to understand perception, focus groups to explore why something isn't landing and analytics to check whether behaviours have shifted.

Here is a worked example.

TABLE 11.3 Mapping intent: worked example

Dimension	What it means	Example 1	Example 2 (Onboarding)
Intended	What are we trying to do or achieve through our communication?	Provide a consumer-grade IC experience.	Deliver a brilliant onboarding comms experience that connects people to our values.
Implemented	What have we actually done?	Implemented an AI tool to personalize the comms experience – think Netflix for IC.	Created a two-week onboarding comms journey with videos, welcome events and manager guides.

(continued)

TABLE 11.3 (Continued)

Dimension	What it means	Example 1	Example 2 (Onboarding)
Perceived	How do employees experience what we've delivered?	'I really feel like the company understands me and what I need to do my job.' 'I'm relieved I no longer have to spend time wading through content and old emails to find what I need.'	'It felt rushed.' 'Videos were useful, but I still felt overwhelmed.'
Outcome	What happened as a result?	Productivity improved and significant increase in employees' perceptions of IC at the company.	Retention only slightly improved but confidence in values increased. Team feedback still suggests gaps.

2. COMMUNICATION EXPERIENCE LAYERS

Thinking about the different layers of IC experience (adapted from Emma and Belinda's book *Employee Experience by Design*) is a valuable thinking tool to design an IC audit because it ensures a more holistic and people-first approach. Rather than focusing solely on channels or outputs, it helps explore how communication is actually experienced across different dimensions. From basic access and clarity (hygiene), to key employee lifecycle moments (often overlooked in IC), everyday cultural signals and deeper motivational drivers like purpose and pride. By structuring your audit around these layers, you can identify gaps, generate richer insights and uncover how communication truly shapes the employee experience. For example:

TABLE 11.4 Exploring communication experience layers

Experience layer	What to explore	Example questions
Hygiene factors	The basics people expect. For example, channels and content.	Do I have access to the information/tools I need? Is comms accessible and timely?

(continued)

TABLE 11.4 (Continued)

Experience layer	What to explore	Example questions
Life cycle comms	Key IC touchpoints and moments that matter across the employee life cycle. For example, onboarding comms, comms around performance management.	Did onboarding comms help me feel welcome? Do comms around performance management make sense?
Everyday IC experience	Culture and daily connection. For example, values, purpose, employee voice and line-manager comms.	Does our comms reflect who we say we are? Does my line manager communicate our purpose effectively with me?
Mindset and motivation	Belief and contribution. For example, what role does the employee play as an active member of the organization?	Do I see how my work connects to the bigger picture? Can I make a difference here?

3. CONTEXTUAL CONSIDERATIONS

Remember to tailor your audit to reflect your organization's strategy, brand and priorities. For example:

- In customer-centric organizations: Do employees understand and live the customer promise?
- In tech organizations: Are digital tools usable and enhancing communication?
- In values-led organizations: Are values visible in how we communicate and make decisions?

4. PEOPLE-FIRST AUDIT FOCUS

In addition to the guidance above, the following areas provide further inspiration to help you explore the IC experience:

- What is the current communication experience like, from the employee's perspective?
- What makes that experience positive or frustrating?
- How important is this experience to employees?
- What would an ideal experience look and feel like?
- Are our intentions and outcomes aligned?

- What beliefs or behaviours are shaped by our communication right now?
- What would need to shift for better outcomes?

Designing great audit questions is both an art and a science. Don't underestimate the skill and insight needed to develop questions that are meaningful, unbiased and actionable. Fortunately, AI tools can now help with crafting and testing questions, giving communicators more confidence in how they gather insight.

Worked example: a People-First IC audit in action

CONTEXT

A global logistics company has been through a period of significant change – a merger, a tech roll-out and a new leadership team. The IC team suspects communication is no longer landing as intended, with signs of disengagement and rising attrition in front-line roles. Leadership requests an internal communication audit to help 'get things back on track'.

STEP 1: CLARIFY THE PURPOSE

Before launching the audit, the IC team defines its purpose:

Audit goal: Understand how employees across the business are experiencing internal communication post-change and identify where communication is helping or hindering trust, clarity and connection.

STEP 2: DESIGN A PEOPLE-FIRST AUDIT

They use the **Intent → Implementation → Perception → Outcome** framework to guide their design. They also map communication experience layers (hygiene, life cycle, culture, mindset).

METHODS USED

- Eight listening groups (front line, HQ, people managers, leaders, remote workers)
- Online pulse survey (20 questions, experience-focused)
- Empathy mapping sessions (focusing on line manager communication and remote workers)
- Review of comms metrics (open rates, intranet use)
- Thematic analysis of exit interviews and engagement survey comments

STEP 3: EXAMPLE OF INSIGHTS SURFACED

TABLE 11.5 Example audit insights

Theme	What employees experienced
Mismatch in moments that matter	IC team prioritized town halls and quarterly cascades. But employees said these felt too abstract and removed from their day-to-day. What *really* mattered were the small, informal moments: weekly stand-ups, shift handovers and manager 1:1s – where clear communication was often missing or inconsistent.
Emotional experience of comms	Employees described feeling *spoken at* rather than *spoken with*. Communication felt polished, generic and 'corporate' – not human or relevant. As one front-line worker put it: 'It's like they're talking to someone else, not me.'
Access vs usefulness	While communication was technically 'accessible' (on the intranet or via email), many employees didn't have the time or habits to check in with these sources. The most useful comms were short, verbal updates from team leads, but these were inconsistent and lacked structure.
Intended message vs perceived reality	A senior leader's video explained the benefits of the transformation, but in listening sessions, employees said they felt confused and anxious. The intent was motivation; the impact was mistrust – largely because key questions ('Will my job change?') were unanswered.
Clarity gaps at key transition points	Employees consistently flagged that communication was worst at critical transition moments: before role changes, during team restructures or when systems went live. These were high-stakes moments with low support, the opposite of what the IC team had assumed.

STEP 4: OUTPUT: FROM FINDINGS TO ACTION

The audit led to a powerful, insight report that didn't just summarize activity; it told the real story of how communication was experienced across the organization. It highlighted blind spots, reframed priorities and provided clear direction for a more human-centred, impact-driven internal communication strategy.

STRATEGIC SHIFTS IDENTIFIED

1 **Refocus on 'moments that matter'**
   Prioritize communication at key transition points (e.g. role changes, restructuring, new system roll-outs), rather than relying solely on scheduled, top-down comms moments. Design communication journeys around employee touchpoints, not organizational calendars.

2 Shift from cascade to conversation

Move away from the assumption that a well-polished cascade = alignment. Instead, equip line managers to have meaningful, two-way conversations. Introduce briefing toolkits, quick comms primers and structured Q&A support.

3 Design for real access, not just availability

Recognize that 'available on the intranet' is not the same as 'useful in the flow of work'. Simplify, shorten and repackage key messages into bite-sized formats that work in front-line and time-poor contexts – think floor huddles, shift briefings, mobile formats.

4 Humanize the tone and build emotional clarity

Strip back jargon. Move from performative messages to transparent, empathetic communication that directly addresses the concerns people actually have. Be real, even when the answers are imperfect.

5 Embed measurement into key comms moments

Introduce lightweight feedback loops for high-impact comms moments, e.g. pulse questions after team briefings or quick sentiment polls during change. Use real-time insight to continuously adapt.

6 Redefine the role of the IC function

Evolve from 'content creator' to 'communication experience designer'. IC becomes a strategic enabler, shaping the conditions for trust, clarity and connection across the employee journey.

THE IMPACT

By shifting from a traditional audit to a people-first lens, the IC team didn't just uncover gaps, they reconnected with the lived experience of employees. The insight gathered helped move from assumptions to evidence, from broadcasting to designing, and from content delivery to genuine impact. The resulting strategy was not only more relevant and trusted, it also repositioned internal communication as a core driver of culture, change and employee experience. In short, the audit didn't just measure comms, it provided a mandate to transform it.

Building muscle in data literacy and analytics in IC

In Chapter 4, we argued that data literacy and analytics are no longer optional skills for the IC pro; they are fast becoming essential. The ability to interpret, question and act on data is what elevates IC from a tactical function to a strategic one. Let's be clear, most of us working in IC are not, and may never be, data scientists, and that's OK. Being data literate is about having the confidence and capability to ask the right questions, work out what the data is telling you (and what it isn't) and know how to turn insight into action. Adopting a people-first approach naturally helps you build these skills because it's about curiosity, listening, sense-making and iteration. The process invites you to explore what really matters to people, develop hypotheses, test ideas and learn from what the data reveals. Over time, using this approach not only improves your IC practice, it strengthens your data literacy muscle in a way that feels grounded, purposeful and human.

In the context of measuring IC, data literacy might look like:

- Understanding the difference between lead and lag indicators.
- Knowing how to interpret survey data, feedback trends and open text responses.
- Being able to read basic HR dashboards and extract relevant IC insights.
- Asking 'what does this data really tell us about the experience?' rather than jumping to conclusions.
- Identifying significant relationships between communication experience and outcomes (e.g. onboarding comms and early attrition).

While you don't need to know everything, you do need to know when to collaborate and seek deeper expertise. This might involve partnering with:

- people analytics teams for strategic data on engagement, attrition and productivity
- IT or digital workplace leads for platform analytics and usage data
- HR and L&D colleagues for feedback and performance insights
- external research or insight agencies if deeper data analysis or benchmarking is needed.

In addition, AI can now play a powerful role in IC measurement and insight. It can help you:

- Design smarter surveys that avoid bias and deliver more meaningful responses.
- Analyse large volumes of feedback (e.g. open text from listening groups or exit interviews).
- Spot patterns or sentiment in real time from pulse data or social tools.
- Generate visual summaries or dashboards that help you tell the story of your impact.

Rather than replacing your judgement, AI gives you faster access to better insight – freeing you up to focus on what matters most: listening, sense-making and designing more human-centred communication experiences.

FROM NOISE TO NOTICED: PERSONALIZED INTERNAL COMMS POWERED BY DATA AND AI

Chris Manning is an HR and workforce transformation consultant with deep expertise in shaping experience-led people strategies and transformation programmes. He specializes in designing operating models, digital solutions and data-driven insights to drive organizational performance. Here, Chris shares his thoughts on how AI, analytics and intelligent systems can offer radically new possibilities for IC pros.

Internal communications (IC) as a function and capability has reached somewhat of a paradox. Organizations have never had more channels to reach their people, yet employees have never felt more overwhelmed, disengaged or unheard. The average worker reportedly receives 120 emails a day, juggles half a dozen collaboration tools and still misses what matters most in the mix of it all.

Meanwhile, employee expectations are more demanding than ever, especially post-pandemic and with Gen Z in play. People want more than information; they want meaning and purpose. Two subjects deeply personal. They want to be seen, understood and communicated with as individuals, not job roles. In the age of Netflix, Spotify and Amazon, the benchmark isn't the corporate intranet. It's consumer-grade personalization and frictionless experiences. IC, much like the rest of the enterprise, hasn't kept up with external customer experience innovation around hyper-personalization through data.

Traditional IC models today can't meet these demands anyway. They rely on mass messaging, hierarchy and broadcasting tactics. These approaches assume relevance can be engineered through creative copy and a basic channel strategy. But they fail to answer a fundamental question: *What makes this message matter to this specific person right now?*

This is where internal comms faces its inflection point. AI, analytics and intelligent systems now offer radically new possibilities. We can finally shift from one-size-fits-all comms to individualized experiences designed around data, behaviour, sentiment, tone and context. But most IC functions aren't structured, skilled or equipped to deliver this future. Yet!

So what's the result? Employees generally tune out. Quick skim (if you're lucky) and a muscle-memory delete. Trust and care erode. Critical messages get lost in the noise. IC loses its value, and not because its mission isn't aligned, but because its delivery methods are outdated.

So how can IC use data and AI to create personalized, human-centred experiences that cut through the daily organizational noise, build trust and meet employees where they are at that very moment in time?

We need to reframe IC as a *data-driven experience engine* linked to the very fabric of the enterprise – a function that uses technology to scale empathy, design for individual journeys and enable meaning-making in real time. This isn't about automating copywriting or adding chatbots. It's about architecting comms from the vast riches of employee data at our disposal, while enabling preferences and amplifying moments that matter.

Here's what that looks like in practice.

1. Start with data, not assumptions

Today's IC is still relatively reactive. Annual plans and themes may be pre-planned, but they're often sidelined by emerging leadership priorities. New campaigns are based on instinct, not insight into what employees care about or how they engage. That has to change.

Take this use case: one global energy firm integrated behavioural analytics into its IC platform. By tracking open rates, scroll depth, click paths and sentiment responses, it segmented its workforce into six dynamic engagement personas. Comms were then tailored by persona, resulting in three times higher engagement with safety bulletins and policy updates.

Workday, Microsoft Viva Insights and Qualtrics EX now offer employee listening and behavioural analytics that can feed real-time comms targeting. So ask yourself:

- What signals do we have about employee attention, sentiment and preference?
- Are we using data to shape the *why*, *what* and *when* of our comms?

2. Design for journeys, not just messages

Great communication doesn't exist in a vacuum. It's part of a dynamic experience. Yet most internal comms are static. AI can help us stitch together communication journeys that anticipate need, context and timing.

A US government department recently rolled out an AI-powered onboarding journey using a low-code platform. Based on role, location, manager and prior experience, new joiners received nudges, videos and policies spaced out over 45 days. Comms adapted dynamically based on user behaviour. The result was a

40 per cent increase in early engagement and a 20 per cent drop in early attrition. This is experience design, not content planning. There are lots of available tools out there, too. Journey orchestration tools like Salesforce Marketing Cloud, Adobe Journey Optimizer and even simple Power Automate flows can deliver this today with the right configuration and integration.

3. Make AI your analyst, not your ghostwriter

AI can now generate IC content in seconds. But the opportunity isn't just speed. It's augmentation. Think of AI as your pattern spotter, insights synthesizer and experiment enabler.

A leading recent use case saw a professional services firm use GPT-based tools to test message variants across different employee groups. AI flagged which tone, format and structure resonated most, then auto-generated suggestions for future iterations. This created a feedback loop between comms and employee preferences. The result wasn't just better copy. It was continuous improvement based on real employee behaviour. If you want to build trust and care, then crowdsource it. And if you want to augment that, combine AI generation with human review to ensure your tone stays empathetic and culturally attuned. Use AI to scale what you do best.

4. Build a personalization engine

It would be amazing if enterprises today had a fully integrated 360-degree employee view and a data engine to hyper-personalize end-to-end experiences. But until that capability exists, we have to build organically. And you *can* start small. Even basic segmentation by role, location, tenure or learning style can transform impact. Take the Microsoft Graph, for example. You can leverage its data to dynamically personalize weekly updates based on roles, locations, seniority, location and team. Imagine the engagement uptake from that opportunity alone. It's already at your fingertips (Azure users).

Imagine if your comms adapted like Spotify:

- 'Because you're leading a new team...'
- 'Since you've just relocated...'
- 'As part of your career goal to become a people manager...'

The holy grail is real-time personalization based on intent and context. It's taking the LXP (learning experience platform) concept of integrated learning experiences and applying it to IC.

5. Redefine the IC skillset for the AI era

This shift isn't just technological. It's cultural and human. The future IC team looks less like a newsroom and more like a cross-functional product squad, blending empathy, design thinking, data literacy, AI fluency and behavioural science. Think of it as moving from your traditional roles of comms manager, copywriter and digital comms analyst and towards an IC journey designer, a comms data analyst, an EX product owner and an AI content orchestrator. It's less 'feels', more 'facts'.

Upskilling is critical here. IC professionals must learn to work *with* AI; interpreting outputs, guiding tone and bringing ethical judgement. But their human superpowers of empathy, narrative insight and ethical reflection will be even more vital.

The thing to ask now is, are you building a team of storytellers, technologists and experience designers? Do you understand the data you need and the AI tools that can amplify you?

Internal communication is no longer just a function. It's moving towards an experience platform, powered by data, shaped by AI and anchored in human need. IC isn't here to push messages; it's here to create meaning and to sew the fabric of purpose to people. Meaning and purpose are only found when communication meets people in their moment, on their terms.

If this is done right, IC won't just be more efficient, it'll make work more human *through* AI.

Making measurement better

Measurement has long been the Achilles' heel of internal communication, but it doesn't have to be. We can move beyond vanity metrics and tick-box audits, and instead use meaningful insight to shape strategy, improve outcomes and prove value. Adopting a People-First IC approach can help to make this shift. When we start with people's lived experiences, get clear on the problems we're solving and define tangible outcomes from the start, measurement becomes not just easier, it becomes purposeful.

When we take this approach it stops being something we dread and starts becoming a tool for learning, influence and progress. It's how we prove value. It's how we earn our seat at the table. And most importantly, it's how we make a difference that lasts. Now is the time to stop measuring what's easy and start measuring what matters.

CHAPTER IN SUMMARY

- Measurement has long been a weak spot in IC, often limited to vanity metrics like clicks and open rates that fail to show real impact or influence.

- The People-First IC approach changes the game by embedding measurement from the start – asking better questions, setting clearer objectives and tracking outcomes that reflect real human experience.

- Most measurement challenges stem from unclear problem definition. When we rush to solutions without understanding the 'why', meaningful measurement becomes impossible.

- People-First IC ties communication objectives directly to business outcomes like retention, trust, confidence and performance, creating clarity for both IC teams and stakeholders.

- OKRs (Objectives and Key Results) provide a useful, practical framework to define measurable, people-first outcomes.

- Effective measurement happens at three levels:

  o Process (perception of comms experience).

  o Impact (immediate changes).

  o Outcome (longer-term behavioural or business shifts).

- The People-First IC audit reimagines traditional audits by shifting focus from channels and content to how communication is experienced, perceived and acted on.

- Building data literacy is now a core IC skill, not a nice-to-have.

- Ultimately, people-first measurement isn't about more data; it's about better insight. It's how we show impact, earn influence and design communication that truly makes a difference.

References

Boon, C (2019) How to best approach HR strategy implementation, Amsterdam People Analytics Centre, https://apac.uva.nl/publications/publications.html (archived at https://perma.cc/X439-R56S)

CIPR Inside and Institute of Internal Communication (IoIC) (2019) Measurement and ROI for Internal Communication, CIPR Inside, www.ciprinside.co.uk (archived at https://perma.cc/DBX2-6PDG)

Doerr, J (2018) *Measure What Matters: How Google, Bono, and the Gates Foundation Rock the World with OKRs*, Penguin Business, London

Gallagher (2024) State of the sector 2024: The definitive global survey of the internal communication and employee experience landscape, Gallagher Communication, www.ajg.com/employeeexperience (archived at https://perma.cc/M28X-3FY3)

Gallup (2015) *State of the American Manager: Analytics and Advice for Leader,* Gallup, Washington, DC, www.gallup.com/workplace/236441/state-american-manager-report.aspx (archived at https://perma.cc/85C6-QERM)

Glassdoor (2015) Why good onboarding leads to better employee retention, www.glassdoor.com/employers (archived at https://perma.cc/D32E-SLTH)

Kotter, J P and Heskett, J L (1992) *Corporate Culture and Performance*, Free Press, New York

Staffbase and USC Annenberg School for Communication and Journalism (2024) Employee communication impact report 2024, Staffbase, staffbase.com/en/pressreleases/communication-breakdown-61-of-employees-unlikely-to-stay-in-their-job-cite-poor-communication-among-top-reasons (archived at https://perma.cc/DGM5-UJTN)

12

This is our moment

This is our moment. Right here, right now, is where a next chapter of our profession's long and rich history begins. But it's also your moment, as this is a future we'll be writing together.

Where we go next is up for grabs, but what is certain is that what comes next will be very different from what has come before. And it will demand a very different type of internal communicator.

We have a once-in-a-generation opportunity to reposition internal communication as the beating heart of the organization and champion of human connection in the workplace. Or we can stand by and watch as AI takes over more and more of what we currently do, leaving those practitioners who survive as little more than AI carers and glorified prompt engineers. It's a stark choice, but that is the nature of revolution.

Our hope is that we'll look back at this moment as the turning point. The point where internal communication stopped being the mouthpiece of management and became the conscience of the organization. The point where internal communicators changed course.

At the start of this book, we made it clear that this is a work of optimism. Our intent is absolutely not to push a doom-and-gloom scenario but to show how, in the face of truly momentous change, we have the opportunity to reimagine our profession, recalibrate our roles and refocus our activity around people. An opportunity to press reset.

In this final chapter, we have come full circle; it's time to reconnect with those early human-centred IC pioneers. We'll revisit the key themes we've explored and set out our bold vision for the future of IC. We'll show you how your human 'superpowers' really are the key to your future as a communicator. This will be our rallying call too – an invitation to you to join your fellow professionals as we usher in the era of People-First IC.

History repeating

In the early 1800s, a group of skilled textile workers in England, known as the Luddites, started smashing up machines. Not because they hated technology but because those machines were being used to cut wages and erode the value of their core skills.

Fast forward to today, and we're facing our very own Luddite moment. But AI isn't just taking over the 'craft' aspects of our work, it's quietly reshaping our entire profession. If we cling to our old ways – channels, control, content, campaigns – we will quickly become irrelevant.

Unlike the Luddites though, we don't need to destroy the tools. We need to redefine our value by doing the deeply human work machines can't. Today's world of work is a far cry from the 19th century and yet the transformation that is underway is arguably bigger and more profound than the Industrial Revolution.

According to HR thought leader Josh Bersin: 'We are in unprecedented times. The impact of business and societal issues, including the pandemic, continuous disruption due to AI and ongoing talent-related issues… result in a pivotal moment for both opportunity and change' (Bersin, 2024).

A pivotal moment

Technology is only one part of this.

The Covid-19 pandemic may feel like a distant memory, but its impact is still being felt. Change was already happening, but that was the moment employee expectations transformed, the balance of power shifted and many of us started to re-evaluate our relationship with work.

The multi-generational workforce is here – ageing baby boomers like us now work alongside Gen Z employees.

Trust has eroded, yet people increasingly look to employers to lead with honesty and behave with integrity.

Climate, equity, social justice – work now sits in a bigger ethical and cultural context.

Employees are now demanding a consumer-grade experience at work – tools, communications and services that are as intuitive, seamless and satisfying as the best consumer apps and brands.

Add AI into the mix and you have the perfect storm.

The impact of AI will be way bigger than many of us can imagine – it's what Angelique de Vries Schipperijn, EMEA President for Workday, recently called an 'incredible tectonic event' (Daisley, 2025).

A report published in summer 2025 by Ravio shows entry-level job openings in the tech space are down 73 per cent year-on-year, while admin roles are down 35 per cent over the same period. Many are interpreting this as a sign of things to come – a clear indication that AI is starting to take over routine tasks (Cranenbroek, 2025).

The pace of this change is truly staggering. In the next five years, 44 per cent of workers' core skills are expected to change – nearly half of the skill set needed for any given job today will either shift in priority, be replaced or require updating within five years (WEF, 2023). What we know today is becoming obsolete faster than ever.

If you need a further wake-up call, check out the AI 2027 scenarios, which predict the impact of AI over the next decade will far exceed that of the Industrial Revolution (Kokotajlo et al, 2025). A detailed near-term forecast from a credible group of researchers, it's sobering reading and suggests that we're woefully unprepared for what's about to hit us.

Over the coming years, the reinvention of work will accelerate as generative AI transforms organizations.

By 2030, the world of work will look very different to today. AI will be embedded into daily work and teams will comprise humans and bots, working side by side. Hybrid work will be the norm, flexibility standard. Offices will be used intentionally for collaboration. Our careers will be non-linear, fluid and self-directed. Human skills and strengths will increasingly define our success. Trust and well-being will become core business metrics as organizations are held accountable for their impact on mental health, equity and sustainability. The world of work will be faster, flatter, more digital – and hopefully also more human.

A choice to make

We can't choose whether to embrace this change or not – AI is already upon us. But what we can do is choose how we respond to it. We're standing at a professional crossroads and the direction we choose will not only dictate whether we survive or not, it will also shape the future of work. The opportunity has never been greater, but nor have the dangers.

Throughout this book, we've made the case for change. We've asked difficult questions about our profession and shown why People-First Internal Communication is the right way forward. And we've showcased the tools, insights and evidence that underpin this approach. Now it's down to you, the practitioner, to take it forward.

Every one of us has a clear choice to make. We can put this book down and return to our old ways of working or we can seize the moment and reshape IC as a human-centred, experience-driven discipline that drives culture, trust and performance. We can stand on the sidelines and watch as the world of work transforms around us or we can get stuck in and lead that transformation. One thing is certain though – if we put our heads in the sand, we will almost certainly suffocate.

People-First IC isn't a new campaign or a comms plan with bells and whistles; it's a fundamental shift in how we define our roles:

- from content creators to experience designers
- from message experts to sense-makers
- from order-takers to culture-shapers.

Change of this magnitude won't be easy. It takes strength and resilience to swim against the tide. And it will be uncomfortable, too. Because it means letting go of the belief that we must have all the answers, need to control the flow of information or polish content before anyone else sees it. Instead, it asks us to dive into the unknown with curiosity and courage.

Already there?

Of course, some of you might argue you're already there.

As we have been researching and writing this book, we've noticed an increase in those using people-first language. Industry reports now focus on employee well-being, trust-building and hyper-personalized messaging; the professional bodies are shining the spotlight on human connection. Even Google has introduced 'helpful, reliable, people-first content' guidelines, reflecting a broader shift towards human-centric thinking.

Certainly, there are an increasing number of us who care deeply about people and want to do the right thing for employees. Having picked up this book, the chances are you're one of them. You write with empathy. You're tuned into emotions. You listen and respond to feedback. You capture and share stories that matter. You get out regularly and talk to front-line employees. You might even use tools like personas and journey mapping. You're already putting people first.

But the painful truth is this: caring about people isn't the same thing as designing with them. Being aware of other people's feelings isn't the same as co-creating with them. And listening after you've launched something isn't the same as involving people from the very start. And that's the leap we need to make.

It's easy to convince yourself that you've already made this shift – when in fact, you're still working inside a system built for control, not collaboration. You may well be doing the best work of your career, bagging awards for campaign excellence and winning the respect of your senior leaders, but still doing it within a frame that is no longer fit for purpose.

The uncomfortable truth is that internal communication, as it stands, is broken. There are pockets of excellence and growing numbers of professionals who believe there is a better way, but all too often it's expert-led, message-first, channel-fixated and stuck in a cycle of output over impact.

A new operating system built on timeless principles

That's not because you're doing it all wrong – it's because the entire IC operating system was built for yesterday.

People-First Internal Communication is your new operating system. It's a collection of ideas, principles, tools and techniques that enable you to recalibrate your role.

The sceptics will say there's nothing new here – and we have to confess, they are absolutely right! People-First IC is not some radical, off-the-wall, conceptual idea but rather a tried and tested approach built on timeless principles. It draws on longstanding, deeply human ideas and a set of tools and methods that have been used and refined for decades. What is different, though, is that this is the first time these ideas have been applied comprehensively to the world of internal communication. We've reclaimed them for the AI era and in doing so, created a bold, new, human-centred operating model for our profession.

Respect, listening, belonging, involvement, shared meaning – these aren't new trends; they are the human fundamentals that, sadly, we have lost sight of. Cadbury and Rowntree knew that care, communication and community were foundational to performance. We have been here before, briefly, but we lost our way. Ultimately, People-First IC is a return to what truly matters in a world that needs it more than ever.

A higher purpose

When we're operating at our best, internal communicators deliver enormous value to organizations by aligning, engaging and enabling employees to drive business success. Great IC connects people to strategy, builds trust, unlocks engagement, strengthens culture, brings values to life, facilitates change and enhances performance. It helps organizations adapt faster and retain talent. It's a strategic enabler, not a support function.

But it's so much more than that. Internal communication is not just a central and critical component of the overall employee experience – it creates that experience. Communication is the lifeblood of the organization and shapes how people feel, think and act at work every day. It creates clarity and connection, builds trust through transparency, listens and involves, supports the moments that matter and shapes the 'everyday EX'.

This book is a call to a higher purpose. It's about reimagining what internal communication is and can be, what we are here to do and how we should go about our work. It's about shifting the emphasis from the organization itself to the people who comprise it – for an organization is nothing more than a group of people pursuing a common aim. It's about creating a better world of work.

We believe passionately that employees deserve better. We believe that one of the most dominant aspects of our lives, work, should be uplifting, stimulating and enjoyable, not something to be tolerated.

For far too many of us, our experience of work is a poor one – evidenced by static engagement data, declining levels of trust, the loneliness epidemic and dozens of other negative indicators. We spend around a third of our adult lives working – and that experience permeates every aspect of our lives, impacting our health, happiness, relationships and self-identity. Work shapes lives.

It's time to recognize that employees are not a means to an end – they are not 'human resource' – they are individuals with their own hopes, dreams, needs and wants. They deserve to be seen, heard and respected. They deserve to be involved. They deserve to matter.

They also deserve to be treated with dignity and fairness, to have a voice and to feel safe enough to speak out. They deserve to be respected.

This is far from 'soft and fluffy' though. Creating a positive employee experience is good for business. When people feel like they matter, they perform better, stay longer and care more. Engagement, innovation, performance, productivity – whatever your measure of success, it will follow.

The world of work has changed, but many workplaces have remained stuck in the past. Until now, they could get away with it, but the ground beneath us has moved. Ever so slowly at first, then accelerated by a global pandemic – and now the very foundations of work are shaking.

Expectations have shifted and employees now demand more – meaning, flexibility, fairness and belonging. The experience we create – the experience we design together – must align with those expectations.

And of course, the monumental game-changer that is AI has arrived. This is the burning platform and the reason we have to change now. It is the reason we wrote this book. There is a small window of opportunity – a brief moment – to ensure that AI becomes a force for good, helping shape better experiences by freeing up people to do more meaningful, human work.

But that won't be easy. The battle between experience and efficiency has only just started and internal communicators are on the front line. And we will be impacted just as much as any other function, perhaps more so. Despite this, it's our duty to show that AI is not the enemy of people-first work; it's the enabler. Used intentionally and implemented with care, it can enhance the experience, not erode it.

Our ability to influence all this is without question.

The communication experience we create shapes the wider employee experience. From onboarding to departure, team meetings to CEO updates, every interaction is a communication experience – and an opportunity to shape how people feel. It's the thread that runs through every moment.

What people see, hear and feel becomes the culture of the organization. Values statements on a poster do nothing – employees judge the culture based on what's communicated day-to-day and especially during key moments of feedback, change, recognition or conflict. Research consistently shows that most of what employees believe comes not from formal channels, but from what they see, hear and experience – particularly through conversations with managers and peers (Edelman Trust Barometer, 2023). It's all about human connection.

It's also about risk management. When communication is unclear, inauthentic or absent, things start to fall apart – trust erodes, engagement drops, productivity nosedives, confusion increases and well-being suffers.

For all these reasons and more, internal communication has a central role to play in the future success of every organization. But this value will only be unlocked through human connection and that is what People-First Internal Communication is all about.

A manifesto for change

To help crystallize our vision for People-First IC, we've drafted a manifesto. More than just a set of words, it's a strategic and symbolic act. A declaration of intent – a bold, public commitment to show up differently.

In the past, internal communication has been seen as a support function – tactical, reactive, output-focused. The manifesto reframes it as something much more than that: a human-centred, strategic practice that can shape culture, build trust and improve lives. It's not just about doing things better, it's about doing better things.

The manifesto is designed to inspire alignment and action. It provides a reference point – something teams and individuals can rally around, reflect on and use to guide decisions. It helps align day-to-day actions with bigger principles.

In a world of AI, automation and noise, People-First IC is the differentiator. A statement like this helps raise the bar, inviting others to hold the work (and themselves) to a higher, more human standard.

The manifesto is intended as a compass, not a rulebook. It doesn't tell you what to do, but it reminds you why you're doing it and who it's for.

In line with our people-first principles, we are seeing this very much as a first draft, an open-source beta version for others to shape, finesse and make their own.

A MANIFESTO FOR PEOPLE-FIRST INTERNAL COMMUNICATION (BETA VERSION)

We believe that internal communication is not about control, but about connection. We reject the idea that communication is something we do to people, but rather something we design and deliver with them.

We design experiences, not deliver messages. We don't just write comms. We shape how people feel at every touchpoint – across journeys, moments and milestones that define the employee experience.

We co-design, not cascade. People-First IC is built with people, not for them. Employees are not an audience – they are collaborators, contributors, co-authors of the story.

We lead with listening, always. We don't wait until the end to gather feedback. We begin with it. Insight is our starting point, not a box to tick after launch.

We put purpose before polish. Done-with is better than perfect. We prioritize authenticity, clarity and care over corporate spin or surface shine.

We prototype, test and learn. We don't default to 'big bang' campaigns. We build small, test early, learn fast and adapt based on real employee input.

We design for real lives, not ideal users. People are busy, distracted, emotional, overwhelmed. We meet them where they are – with empathy, clarity and respect.

We shape trust, not just content. We see every communication as a moment of truth. We hold space for vulnerability, hard conversations and real connection.

We influence systems, not just outputs. We don't just 'do comms'. We question assumptions, shape behaviours and shift culture – from the inside out.

We are experience designers, sense-makers and culture-shapers. We reject the narrow definition of IC as messaging. Our value lies in understanding, facilitating and making work feel more human.

We don't serve the system. We humanize it. That's our responsibility. That's our power. That's what People-First IC is here to do.

Your invitation to step into a new role

The shift to People-First Internal Communication won't come from fancy job titles or formal strategies. It won't come from those with the best writing skills, the most polished presentations or guru-like professional knowledge. It will come from small, intentional choices made every day – by people like you.

You don't need permission. You don't need a blank slate. You just need to begin.

Here's how to get started – using the People-First IC Design Loop as your guide.

1. Discover

Start with people, not problems.

- Run a few short *empathy interviews* with colleagues – especially those often overlooked.

- Shadow a front-line team or walk through a comms experience as if you were them.
- Ask 'what's it like to receive communication here?' and really listen.

2. Define

Don't jump to solutions – reframe the challenge.

- Use what you've heard to build a quick *persona* or *empathy map*.
- Write a 'How might we...' question that focuses on real needs, not outputs.
- Challenge yourself to define the communication *experience* to be shaped, not just the content to be delivered.

3. Design

Co-create solutions, don't just write messages.

- Involve employees in shaping messages, toolkits or visuals – *before* launch.
- Use *storyboards, scripts or role-plays* as low-fi prototypes to test ideas.
- Bring others into your process – not for approval, but for co-ownership.

4. Deliver

Focus on connection, not perfection.

- Design for real lives: simplify copy, respect attention, time and context.
- Use *moments that matter* to create impact, e.g. how a message is received during a restructure or recognition moment.
- Support managers with prompts and give them the space to be human, not just push messages.

5. Measure and learn

Ask better questions. Measure what matters.

- Set people-centred outcomes from the start: clarity, confidence, connection.

- Collect feedback continuously, not just post-launch.
- Use insights to improve *with* employees – and share what you're learning.

Start small. Think big. Keep moving.

This isn't about doing more – it's about doing differently. One step at a time.

As these examples show, People-First IC isn't a one-off initiative. It's a new operating system. And the best way to install it is to start living it – today.

Join the movement

The life of a revolutionary can be hard and lonely. To succeed, you'll need to surround yourself with fellow fighters and arm yourself for the battle.

That's why we've created the People-First IC Movement, a collective of IC pioneers, senior leaders and practitioners who want to lead with people-first principles.

It's completely free to join and as part of the movement, you'll have access to new tools, frameworks and professional resources, exclusive content drops, invitations to our events and the chance to shape what comes next.

Please join us and together, let's shape the future of IC. Just scan the QR code to sign up.

FIGURE 12.1 Join the People-First IC Movement

CHAPTER IN SUMMARY

- **This is our moment, a time to choose** – adapt and lead or risk irrelevance in an increasingly AI-driven future.

- **We must move from content delivery to championing human connection** – from being message-makers to experience designers, sense-makers and culture-shapers.

- **AI is accelerating change at an unprecedented pace** – transforming work faster than the Industrial Revolution.

- **People-First IC is your new operating system** – rooted in timeless principles: empathy, respect, belonging and involvement. It replaces old frameworks built around control, channels and campaigns.

- **Simply caring about people isn't enough** – we must design *with* them, not *for* them.

- **The People-First IC manifesto** calls for communication that connects, involves, listens and builds trust.

- **AI isn't the enemy of people-first work** – it can be an enabler if implemented with care and intention.

- **You don't need permission to lead this change** – start small, start today, think differently and take action.

- **A new movement is forming to support this shift** – join us and be part of the collective.

References

Bersin, J (2024) *Welcome to the Post-Industrial Age*, Josh Bersin Insights, https://joshbersin.com/post-industrial-age (archived at https://perma.cc/AK8T-4NWE)

Cranenbroek, P (2025) AI eliminates entry-level jobs, *LinkedIn News*, 10 June, www.linkedin.com/news/story/ai-eliminates-entry-level-jobs-6443308/?utm_source=chatgpt.com (archived at https://perma.cc/FJB6-M5DL)

Daisley, B (2025) Getting to grips with workplace AI, *Eat Sleep Work Repeat* [podcast], season 12, episode 207, 6 June, https://eatsleepworkrepeat.com/getting-to-grips-with-workplace-ai (archived at https://perma.cc/YM9V-HEH7)

Edelman (2023) 2023 Edelman trust barometer, Edelman, https://www.edelman.com/sites/g/files/aatuss191/files/2023-08/2023-Edelman-Trust-Barometer-Special-Report-Trust-Work.pdf (archived at https://perma.cc/2ZWF-F3FV)

Kokotajlo, D, Alexander, S, Larsen, T, Lifland, E and Dean, R (2025) AI 2027: We predict that the impact of superhuman AI over the next decade will be enormous, exceeding that of the Industrial Revolution, AI Futures Project, ai-2027.com (archived at https://perma.cc/J7P4-EQTY)

Ravio (2025) *The Tech Job Market in 2025*, Ravio, Summer 2025 report, www.linkedin.com/posts/ravio-com_entry-level-hiring-has-shifted-dramatically-activity-7338848803413745665-iD_C/?utm_source=chatgpt.com (archived at https://perma.cc/N4LP-K3U6)

World Economic Forum (WEF) (2023) *The Future of Jobs Report 2023*, World Economic Forum, Geneva, www.weforum.org/publications/the-future-of-jobs-report-2023 (archived at https://perma.cc/9JGB-GQNK)

INDEX

Note: Page numbers in *italics* refer to figures or tables.

Looking for another book?

Explore our award-winning
books from global business
experts in Human Resources,
Learning and Development

Scan the code to browse

www.koganpage.com/hr-learning-
development

More from Kogan Page

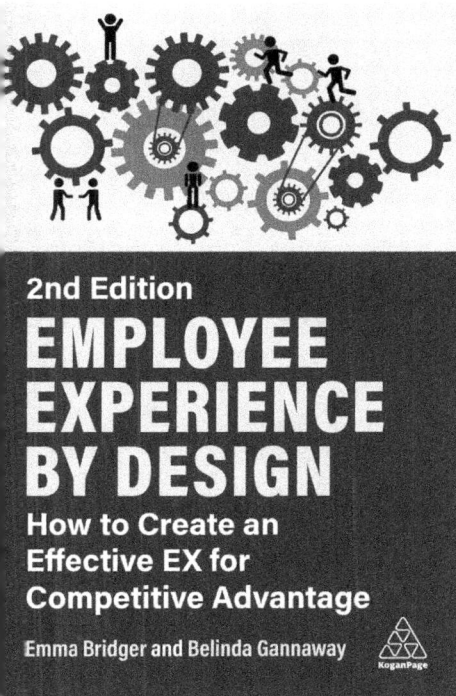

BN: 9781398614369

ISBN: 9781398614642

www.koganpage.com

From 4 December 2025 the EU Responsible Person (GPSR) is:
eucomply oÜ, Pärnu mnt. 139b – 14, 11317 Tallinn, Estonia
www.eucompliancepartner.com

www.ingramcontent.com/pod-product-compliance
Lightning Source LLC
Chambersburg PA
CBHW071539210326
41597CB00019B/3053